VOLUME TWO

ADVANCES IN TRANSPORT POLICY AND PLANNING

Population Loss: The Role of Transportation and Other Issues

VOLUME TWO

ADVANCES IN TRANSPORT POLICY AND PLANNING

Population Loss: The Role of Transportation and Other Issues

Edited by

RACHEL S. FRANKLIN

Newcastle University,
Newcastle upon Tyne, United Kingdom

EVELINE S. VAN LEEUWEN

Wageningen University & Research,
Wageningen, The Netherlands

ANTONIO PAEZ

McMaster University,
Hamilton, ON, Canada

ELSEVIER

ACADEMIC PRESS

An imprint of Elsevier

Academic Press is an imprint of Elsevier
50 Hampshire Street, 5th Floor, Cambridge, MA 02139, United States
525 B Street, Suite 1650, San Diego, CA 92101, United States
The Boulevard, Langford Lane, Kidlington, Oxford OX5 1GB, United Kingdom
125 London Wall, London, EC2Y 5AS, United Kingdom

First edition 2018

Notices
Knowledge and best practice in this field are constantly changing. As new research and experience broaden our understanding, changes in research methods, professional practices, or medical treatment may become necessary.

Practitioners and researchers must always rely on their own experience and knowledge in evaluating and using any information, methods, compounds, or experiments described herein. In using such information or methods they should be mindful of their own safety and the safety of others, including parties for whom they have a professional responsibility.

To the fullest extent of the law, neither the Publisher nor the authors, contributors, or editors, assume any liability for any injury and/or damage to persons or property as a matter of products liability, negligence or otherwise, or from any use or operation of any methods, products, instructions, or ideas contained in the material herein.

ISBN: 978-0-12-815454-0
ISSN: 2543-0009

Publisher: Zoe Kruze
Acquisition Editor: Sam Mahfoudh
Editorial Project Manager: Shellie Bryant
Production Project Manager: James Selvam
Cover Designer: Alan Studholme

Typeset by SPi Global, India

Contents

Contributors

Aldo Arranz-López
Department of Geography and Spatial Planning, Universidad de Zaragoza, Zaragoza, Spain

Ricardo Badía-Lázaro
Department of Geography and Spatial Planning, Universidad de Zaragoza, Zaragoza, Spain

Anastassios Dardas
School of Geography & Earth Sciences, McMaster University, Hamilton, ON, Canada

Tiago Fioreze
University of Twente, Enschede, The Netherlands

Rachel S. Franklin
Newcastle University, Newcastle upon Tyne, United Kingdom

Martina Fromhold-Eisebith
Chair of Economic Geography, Department of Geography, RWTH Aachen University, Aachen, Germany

Joanna Ganning
Department of Urban Studies, Levin College of Urban Affairs, Cleveland State University, Cleveland, OH, United States

Karst T. Geurs
University of Twente, Enschede, The Netherlands

Konstantinos Gkiotsalitis
University of Twente, Enschede, The Netherlands

Christopher Graziul
Spatial Structures in the Social Sciences, Brown University, Providence, RI; Department of Comparative Human Development, University of Chicago, Chicago, IL, United States

Sophia Gross-Fengels
Chair of Economic Geography, Department of Geography, RWTH Aachen University, Aachen, Germany

K. Bruce Newbold
School of Geography & Earth Sciences, McMaster University, Hamilton, ON, Canada

Antonio Paez
McMaster University, Hamilton, ON, Canada

Aisling Reynolds-Feighan
University College Dublin, Ireland

Daniel Schleith
Spatial Structures in the Social Sciences, Brown University, Providence, RI, United States

Eric Seymour
Spatial Structures in the Social Sciences, Brown University, Providence, RI, United States

Julio A. Soria-Lara
Transport Research Centre (TRANSyT), Universidad Politécnica de Madrid, Madrid, Spain

Eveline S. van Leeuwen
Wageningen University & Research, Wageningen, The Netherlands

Mettina Veenstra
Saxion University of Applied Sciences, Enschede, The Netherlands

Gideon Visser
HAN University of Applied Sciences, Arnhem, The Netherlands

Allison Williams
School of Geography & Earth Sciences, McMaster University, Hamilton, ON, Canada

CHAPTER ONE

Transportation where people leave: An introduction

Rachel S. Franklin[a,*,†], **Eveline S. van Leeuwen**[b], **Antonio Paez**[c]
[a]Newcastle University, Newcastle upon Tyne, United Kingdom
[b]Wageningen University & Research, Wageningen, The Netherlands
[c]McMaster University, Hamilton, ON, Canada
*Corresponding author: e-mail address: rachel.franklin@newcastle.ac.uk

Contents

Abstract

Transportation means access: to jobs, information, communities, and services. When depopulation occurs a number of questions arise around the central query: what was and will be the role of transportation? This volume engages with several aspects of the depopulation-transportation topic and at multiple geographic scales—from the national and regional to the city- and neighborhood-level. In this chapter, we provide an overview of the challenges associated with population loss and how various aspects of transportation research intersect with these issues. We then summarize the chapters included in this volume, showing how they connect to larger emerging research themes, as well as to each other.

Keywords: Population loss, Transportation, Demographic aging, Rural, Suburbia, Exurbia, Cities

According to the archeological record, for most of history humans lived in small bands as hunter-gatherers, traveling slowly on foot while following game and nuts possibly into new regions of the world. Population during this period of time grew only at a sluggish rate and was kept in check by several natural—and frequently violent—controls. The first agricultural revolution (ca. 10,000 BC) allowed humans for the first time to settle, but even

† Rachel Franklin's contribution to this chapter was supported by NSF Award 1561060.

ISSN 2543-0009
https://doi.org/10.1016/bs.atpp.2018.09.008

then, population growth remained relatively tame—between 10,000 BC and 1800 CE it could take anything from millennia to centuries for the world population to double. In the late modern period in contrast, as conditions dramatically changed with several technological revolutions (e.g., the invention of science, the industrial revolution, and the third agricultural revolution) life conditions and expectancy improved, with the consequence that in the 20th Century it took less than a hundred years for the world's population to double twice over.

With population growth the patterns of human settlements also changed. Although the oldest known human settlements date from at least 8000 BC, and cities with populations of hundreds of thousands had already emerged in the ancient and premodern world (for instance, Rome in the 1st Century AD, Chang'an in China in the 7th Century AD, and Baghdad in the 11th Century AD), most of the world's human population remained rural until relatively recent times. It was only in the first half of the 20th Century that North America, Western and Northern Europe, and Japan turned mostly urban. By the turn of the 21st Century, most regions in the world had turned urban, and there is every indication that, barring major (and possibly catastrophic) changes, the process of urbanization will continue well into the future.

The transition from a mostly rural to a mostly urban world population in the 20th Century was a consequence of several factors, including declines in the natural growth of population, outmigration from rural areas particularly by the young, and reclassification of previously rural areas as urban (United Nations, 1980). For most developed regions of the world, where this phenomenon first emerged, total fertility rates have long been at or below replacement levels and population increases are due to immigration and, at the sub-national scale, internal migration. This has entailed a net population loss for many "sender" regions in recent decades, in particular rural areas and even in some cases larger cities—leading to an aging population structure and decreased population density, but also, at least in the case of US metropolitan areas, different patterns of racial/ethnic diversity and residential segregation (Bellman et al., 2018). The process, however, has not been uniform, and during the second half of the 20th Century there were regions where rural population decline was accompanied *simultaneously* by decline in traditional urban population (e.g., Beauregard, 2009; Catalan et al., 2008; Lee et al., 2016). In many regions, an intermediate ground for population growth was suburbia and even exurbia (Clark et al., 2009; Theobald, 2005)—peri-urban regions with low density patterns of development covering extensive areas.

It is well understood that suburban development in the past century was made possible by relatively inexpensive transportation. Indeed, urban economic theory (Alonso, 1964) explains the effect of transportation on land rent and subsequent development. In this way, even as the world became increasingly urban in the 20th Century, a major source of growth was low density development around traditional cities, fueled by historically inexpensive transportation in the form of mass automobility. Underlying these processes of development too was the explosive growth of population since the Industrial Revolution—a phenomenon that may be on the cusp of naturally reaching a limit. Indeed, by some estimates, population may stabilize in most regions of the world, and rapid growth is only expected to happen in Africa (Gerland et al., 2014). While a global population of approximately 11 billion is a figure substantially larger than the population circa 2020, it no longer reflects the type of exponential growth seen over the past 200 hundred years. This happens at a time when the fossil fuels that sustained a decades-long period of cheap transportation will become scarcer (Almeida and Silva, 2009), and their continued use grows increasingly inadvisable (Chapman, 2007). Future technologies for clean transportation remain speculative (Yang, 2009), and even if they were realized at the scale needed to mitigate an environmental crisis, it remains questionable whether they would achieve much in terms of reducing congestion and sprawl (Zakharenko, 2016). As a consequence, demand for peri-urban development may stall, especially in the developed world.

Putting these trends together it is possible to envisage a number of emerging challenges for the field of transportation. On the one hand, there is the loss of population and demographic aging in rural regions. At the very least, this process of decline should be managed in such a way that the quality of life of inhabitants in rural regions does not suffer. Maintaining life standards and ensuring social inclusion is an acknowledged policy goal in many regions in the world (Stanley and Lucas, 2009), from the UK (Lucas, 2006) to South Africa (Lucas, 2011), the Czech Republic (Musil and Muller, 2008), Australia (Currie et al., 2009), and Canada (Páez et al., 2009). A challenge with rural regions is that their low density makes it expensive to provide traditional public transportation. While automobility currently can serve the mobility needs of perhaps a majority of rural residents, it does not necessarily help those who lack access to private vehicles, including individuals with disabilities or lower incomes. Furthermore, it may in the future become insufficient for many more residents as they age and lose the ability to drive (Davey, 2007; Yagi and Managi, 2016), or alternatively if, as it seems likely, the cost of transportation continues to increase as world oil reserves dwindle (Mattioli et al., 2018; Shapiro et al., 2012). There may be other reasons to ensure that transportation contributes to making rural regions livable—for instance, in order to help them retain their population or to attract new residents and economic activity (McArthur et al., 2014; Musil and Muller, 2008). In a world with a stable population, this would imply slower growth in urban regions, or even population loss there. Whatever the ultimate goal, whether to manage the decline of rural regions or to mitigate it, it is clear that to achieve it there is a need to provide mobility and accessibility solutions that will challenge much of the way that transportation has operated in the last century.

Another area of concern is the future of peri-urban areas, neighborhoods characterized by a form of development that has sought to combine the best aspects of both rural and urban life: living large in proximity to nature while at the same time maintaining accessibility to employment centers, shopping, amenities, and recreation (Leichenko and Solecki, 2005). In several countries the uneasy compromise between rural life and urban accessibility resulted in increasing levels of congestion that choke many major urban regions in the world. The trade-off between suburban life and commuting time and cost in those regions already takes a toll in economic (e.g., productivity losses), environmental (e.g., emissions, land consumption, use of non-renewable resources), and social terms (e.g., impacts on health, loss of social contact). Moreover, it is important to ponder what would happen if suburbia and exurbia, which are already difficult to serve by public transportation, started to lose population, either because of a renaissance in rural life (Argent et al., 2013), or simply trends that favored a return to a more urban lifestyle (Jacobsen, 2004), a development already observed in Japan (Buhnik, 2010). At first glance, it would seem that the challenges are similar to those of rural regions, but for one important difference: the vastly larger suburban populations relative to rural populations. Given the size of suburban and exurban populations, managing decline would appear to be a considerably more difficult problem than it would be for rural regions—keeping in mind, however, that despite their low density, in these suburban/exurban regions there might be sufficient demand/critical mass to provide alternative transportation solutions, such as on-demand services (e.g., Alshalalfah and Shalaby, 2012; Cervero, 2017)

There is, in addition, yet another possibility for suburban regions: that peri-urban commuting fields shrink due for instance to increases in the cost of transportation (Boussauw et al., 2011; Dodson and Sipe, 2007). Just as suburban and exurban development have been made possible by relatively inexpensive transportation, increases in the cost of transportation may make already developed areas lose value—which might lead to population relocation closer to traditional cities, or alternatively population displacement, as wealthier households out-bid lower income ones for more accessible locations in traditional cities (Tighe and Ganning, 2016). The outcome of one scenario would be akin to population loss. The other would be a possibly stagnant population of the economically vulnerable located in regions that are difficult to serve by traditional public transportation services. In either case, again, there is a need to think of innovative solutions to minimize the disruptive potential of such developments.

Cities themselves have also been the site of population loss over the past several decades. The twin processes of suburbanization and shifts in employment centers have resulted, in many places, in a hollowing out of the central city. In the United States context, in particular, these redistributions of urban populations have also led to urban concentrations of poverty and racial minorities, often in a larger fiscal context of falling tax revenue and tighter municipal budgets. In many of these cities, pockets of gentrification juxtapose "haves" and "have nots" and also lead to potential displacement of remaining (disadvantaged) residents, heightening disparities in access to jobs, schools, and services

Whether rural, urban, or in between, at the nexus of demographic change and transportation also lies the issue of equity. The numbers and characteristics (demographic, but also socio-economic) of individuals are not uniformly distributed in space. The poor, the unemployed, the elderly, and the otherwise socially disenfranchised are not uniformly distributed in space. At every spatial scale, as population loss occurs, the impacts may fall disproportionately on the already vulnerable. That is, to the challenges of good transport provision and policy that arise from decreased population density and falling revenues are added those related to inequity of accessibility and service provision. In areas that are geographically isolated, whether neighborhoods or regions, there is a triple jeopardy effect for those living in affected places.

As the preceding paragraphs suggest, there are a number of trends that could pose novel challenges for transportation professionals. It is important, therefore, to develop a knowledge base with which to confront any emerging challenges. Clearly, for the understanding of decline we need conceptual and analytical tools that allow space and time to be considered simultaneously (Franklin and van Leeuwen, 2018). This includes, for example, con ceptual work to understand the degree of heterogeneity among places that depopulate (e.g., Osti, 2010) and indeed what are reasonable accessibility expectations in rural areas (Farrington and Farrington, 2005). It is necessary also to document population trends along with the evolution of travel and locational behaviors in such regions (e.g., Howe et al., 1998). Finally, projecting the potential impact of these trends can provide valuable information to prepare for and best manage them if/and when they emerge (e.g, Silhan et al., 2017; Wiersma et al., 2017).

In order to confront some of these emerging challenges a range of different policy interventions have been proposed in the literature. Chief among these interventions are those that rely on physical planning, that call for a greater use of information and communications technologies (ICT), or that try to effect behavioral change. Moving forward, it is important to discern which interventions work and understand how they work. For instance, in research by Lee et al. in South Korea (2016), it was found that institutional responses to urban shrinkage, including transportation infrastructure and strict regulations on urban form, did not halt the process and may even have contributed to its acceleration through a loss of securely-enclosed residential areas and adaptable market-spaces. Why did transportation infrastructure in this particular situation fail, and how can such experiences be avoided in the future? Research by Anderson et al. (2015) examined the potential of ICT to enable rural businesses in Scotland. These authors discovered that broadband fostered new ways of achieving small country life but did not lead to a creative transformation of rural regions. Could ICT prove more effective in combination with other interventions that increased not only cyber-accessibility but physical accessibility as well (e.g., Kwan and Ren, 2008)? Then, there is the question of who benefits from interventions. For example, Knight et al. (2018) found that fragmented cityscapes are associated with an uneven distribution of benefits in Buffalo, New York, a classic American shrinking city—and consequently that social justice must be an important element in redevelopment strategies in such context. In another case, research by Šťastná et al. (2015) confirmed for the South-Moravian Region, that integrated transport systems provide reasonable levels of accessibility, albeit at a high fiscal cost. Will the public continue to support these systems in similar regions? What are the trade-offs? Or are there alternatives that would be more fiscally palatable to the public and still provide reasonable levels of accessibility to users, as is the case of on-demand transport in rural areas of Castilla y León, in Spain (Urrecho and Fernandez, 2016)?

Clearly, there are multiple interesting and pressing questions. The objective of this volume is less to provide a comprehensive snapshot of the diversity of challenges ahead and ways of addressing them, and more to offer a sample of recent research that touches on several of these themes. In this way, the book collects recent research on the theme of transportation in the face of demographic change. The research is international, albeit circumscribed to more developed economies—with examples from Spain, Canada, Germany, The Netherlands, and the United States. The book is organized following a macro- to micro-perspective, taking a look first at the links between depopulation and accessibility by air transport. Following this chapter, the issue of aging in a rural context is addressed. The following three chapters offer case studies on transportation in a declining region context from the Netherlands, Spain, and Germany. Finally, the volume closes with two chapters at the city and neighborhood scale, this time in a United States context. Recurring themes of accessibility, equity, aging, and policy innovation echo across all chapters. Importantly, taken as an ensemble, these chapters highlight how these challenges—which are, after all, widely recognized—resonate at the national, regional, and local scales.

1. The national level

In her chapter, Aisling Reynolds-Feighan focusses on the link between depopulation at the EU state level and changes in accessibility by air transport. In the EU, air transport is strongly linked to a core value: "freedom of movement of labour, goods, services and capital" (Favell, 2011). Causality is however difficult to establish. Also, the link between depopulation and the amount of air traffic is not as straightforward as it might seem: if depopulation is mainly caused by a negative natural increase, less air traffic is expected. However, when depopulation is mostly driven by (longer distance) emigration this might generate extra demand between host and receiving regions (see chapter "Air transport accessibility changes in depopulating European states" by Reynolds-Feighan).

Indeed, Reynolds-Feighan finds that there is a strong link between the development of new route structures and the location of the host and receiving regions of EU migrants. In particular, low-cost carriers quickly responded to this kind of emerging demand. In addition, many higher cost "national flag carriers," which often provided global hubs went bankrupt. Unfortunately, most low-cost carriers mainly offer point-to-point services, with little opportunities for connecting (inter-national/continental) flights. As a result, in particular depopulating post-2004 EU member states in Central Europe face challenges in capitalizing the benefits of global accessibility. This chapter emphasizes an oft-neglected aspect of depopulation:

when it occurs at the national scale, what are the implications for connectivity and flows of people, goods, and information? This remains an open question, but one that is likely to be posed to an increasing number of developed countries in the coming decades.

2. The regional level

Several chapters in this volume draw insights from particular regional cases, whether Canada, The Netherlands, Spain, or Germany. In general, when looking at the regional level, we can identify a major difference between urban and rural areas in how depopulation impacts (public) transport opportunities and thereby accessibilty. In rural areas, the combination of lower and changing demand (e.g., due to aging), relatively high fuel and labor costs due to longer distances and the increasing competition of cars and electric bikes makes it increasingly difficult to offer profitable public transport services. Karst Geurs and his co-authors focus on how Mobility-as-a-Service (MaaS) can be used to face the challenges in providing transport services in low-density depopulating areas in the Netherlands. In order for public transport to compete with private transport modes, they argue (following Cervero, 1997, and Daniels and Mulley, 2010) (following Cervero, 1997; and Daniels and Mulley, 2010) that public transport should be much better able to sustain the demand for spontaneous travel. By offering a variety of transport options in a single platform, MaaS might be just the way to tackle this. In chapter "The potential of a mobility-as-a-service platform in a depopulating area in the Netherlands: An exploration of small and big data" by Geurs et al. use a revealed preference survey approach to better understand the potential of MaaS in the municipality of Oost-Gelre, a rural municipality with 30,000 residents divided of two main cores and several smaller communities located in the East of the Netherlands. In addition, they used big-data information from smart cards and mobile phones.

The data showed that only 5% of the respondents use public transport on a daily basis. However, the survey results do show that the residents are in general satisfied with the current public transport services for fixed, re-current trips, but that they are dissatisfied in the case of infrequent trips to varying destinations (Geurs et al., this book). In order for MaaS to be successful in this region, it should target in particular students and infrequent trips of residents.

Julio Soria-Lara and his co-authors focus on a depopulating rural region in Spain, "the Maestrazgo"—a very rural and relatively poor region of

15 municipalities, home to 20,600 persons, with the largest settlement consisting of 688 residents. The concern of the authors is inequality in accessibility to retail services among different socio-economic groups. Not only do people with different socio-economic backgrounds face different transport opportunities, based on cultural norms, habits, and physical abilities—they also have a different "willingness to cover distances." Based on a face-to-face survey asking about the willingness to travel a certain number of minutes for daily- and non-daily shopping activities, in chapter "Evaluating relative accessibility to retail in depopulated areas: Case study of the Maestrazgo region in Spain" by Soria-Lara et al. distinguish three main groups of people: the young, with higher incomes, the adults with lower incomes and the seniors, also with relatively low incomes. Based on the opportunities and preferences of those three groups, it appears that retail accessibility for seniors is significantly different from the other two groups, in particular because they very much depend on shops within walking distance for their daily purchases and on the help of others to obtain their non-daily purchases at a longer distance. In most cases, and for all three groups, public transport was not an option to access stores beyond the own municipality. The authors strongly advocate the need for regional connections, not only in terms of physical transport and on demand transportation services, but also related to ICT and the required internet connectivity.

In chapter "Older drivers in rural areas: Implications for health, social inclusion and caregiving" by Bruce Newbold et al. focus on a group of older people, and in particular on the drivers among them, in their chapter. As Soria-Lara and co-authors noticed as well, aging people develop different—in space and time—travel demands, opportunities and constraints. This is partly due to decreasing health conditions that limit the opportunities of using public transport, as well as driving a car. Earlier research showed that most older persons prefer the car over public transit services (Newbold and Scott, 2017). Given that also in depopulating areas elderly want to "age in place" additional transportation options are very important to prevent social exclusion and limited access to (health) services. Newbold and his co-authors focus on how transportation preferences and behavior among the elderly in Canada differ between urban and rural areas. They base their results on the 2009 Canadian Community Health Survey from Statistics Canada and find that, indeed, the rural population depends more on cars, as is shown by a higher licensure rate. In addition, those rural residents without a driving license make fewer trips than their urban counterparts. Giving the decreasing rate of driving licenses among the older population, and in particular among older females, insufficient transportation services are likely to result in either out-migration or social exclusion.

In their chapter on Information and Communication Technologies (ICT), or "Smart Mobilities", and rural depopulation, Gross-Fengels and Fromhold-Eisebith reflect on issues similar to those addressed by Geurs in his chapter on Mobility-as-a-Service in the Netherlands. Here, Gross-Fengels and Fromhold-Eisebith use a case study from the Heinsberg region in Germany to illustrate how transportation contributes to well-being in a declining rural region and to highlight some of the challenges that lie in the way of successful implementation. In their opening, the authors note that, ideally, improved transport provision does more than simply facilitate inhabitants leaving the area. In fact, good transport policy should not only maintain or even improve the well-being of remaining inhabitants, but also hopefully make the area a more desirable place for others to locate (the authors do not discuss, however, the fact that in a stable or shrinking country such as Germany, attracting migrants is in effect a zero-sum game at the national scale: some region has to lose population in order for Heinsberg, for example, to grow.) Smart Mobilities—flexible transportation solutions that help connect sparsely populated and often older areas to jobs and services—offer one possible way forward. Importantly, Gross-Fengels and Fromhold-Eisebith note that barriers to uptake of these options exist at multiple levels. For example, while political intervention is likely necessary at the national scale (in terms of allocation of resources and policy), regional level challenges such as access to broadband and wifi are also important. Finally, just as in an urban context, the "last mile" of transport provision is tricky, particularly in case where solutions must be negotiated with land owners over a largely geographic area. The authors conclude on a hopeful note, however, offering numerous suggestions for successful "Smart Mobility" programs in rural areas.

3. The city and neighborhood levels

As already noted, depopulation affects cities as well as rural areas. In the United States, Ganning and Tighe (2018) in fact identify 80 shrinking cities, and this in a country that grew overall by approximately 10% between 2000 and 2010. As in rural areas, a key question related to transportation and population in an urban context is how to guarantee access to jobs. This practical transport question, how to create and maintain links between workers and workplaces, can be confounded when the locations of jobs are shifting over time. And when cities lose population, the already-delicate balance between workers and employment may be especially vulnerable. This conundrum is the subject of Ganning's contribution. Using block group-level data for principal cities located in 349 metropolitan statistical areas in the United States, Ganning uses the lens of the spatial mismatch hypothesis (the gap between job and residence location experienced disproportionately by some population sub-groups more than others) to assess how job accessibility is affected by shrinkage or depopulation. She finds that the dual processes of depopulation and job loss in shrinking principal cities result in substantial decreases in job accessibility (about 6.9 and 13.5%, in the two analytical approaches employed), whereas job growth in growing cities tends to be shared between suburbs and central cities, mitigating negative impacts on central city residents. Her results suggest that any endeavors at the city or metropolitan scale to ease spatial mismatch should take into consideration the larger context of growth and shrinkage.

Much of this volume is concerned with how innovation in transportation modes and policy can mitigate the effects of population loss that has already occurred. Good transport provision might also serve to inoculate against population loss, however. Similar to Gross-Fengels and Fromhold-Eisebith, who suggest in their chapter that innovations in transportation provision might attract new residents, Graziul, Seymour, and Schleith ask whether "commuter culture" is a predictor of neighborhood loss. Using census tract-level data for the largest metropolitan areas in the United States, they estimate the association between neighborhood modal choice and subsequent population change. The relationship is difficult to estimate: the authors do not directly observe availability of transportation alternatives. Instead, it is assumed tract residents only walk or bike or use light rail when these choices make the most sense. Their results suggest that use of light rail, for example, is associated with population increase. Use of bicycle or bus, in contrast, is only associated with neighborhood population growth in high-density tracts; in lower density tracts higher usage of these transport modes is associated with population loss. A similar result is observed for walking. These findings suggest that neighborhood characteristics, particularly access to alternative modes of transportation, may well help determine a neighborhood's short- or medium-term fate—but that further research is required.

The population trends driving some of the challenges discussed in this collection are already underway and appear to be on track to shape how we live, travel, work, and play in the future. It is our hope that the research presented in this volume will contribute to improve our understanding of the road ahead and inspire further research on this important topic.

References

Almeida, P., Silva, P., 2009. The peak of oil production—timings and market recognition. Energy Policy 37, 1267–1276.

Alonso, W., 1964. Location and Land Use. Harvard University Press, Cambridge.

Alshalalfah, B., Shalaby, A., 2012. Feasibility of flex-route as a feeder transit service to rail stations in the suburbs: case study in Toronto. J. Urban Plann. Dev. 138, 90–100.

Anderson, A.R., Wallace, C., Townsend, L., 2015. Great expectations or small country living? Enabling small rural creative businesses with ICT. Sociol. Rural. 56, 450–468.

Argent, N., Tonts, M., Jones, R., Holmes, J., 2013. A creativity-led rural renaissance? Amenity-led migration, the creative turn and the uneven development of rural Australia. Appl. Geogr. 44, 88–98.

Beauregard, R.A., 2009. Urban population loss in historical perspective: United States, 1820–2000. Environ. Plan. A 41, 514–528.

Bellman, B., Spielman, S.E., Franklin, R.S., 2018. Local population change and variations in racial integration in the United States, 2000-2010. Int. Reg. Sci. Rev. 41, 233–255.

Boussauw, K., Neutens, T., Witlox, F., 2011. Minimum commuting distance as a spatial characteristic in a non-monocentric urban system: the case of Flanders. Pap. Reg. Sci. 90, 47–66.

Buhnik, S., 2010. From shrinking cities to Toshi no Shukushō: identifying patterns of urban shrinkage in the Osaka metropolitan area. Berkeley Plan. J. 23, 132–155.

Catalan, B., Sauri, D., Serra, P., 2008. Urban sprawl in the Mediterranean? Patterns of growth and change in the Barcelona metropolitan region 1993-2000. Landsc. Urban Plan. 85, 174–184.

Cervero, R., 1997. Paratransit in America: Redefining Mass Transportation. Praeger, Westport, USA.

Cervero, R., 2017. Mobility niches: jitneys to robo-taxis. J. Am. Plan. Assoc. 83, 404–412.

Chapman, L., 2007. Transport and climate change: a review. J. Transp. Geogr. 15, 354–367.

Clark, J.K., McChesney, R., Munroe, D.K., Irwin, E.G., 2009. Spatial characteristics of exurban settlement pattern in the United States. Landsc. Urban Plan. 90, 178–188.

Currie, G., Richardson, T., Smyth, P., Vella-Brodrick, D., Hine, J., Lucas, K., Stanley, J., Morris, J., Kinnear, R., 2009. Investigating links between transport disadvantage, social exclusion and well-being in Melbourne-preliminary results. Transp. Policy 16, 97–105.

Daniels, R., Mulley, C., 2010. In: Overcoming Barriers to Implementing Flexible Transport Services in NSW. 33rd Australasian Transport Research Forum Conference. Canberra, Australia.

Davey, J.A., 2007. Older people and transport: coping without a car. Ageing Soc. 27, 49–65.

Dodson, J., Sipe, N., 2007. Oil vulnerability in the Australian city: assessing socioeconomic risks from higher urban fuel prices. Urban Stud. 44, 37–62.

Farrington, J., Farrington, C., 2005. Rural accessibility, social inclusion and social justice: towards conceptualisation. J. Transp. Geogr. 13, 1–12.

Favell, A., 2011. Eurostars and Eurocities: Free Movement and Mobility in an Integrating Europe. John Wiley & Sons.

Franklin, R.S., van Leeuwen, E.S., 2018. For whom the bells toll: Alonso and a regional science of decline. Int. Reg. Sci. Rev. 41, 134–151.

Ganning, J.P., Tighe, J.R., 2018. Moving toward a shared understanding of the US shrinking City. J. Plan. Educ. Res. https://doi.org/10.1177/0739456X18772074.

Gerland, P., Raftery, A.E., Ševčíková, H., Li, N., Gu, D., Spoorenberg, T., Alkema, L., Fosdick, B.K., Chunn, J., Lalic, N., Bay, G., Buettner, T., Heilig, G.K., Wilmoth, J., 2014. World population stabilization unlikely this century. Science 346, 234.

Howe, S.R., Allor, D., Bier, T., Finnerty, T., Green, P., 1998. The shrinking central city amidst growing suburbs: case studies of Ohio's inelastic cities. Urban Geogr. 19, 714–734.

Jacobsen, N.L.S., 2004. From depopulation to repopulation: the shift of population development in central city areas. In: Marchettini, N., Brebbia, C.A., Tiezzi, E., Wadhwa, L.C. (Eds.), Sustainable City III: Urban Regeneration and Sustainability. WIT Press, United Kingdom, pp. 379–390.

Knight, J., Weaver, R., Jones, P., 2018. Walkable and resurgent for whom? The uneven geographies of walkability in Buffalo, NY. Appl. Geogr. 92, 1–11.

Kwan, M.-P., Ren, F., 2008. Analysis of human space-time behavior: geovisualization and geocomputational approaches. In: Hornsby, K.S., Yuan, M. (Eds.), Understanding Dynamics of Geographic Domains. CRC Press, New York, pp. 93–113.

Lee, J.S., Won, S., Kim, S., 2016. Describing changes in the built environment of shrinking cities: case study of Incheon, South Korea. J. Urban Plann. Dev. 142.

Leichenko, R.M., Solecki, W.D., 2005. Exporting the American dream: the globalization of suburban consumption landscapes. Reg. Stud. 39, 241–253.

Lucas, K., 2006. Providing transport for social inclusion within a framework for environmental justice in the UK. Transp. Res. A Policy Pract. 40, 801–809.

Lucas, K., 2011. Making the connections between transport disadvantage and the social exclusion of low income populations in the Tshwane region of South Africa. J. Transp. Geogr. 19, 1320–1334.

Mattioli, G., Wadud, Z., Lucas, K., 2018. Vulnerability to fuel price increases in the UK: a household level analysis. Transp. Res. A Policy Pract. 113, 227–242.

McArthur, D.P., Thorsen, I., Uboe, J., 2014. Employment, transport infrastructure, and rural depopulation: a new spatial equilibrium model. Environ Plan A 46, 1652–1665.

Musil, J., Muller, J., 2008. Inner peripheries of the Czech Republic as a mechanism of social exclusion. Soc. Casework 44, 321–348.

Newbold, K.B., Scott, D.M., 2017. Driving over the life course: the automobility of Canada's millennial, generation X, baby boomer and greatest generations. Travel Behav. Soc. 6, 57–63.

Osti, G., 2010. Mobility demands and participation in remote rural areas. Sociol. Rural. 50, 296–310.

Páez, A., Mercado, R.G., Farber, S., Morency, C., Roorda, M., 2009. Mobility and Social Exclusion in Canadian Communities: An Empirical Investigation of Opportunity Access and Deprivation. Report to Policy Research Directorate, Strategic Policy and Research, Human Resources and Social Development Canada.

Shapiro, D., Pearlmutter, D., Schwartz, M., 2012. The emergence of rural transport strategies in response to rising fuel costs. Energy Policy 44, 92–100.

Silhan, Z., Svobodova, H., Binek, J., 2017. Shrinking City Ceska Lipa—Is Strategic Planning a Tool Against Shrinking? https://doi.org/10.5817/CZ.MUNI.P210-8587-2017-68.

Šťastná, M., Vaishar, A., Stonawská, K., 2015. Integrated transport system of the south-Moravian region and its impact on rural development. Transp. Res. Part D: Transp. Environ. 36, 53–64.

Stanley, J., Lucas, K., 2009. Special issue of the journal of transport policy focusing on international perspectives on transport and social exclusion. Transp. Policy 16, 89.

Theobald, D.M., 2005. Landscape patterns of exurban growth in the USA from 1980 to 2020. Ecol. Soc. 10.

Tighe, J.R., Ganning, J.P., 2016. Do shrinking cities allow redevelopment without displacement? An analysis of affordability based on housing and transportation costs for redeveloping, declining, and stable neighborhoods. Hous. Policy Debate 26, 785–800.

United Nations, 1980. Patterns of Urban and Rural Population Growth. United Nations.
Urrecho, J.M.D., Fernandez, L.C.M., 2016. On-Demand-Transport as Alternative Mobility System in Low Density Areas: The Case of Castilla and Leon. Boletin De La Asociacion De Geografos Espanoles. pp. 195–220.
Wiersma, J., Bertolini, L., Straatemeier, T., 2017. Adapting spatial conditions to reduce car dependency in mid-sized 'post growth' European city regions: the case of South Limburg, Netherlands. Transp. Policy 55, 62–69.
Yagi, M., Managi, S., 2016. Demographic determinants of car ownership in Japan. Transp. Policy 50, 37–53.
Yang, C.J., 2009. An impending platinum crisis and its implications for the future of the automobile. Energy Policy 37, 1805–1808.
Zakharenko, R., 2016. Self-driving cars will change cities. Reg. Sci. Urban Econ. 61, 26–37.

CHAPTER TWO

Air transport accessibility changes in depopulating European states

Aisling Reynolds-Feighan*
University College Dublin, Ireland
*Corresponding author: e-mail address: aisling.reynolds@ucd.ie

Contents

Abstract

This chapter examines air transport access for depopulating states in the European Union. Air transport can offer a relatively low cost transport and high speed access solution to communities and regions. It is a flexible and responsive transport mode which can be easily tailored to changing demand conditions. The drivers of variability in access by air for depopulating states are the focus of this chapter. Air services changes and population changes are related for the EU states and the characteristics of those experiencing depopulation are detailed. Extensive use is made of the rich *Official Airline Guide* (OAG) air traffic databases to trace the evolution of air service developments. It is shown that Europe's depopulating states for the most part have seen increased incomes and substantially increased levels of air access. Typically the air transport services are dominated by low cost carriers with destinations often influenced by the locations of migrant populations. The freedom of movement of the populations in these states

Advances in Transport Policy and Planning, Volume 2
ISSN 2543-0009
https://doi.org/10.1016/bs.atpp.2018.09.002

has resulted in an overall westward shift in the population and this is reflected in the westward orientation of the air route networks of many Central European states since their accession to the EU.

Keywords: Air transport, Accessibility, EU depopulated states

1. Introduction

This chapter will focus on the trends, role and impact of air transport in communities and countries experiencing depopulation in the European Union. Air transport plays a vital role in facilitating access to and between regions, and in enabling the mobility of populations. Air transport networks make possible movement of people and freight at a variety of spatial scales and have been essential elements in the globalization of supply chains. In Europe, air transport has played a key role in facilitating the realization of the overarching European Union goals of enabling the "four freedoms": freedom of movement of labor, goods, services and capital. Most of the literature examining the role and impact of air transport has focused implicitly on the growth-promoting effects, as air transport has been the fastest growing transport mode in the last 50 years.

According to Airbus, air traffic in 2017 (as measured by revenue passenger kilometers (RPK) globally) has doubled since 2011 (Airbus, 2018). Air traffic growth and economic growth are closely linked, with GDP being the most important driver of long term trends (see, for example, Button and Yuan, 2013; Button et al., 1999; Chevallier et al., 2011; Hakim and Merkert, 2016; Ishutkina and Hansman, 2009). There is some debate however over the direction of causality. Private consumption, employment, the size of the middle class population, total population and the degree of urbanization are also important factors explaining differential patterns of air traffic among countries and continental regions. When depopulation is experienced, it might be reasonable to expect that air traffic levels might fall, though if the depopulation has been driven largely by emigration, this may generate air traffic demand between host and receiving countries and communities. This chapter aims to explore the role and impacts of air transport in shrinking states in the European Union.

The history of air transport development demonstrates an early appreciation by individual countries of the strategic importance and benefits that this newly emerging 20th century mode of transport could offer. Governments were heavily involved in setting up airlines and developing airport and navigational infrastructure to support the development of air services from the 1920s and 1930s. The early air transport networks grew from the capital cities or largest cities and connected with other states via routes negotiated by governments and set out in bilateral air service agreements. Historical political and economic relationships, migration flows as well as financial resources and national ambitions drove the growth and scale of international air services between nations. In Europe, each state developed a national airline and funded the long-term growth and development of scheduled air transportation, as well as establishing a legal framework for the standardization and operation of international air transport through participation in the International Civil Aviation Organization (ICAO).[1] In analyzing the development of air transport services and operations, the appropriate scale of analysis is at the nation state level: air transport operations (carrier registrations, aircraft registrations, air space management, navigational services, airport developments, etc.) have been regulated and negotiated by each state.

Depopulation has become a significant feature of population dynamics worldwide in the 21st century, with an expected 43 countries set to experience shrinkage in population terms by 2050 (United Nations, 2015). Within countries, rural migration and depopulation have been fueling the growing rates of urbanization. Rural depopulation and regional population decline are usually observed before national population declines are recorded (McMillan, 2016). In Europe, Eurostat report that 505 of the 1342 NUTS3[2] regions showed population decline between 2015 and 2016, with a strong capital city/urban region—rural region split; urban regions generally showed increases in population, while peripheral, rural and post-industrial regions were more likely to have experienced population decline. Surface transportation systems will facilitate interregional movements between contiguous regions. Air transport becomes the dominant option when distances exceed the range of surface transport thresholds. In this chapter, the focus will be on national level analysis rather than regional analysis in order to examine the relationship between air transport evolution and negative population change.

1 ICAO is a UN agency founded in 1944 and charged with regulating and coordinating international air transportation. ICAO was established through the Convention on International Civil Aviation (also known as the Chicago Convention) which set out as a starting point, recognition that each state had complete and exclusive sovereignty over the airspace above its territory.

2 NUTS3 is the EU's hierarchical and exhaustive nomenclature of territorial units for the purposes of recording and reporting statistical data at different spatial scales.

The chapter is organized as follows. Section 2 outlines the development and key characteristics of air transport and summarizes experiences in Europe in the last 50 years. Section 3 examines depopulation and gives some general background on the European Union and its recent economic experiences. Section 4 examines and analyses depopulation at the national level in the EU. Member states with shrinking populations are identified, characterized and analyzed in terms of their air transport experiences in the last 20 years. Airports in these states are identified and traffic patterns (growth, airlines, seasonality, etc.) are described for the period 2006–2017. Section 5 draws some general conclusions and discusses the positive impacts that air transport activity can have on depopulated regions and states. Some suggested further research is also outlined.

2. Development and key characteristics of air transport

Air transportation has been an important contributing factor in the development and growth of national and regional economies and has an important strategic role nationally and internationally for nation states. Air transport can provide a relatively low cost transport solution and facilitate high speed access to peripheral regions and communities. For large countries, air transport can provide political, economic and social cohesion through the facilitation of higher levels of interaction compared to surface transport modes. Air transport has undergone processes of deregulation in national markets or liberalization in international markets and this has enabled rapid growth of air passenger and freight services particularly in the last 20 years. In Europe, the Single European Market required the liberalization of air service agreements in order to achieve the goals of free movement of people and of goods and services.

Access to air transport networks is important for economic growth and development, though establishing causal linkages is difficult because air transport is typically one of a suite of ingredients necessary to enable and sustain economic activities, particularly higher yield activities (Button et al., 1999; Mukkala and Tervo, 2013). Passenger air transport activity, as measured by departure movements, has grown at an annual average rate of 3.2% throughout the 1996–2017 period, and a 3.4% annual average growth in available seats, despite two major global recessions in 2001/2 and 2008–2010. Asia has been the fastest growing region in the recent period and is forecast to continue growing at a faster pace than other major global regions, and as a result, increasing its share of global air traffic. European air traffic grew rapidly during the early 2000s, but growth rates have slowed in the post-2010 period with Europe maintaining a 22–23% share of global air traffic (as measured by departure movements and seating capacity) in 2017. The North American share of global traffic fell steadily following the 2001/2 recession, with American airlines cutting capacity and facilitating traffic growth through better management of existing capacity. The result of this process in the USA was a gradual improvement in load factors and increase in the total number of passengers carried despite reductions in departure movements. In the period since 2012, North American air traffic has expanded substantially in terms of the number of communities served, the numbers of departure movements and available seating capacity.

In the early days of air transport, governments saw the strategic importance and potential of this new 20th century mode of transport and, in most instances, established state-owned airlines to develop scheduled air services. One of the impacts of more liberalized air transport markets has been the long term reduction in the total number of airlines serving the major continental markets. Liberalization has also led to the privatization of government owned carriers. Consolidation and bankruptcies have reduced the number of airlines and resulted in an industry with a small number of very large carriers in North America. In Europe too, there has been considerable consolidation activity during the 2010s, along with the privatization of most of the remaining state-owned airlines. These carriers make important decisions regarding where to fly and the levels of air service to provide on a monthly basis. The decisions by carriers have substantial impacts and consequences for communities of all sizes as community accessibility and the mobility of people and goods in regions can be positively or negatively affected. In this chapter where the focus is on depopulated communities and nations, the role and impact of air transport are examined in light of the problems facing these places. Some general conclusions are drawn to highlight the continued strategic importance of airlines and air transport on the economic wellbeing of communities at varying spatial scales.

The two major aircraft manufacturers, Airbus and Boeing, produce regular global industry forecasts of air traffic activity for a 25–30 year period. The Airbus forecast detailed an econometric model calibrating the basis for air traffic growth by region based on a number of key drivers (Airbus Industries, 2016). The main drivers of air traffic activity are

- Economic growth
- Degree and rate of increase of urbanization and growth of mega-cities (i.e., cities with >10,000 daily long-haul passengers)
- Size and rate of expansion of the middle class

- Rate of growth of international students, migration and tourism
- Trade
- Liberalization and bilateral air service agreements

The propensity to travel will depend on incomes and rates of private consumption which will be higher in countries with a growing middle class (typically defined as households with annual incomes of $20,000–150,000). Geography is also an important influencing factor, with islands and more peripheral locations generally having higher than average air transport activity levels.[3] High speed rail networks are expensive and take many years to build but have been competing with air transport where they have been constructed. Many short-haul air transport routes that would have been important in the 1970s and 1980s have seen substantial falls in air traffic as high speed rail networks have come on stream. For example, London-Paris was consistently ranked as the world's busiest international air route until the Channel Tunnel rail link was opened in 1994.

Air carriers can easily change their networks by adding or cutting air routes as demand conditions change. In liberalized markets, air carriers will be very sensitive to changing market conditions and each quarter decide on the schedule of air services to provide for the next 6 months. These air schedules are commitments to offer air services at specific times and places and with specific aircraft deployed. The available seats are then sold to the public directly via Internet portals or through sales and travel agents. The airlines will be acutely responsive to changes in the air traffic drivers and if sales are below expectations, the air services may be canceled, reduced or see capacity reductions in the form of equipment downgrades (where the airline uses multiple aircraft types). These factors will be examined in relation to the European Union in the next sections.

3. European Union characteristics and the identification of depopulating places

The EU28[4] states vary considerably in every measurable dimension across geography, economy and society: Figs. 1 and 2 capture two summary

[3] Indeed Mukkala and Tervo (2013) demonstrate that there is a causal relationship between air traffic and regional growth in peripheral regions, though this link is less evident in more central or core regions.

[4] The European Union (EU) has expanded significantly since 2000, and in 2018 consisted of 28 member states and over 510 million people. In 2004, the largest expansion of the European Union took place. The number of states grew from 15 to 25 with the accession of 10 new member states, 8 of whom were Central European and former USSR countries. In 2007, Bulgaria and Romania joined, followed by Croatia in 2013.

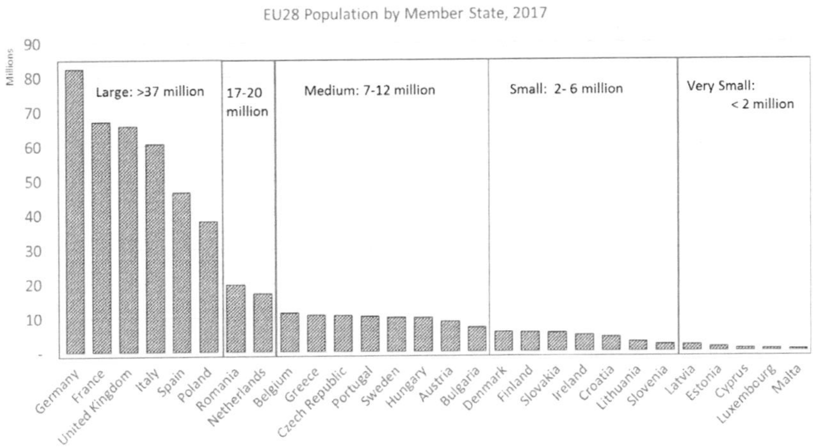

Fig. 1 EU28 state populations in 2017. *Eurostat population estimates 2017 (data series code: tps00001).*

measures to demonstrate this. In Fig. 1, the total population of each EU state is illustrated for 2017. The states are divided into groupings, with 6 large states (Germany, France, UK, Italy, Spain and Poland) with populations in excess of 37 million persons; Romania and the Netherlands have populations of 17–19.5 million; 10 medium-sized states having populations of between 7 and 12 million persons; 7 small states with populations of between 2 and 6 million; and 5 very small states with populations of less than 2 million persons.

Population change occurs because of natural increase (the difference between the birth rate and death rate) and net migration (the difference between immigration and emigration). Depopulation occurs when population change is negative and this can occur because of negative natural increase, negative net migration or both. In this chapter, depopulation will be defined as a sustained decrease in population over a 10-year period. The focus will be at the member state level.

EU membership conferred rights on the citizens of the new member states enabling them to migrate to where economic opportunities and living standards were superior. Labor force migration has been a feature of recent dynamics in the EU28, but migration also takes place for family and social reasons (Benton and Petrovic, 2013). Strong national identity and family networks and relationships before and after relocation generate travel demand requirements that have evolved in tandem with migration flows (Castro-Martín and Cortina, 2015). These relations will be explored in some

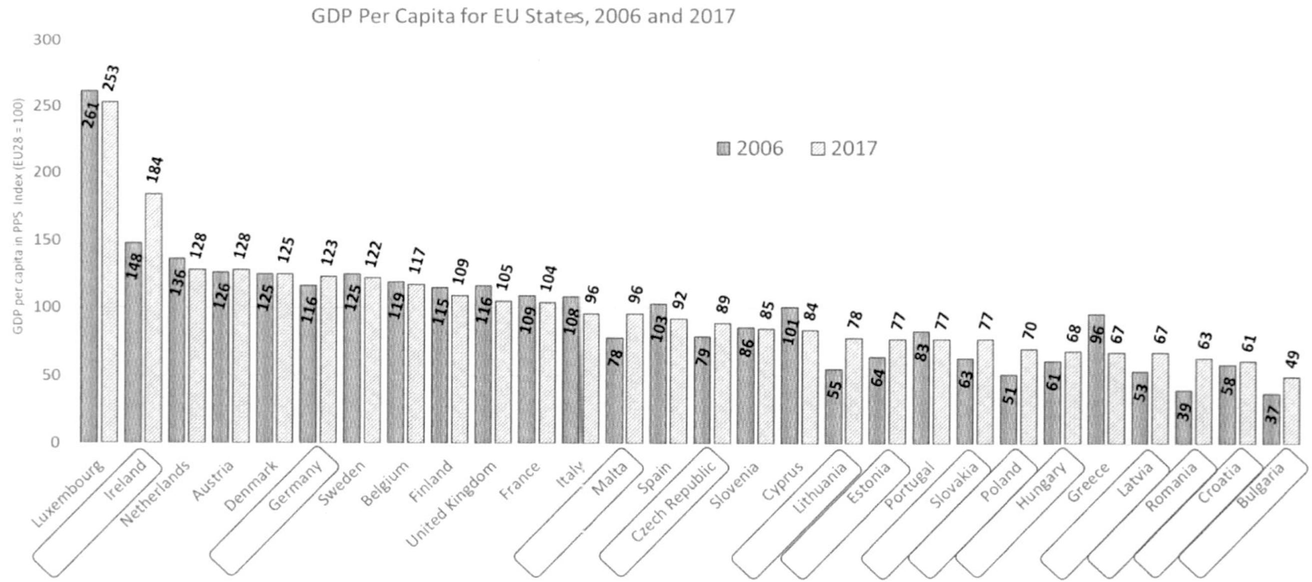

Fig. 2 EU28 state purchasing power adjusted Gross Domestic Product (GDP) per head of population, 2006–2017. *Eurostat data series code: sdg_10_10.*

detail in the next section. Data from the EU member state statistical agencies and from the United Nations Economic and Social Division are examined in order to better understand the potential interactions generated between member states resulting from migration.

Fig. 2 illustrates the variability of gross domestic product per capita (purchasing power of parity adjusted) in 2006 and 2017 across the EU28 states. These data are drawn from the Eurostat databases and indexed to the EU28 average in each year, which has a value of 100. The states that have seen an increase in GDP per capita are highlighted and mostly occur toward the lower end of the distribution. Ireland and Germany are the only two member states that had higher than EU-average GDP per capita in 2006 *and* have seen an increase since the Great Recession of 2008–2010. Eleven of the 13 post-2004 accession member states have seen an increase in GDP per capita, the exceptions being the Slovenia (which saw a 1-point drop) and Cyprus (17-point drop). Substantial investments through the EU's regional policies have focused on the particular set of problems and issues facing the poorer EU states and these policies are targeted at sub-national level. Policies are also in place to address labor market problems (see, for example, Bachtler et al., 2016; Giordano and Dubois, 2018).

In order to achieve the overarching EU goals of freedom of movement of people, goods, services and capital, significant reform and harmonization of European transportation systems needed to take place by 1993 when the Single European Market came into effect. Air transport was liberalized in the period from 1987 to 1997 through a series of policy changes agreed by the then 15 member states and gradually expanded to govern the single European air transport market for 36 countries.[5] This liberalization process radically changed the way in which European air transport operated.

Prior to 1993, Europe's air transport was governed by an extensive system of bilateral air service agreements between member states that set out (and restricted) which airlines could fly, where they could fly and the prices that they could charge. Because of the small size of most European countries,

[5] The European Common Aviation Area (ECAA) was an agreement negotiated between the European Union and several non-member states during the period 2005–2008. The agreement integrated the neighboring states into the EU's internal aviation market, with the full application of the EU's aviation law and uniform application of rules relating to safety and security (see European Union Decision 2006/682/EC, Official Journal of the European Union, 16th October 2006L285/1. Accessed July 2018 at https://eur-lex.europa.eu/LexUriServ/LexUriServ.do?uri=OJ:L:2006:285:0001:0002:EN:PDF).

air transport was largely international, with only Germany, France, the UK and Italy having significant domestic air route networks. Typically, state-owned national carriers were the only carriers designated to operate on international routes, so the scope for privately owned carriers to develop commercially viable networks was limited. The liberalization of European air transport essentially created a large domestic market with free entry and exit to the industry and to individual markets, and complete pricing freedom for carriers. Summary air transport indicators for the EU28 member states are presented in Table 1.

Table 1 shows the very strong growth in air transport since the completion of the liberalization process in 1997. The largest countries in terms of population are also the countries with the largest volumes of air traffic, though in a slightly different order, namely UK, Germany, Spain, France and Italy. The post-2004 accession member states have seen the strongest growth rates, although Ireland and Spain also saw more than doubling of seating capacity in the period 1996–2006. The next section further explores the relationships between air traffic drivers and population, particularly focusing on the depopulating states.

4. European Union depopulation and air transport

EU membership had a dramatic impact on air transport activity in several of the post-2004 entry states, with rapid expansion of air services as illustrated in Fig. 3. In the figure, the change in air traffic between 1996 and 2003 can be seen to be relatively flat for all of the post-2004 Central European member states, with increases thereafter. Poland, Romania, Hungary and the Czech Republic saw at least a doubling of air traffic capacity between 2003 and 2017. Estonia, Latvia, Slovakia and Slovenia saw smaller increases in traffic over the same period, with Slovakia actually experiencing a decrease in air traffic capacity between 2008 and 2017, although as Table 1 shows, this state had experienced dramatic growth in the 1996–2006 period.

The population changes over the period 2006–2017 were compared with the air traffic changes and these are illustrated in Fig. 4.[6] The data are again drawn from the Eurostat and OAG databases. The figure shows

[6] 2006 was selected as the last full year before the financial crisis and ensuing recession, and 2017 as the latest year for which data were available.

Table 1 EU28 air traffic statistics for 1996, 2006 and 2017.

EU state	Total number of available departure seats on non-stop routes			Growth rates (%)		Departure movements, 2017	Number of airports	
	1996	2006	2017	1996–2006	2006–2017		1996	2017
Austria	7,645,273	11,836,950	17,151,194	55	45	107,645	6	6
Belgium	10,560,638	11,454,672	20,122,912	8	76	124,818	3	5
Bulgaria	1,009,626	2,008,713	5,728,044	99	185	34,196	3	4
Croatia	915,369	2,229,360	4,892,527	144	119	30,589	5	9
Cyprus	2,445,950	3,799,395	7,573,986	55	99	41,954	3	3
Czech Republic	2,045,462	6,527,225	8,989,000	219	38	54,307	1	5
Denmark	11,730,688	12,459,651	19,736,522	6	58	123,798	7	7
Estonia	335,460	773,502	1,331,724	131	72	12,545	1	1
Finland	6,360,095	9,346,446	12,280,422	47	31	73,673	15	19
France	66,937,425	84,713,486	104,256,933	27	23	622,416	36	50
Germany	75,463,117	113,172,248	146,798,006	50	30	875,860	24	31
Greece	9,846,020	16,222,636	27,181,603	65	68	151,184	17	27
Hungary	2,621,611	5,578,120	7,457,869	113	34	41,593	1	3
Ireland	7,046,865	16,931,738	18,378,310	140	9	100,224	5	5
Italy	48,066,635	78,280,715	103,165,331	63	32	618,213	30	35

Continued

Table 1 EU28 air traffic statistics for 1996, 2006 and 2017.—cont'd

EU state	Total number of available departure seats on non-stop routes			Growth rates (%)		Departure movements, 2017	Number of airports	
	1996	2006	2017	1996–2006	2006–2017		1996	2017
Latvia	474,190	1,604,502	2,192,935	238	37	15,064	1	1
Lithuania	467,299	744,691	2,769,106	59	272	18,383	3	3
Luxembourg	776,671	1,148,722	1,685,771	48	47	12,388	1	1
Malta	1,182,366	1,401,151	3,522,972	19	151	19,755	1	1
Netherlands	17,275,954	26,805,308	42,774,353	55	60	251,526	3	5
Poland	2,351,071	8,271,435	19,552,753	252	136	127,153	4	14
Portugal	8,738,641	14,786,036	28,567,256	69	93	164,373	9	10
Romania	1,375,850	3,077,998	11,880,203	124	286	72,465	5	12
Slovakia	93,655	1,373,481	1,233,444	1367	−10	6857	2	4
Slovenia	429,087	868,658	1,011,340	102	16	10,004	1	1
Spain	49,880,912	100,846,068	136,230,118	102	35	764,973	34	38
Sweden	17,371,088	17,490,114	26,080,873	1	49	169,921	23	26
UK	73,784,649	132,778,286	157,522,118	80	19	867,774	31	36

OAG databases, compiled by the author from OAG databases.

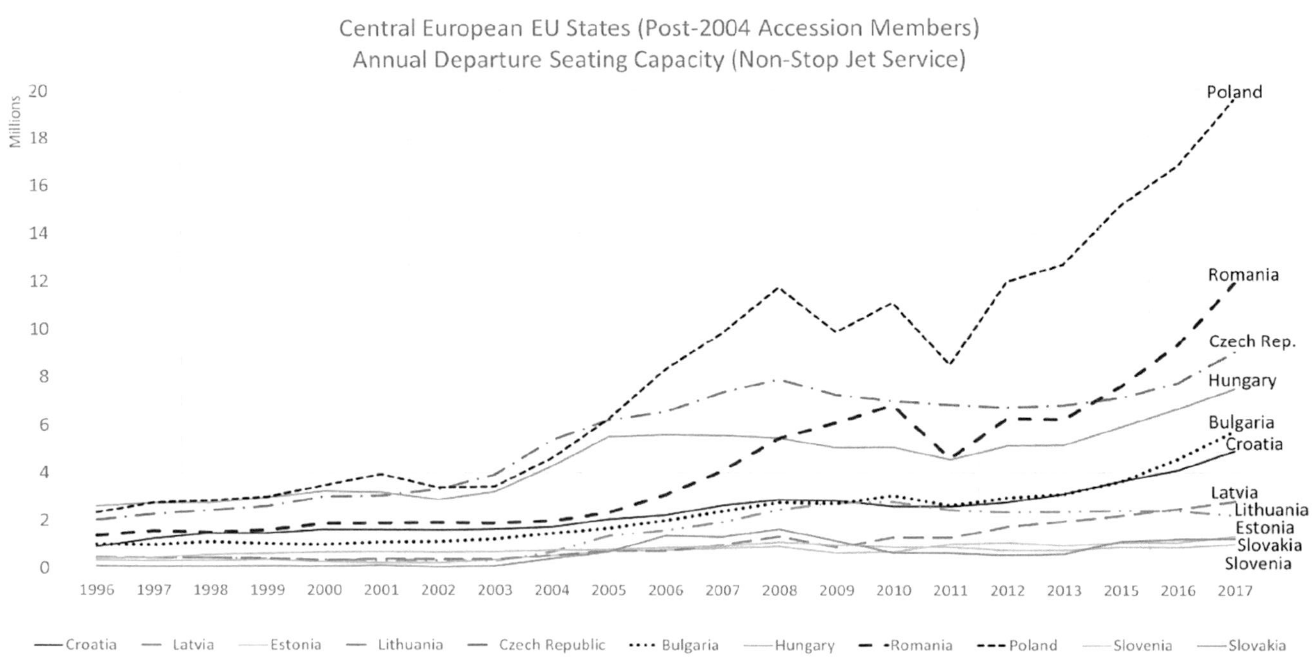

Fig. 3 Air transport activity (as measured by non-stop departing seating capacity) for post-2004 Central European EU states, 1996–2017.

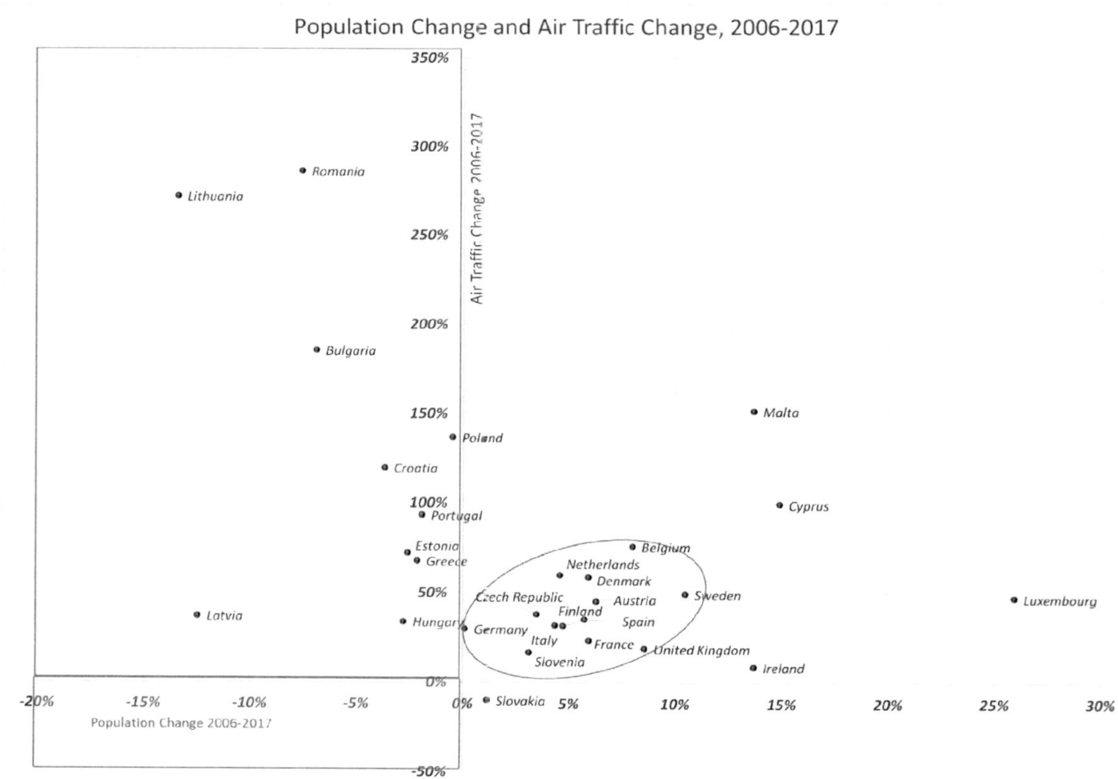

Fig. 4 Population changes and air traffic capacity changes among EU member states 2006–2017.

four quadrants indicating combinations of population change and air traffic change as measured by available departing seating capacity.

Those countries appearing in the upper left quadrant experienced population decline and air traffic increases. No EU state experienced population and air traffic declines (lower left quadrant), with Slovakia being the only member state to experience an air traffic decline over the period (lower right quadrant). Lithuania, Romania and Bulgaria had the largest air traffic increases and were in the top 4 member states experiencing the highest population declines. Poland had a very slight decline in population over the period 2006–2015, with a small population increase between 2016 and 2017. All of the countries in this quadrant except Poland were selected as depopulating states and are examined in more detail to further explore the relationship between air transport and population change.

The clustering of the older EU member states in the upper right quadrant in Fig. 4 is noted indicating smaller levels of population and air traffic increases. The smaller states of Cyprus, Malta, Ireland and Luxembourg saw much larger population increases: relatively small absolute population changes can have a more dramatic effect in these circumstances. Germany had a very low level of population increase over the period 2006–2017 resulting from substantial in-migration as there was a significant negative rate of natural increase.

In order to compare air traffic activity between the new member states and other EU members, the average number of available departure seats per head of population was calculated for four sample years (2005, 2009, 2015 and 2017) and is illustrated in Fig. 5. Population data were drawn from the Eurostat databases, while the air transport activity was collated from OAG daily airline schedules. The figure highlights the clear divide between the post-2004 entrant Central European members and the older western European member states as well as Cyprus and Malta (both of which became members of the EU in 2004). The three island nations of Malta, Cyprus and Ireland have significantly higher traffic volumes per head compared to the other member states reflecting their heavier reliance on air and sea transport to connect to the rest of the EU28 nations. The post 2004-Central European states had very low levels of per capita air traffic in 2004/5 and while these have increased substantially in most cases, they remain significantly lower than the rest of the EU. The expansion observed in Fig. 5 was from a very low air traffic base.

The distribution of air traffic activity across the airports system in the EU is summarized in Table 2. In the table, a hub hierarchy is defined based on

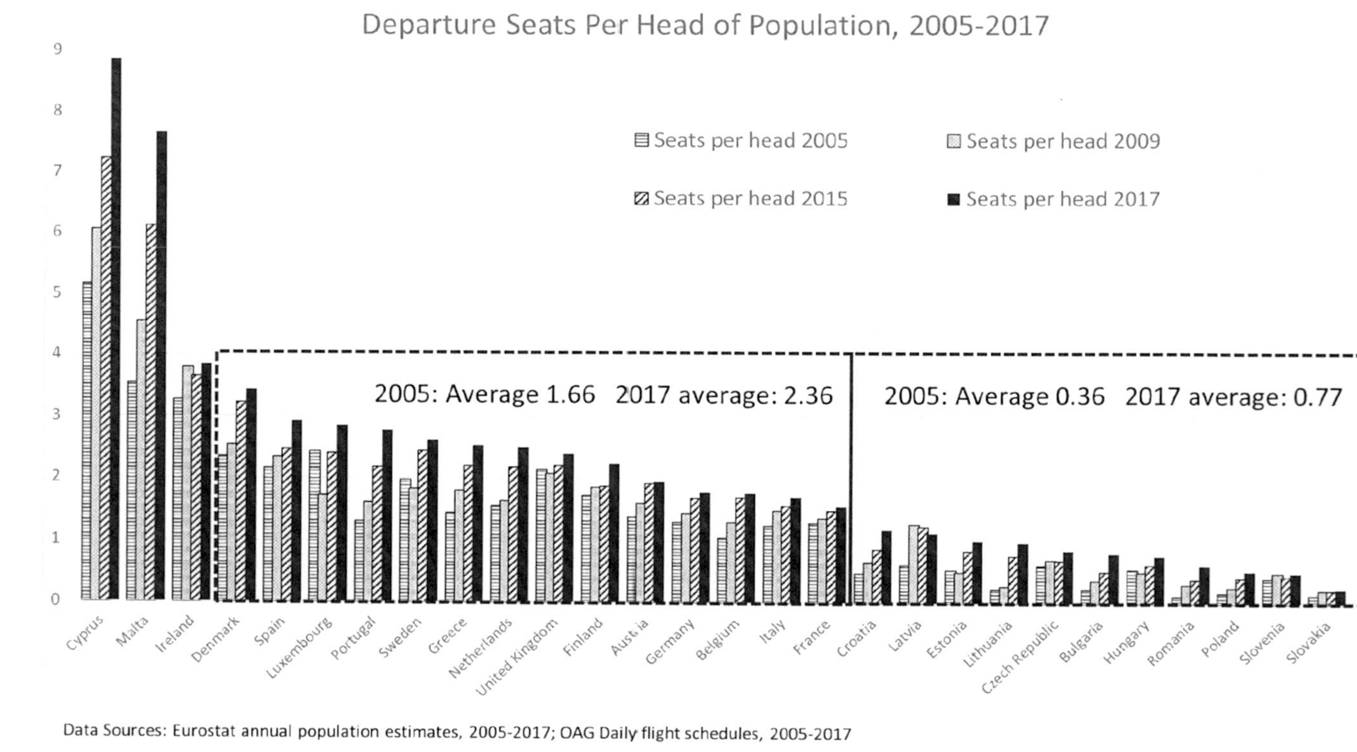

Fig. 5 Per capita available departure seating capacity for EU member states, 2005, 2009, 2015 and 2017.

Table 2 Hub classification scheme for EU member states showing number of each hub type and seasonal Gini Index for available seat capacity in 2017.

	Large hubs		Medium hubs		Small hubs		Non-hubs—Type A		Non-hubs—Type B		Total	
EU state	**Number**	**Gini**	**Number**	**Gini**	**Number**	**Gini**	**Number**	**Gini**	**Number**	**Gini**	**Number**	**Gini**
Austria	1	0.072			3	0.223	1	0.090	1	0.066	6	0.149
Belgium	1	0.069			1	0.314	2	0.183			4	0.187
Bulgaria			1	0.048	2	0.464			1	0.250	4	0.307
Croatia					3	0.367	3	0.401	2	0.205	8	0.339
Cyprus			1	0.180	2	0.138					3	0.152
Czech Republic			1	0.110			2	0.361	2	0.266	5	0.273
Denmark	1	0.048			2	0.099	2	0.133	2	0.239	7	0.141
Estonia					1	0.095					1	0.095
Finland	1	0.034			1	0.068	6	0.209	8	0.394	16	0.282
France	1	0.059	6	0.125	9	0.131	15	0.253	13	0.253	44	0.206
Germany	5	0.100	4	0.108	7	0.115	5	0.238	3	0.370	24	0.168
Greece	1	0.121	2	0.276	7	0.469	6	0.351	9	0.270	25	0.340
Hungary			1	0.073			1	0.107	1	0.240	3	0.140
Ireland	1	0.083			2	0.143	2	0.111			5	0.118
Italy	2	0.070	9	0.120	9	0.183	7	0.175	2	0.264	29	0.159

Continued

Table 2 Hub classification scheme for EU member states showing number of each hub type and seasonal Gini Index for available seat capacity in 2017.—cont'd

	Large hubs		Medium hubs		Small hubs		Non-hubs—Type A		Non-hubs—Type B		Total	
EU state	**Number**	**Gini**	**Number**	**Gini**	**Number**	**Gini**	**Number**	**Gini**	**Number**	**Gini**	**Number**	**Gini**
Latvia			1	0.058							1	0.058
Lithuania					2	0.204	1	0.097			3	0.168
Luxembourg			1	0.095							1	0.095
Malta			1	0.121							1	0.121
The Netherlands	1	0.053	1	0.079	1	0.143	2	0.239			5	0.151
Poland	1	0.081	2	0.065	4	0.068	5	0.089	1	0.121	13	0.081
Portugal	1	0.073	2	0.176	2	0.085	1	0.152	4	0.206	10	0.157
Romania			1	0.058	3	0.065	5	0.148	3	0.125	12	0.114
Slovakia					1	0.192	1	0.198	2	0.187	4	0.191
Slovenia					1	0.092					1	0.092
Spain	4	0.147	9	0.109	12	0.200	5	0.110	7	0.199	37	0.160
Sweden	1	0.102	1	0.062	3	0.076	10	0.101	7	0.273	22	0.151
UK	2	0.096	7	0.115	7	0.138	10	0.109	3	0.110	29	0.116
EU28 total	24	0.092	51	0.117	85	0.187	92	0.188	71	0.251	323	0.183

OAG data; Hubs classes are defined for the EU as follows: large hubs in 2017 had at least 9.4031 million available non-stop departing seats; medium hubs between 2.35078 and 9.4030 million; Small hubs between 470,157 and 2.35077 million; non-hub type A between 500 and 470,156; non-hub type B between 10 and 500.

the percentage of non-stop departing available seats for each community in 2017.[7] Air transport communities may be served by more than one airport, and traffic is combined in these cases. The number of large, medium, small hubs, and of three categories of "non-hubs" are presented in Table 2 for each EU member state. The seasonal Gini coefficient was computed for each airport, and each community and the average score for each hub class and EU state are also included in the table.

The temporal Gini is computed by measuring monthly traffic (measured as either departure movements or available seats) for the year indicated and for each air traffic hub. These are then averaged for hubs in the same class category in each member state and averaged again for all hubs and non-hubs in the state (far right hand side column). The hubs Gini Index scores are adjusted to take account of the number of days per month. If every month has an equal traffic share, the temporal Gini Index takes a value of 0. As the monthly traffic distribution varies, the Gini Index value increases. If all of the traffic takes place in just 1 month, then the Gini Index score will be 1. The Gini Index summarizes the pairwise variability between each month's traffic and every other month's: because there are just 12 month categories, temporal Gini Index scores will be relatively low if there are significant traffic volumes recorded in each month.

Air traffic is highly concentrated in space within the EU, with just 24 large hubs accounting for 64% of all available departing seats. German large hubs account for 12.5% of all available seats, the UK large hubs account for 12%, and Spanish large hubs account for 9%. All but one of the large hubs are in Western Europe, with Poland being the only post-2004 new entrant to have a large air traffic hub. Of the 51 Medium air traffic hubs, only 6 are in the post-2004 entrant member states. The small hubs and non-hubs are widely distributed across the EU, with the highest density occurring in France (44 air traffic communities).

There is a large degree of variation in the extent of seasonality in the air traffic. The large hubs have the lowest average seasonality with Gini Index scores of usually under 0.10. Greek and Spanish large hubs have higher seasonal variability because of the substantial tourism traffic and it can be observed that for the medium hubs also, significantly higher than average seasonal Gini Index scores are associated with major "sun tourism" markets

[7] The hub classification scheme is based on the approach used by the US Federal Aviation Administration (FAA) to classify US air transport communities and allocate funding. Further detail of the scheme and its application in other regions are set out in Reynolds-Feighan (2017).

(Greece, Cyprus and Portugal). Small hubs and non-hubs have higher seasonal Gini Index scores as many of these communities do not have year-round air services. Seasonal Gini Index scores will typically exceed 0.20 when 1 or 2 months have no traffic, or very low levels of traffic compared to the peak months. The relatively low levels of per capita air traffic observed in Fig. 5 are reflected in Table 2 where many of the post-2004 member states have no large or medium hubs (namely Croatia, Estonia, Lithuania, Slovakia and Slovenia). Bulgaria and Romania both have a single medium hub as the largest air traffic community, serving Sofia and Bucharest, respectively.

Tourism traffic is a significant component of air traffic volumes. Where the tourism is dependent on climate, there can be substantial differences between the peak period months and the off-peak or low season. Spain, UK, Italy and France have the largest tourism volumes in the EU as measured by the total number of nights spent at tourist accommodation in 2016. In order to identify those EU states with a high reliance on tourism traffic, Eurostat tourism statistics were computed on a per capita basis and are presented in Fig. 6. The figure shows two indicators: (i) the number of nights spent at tourist accommodation establishments by non-residents per head of population and (ii) the total number of arrivals of residents and non-residents at tourist accommodation establishments per head of population. The two indicators are highly correlated with Malta, Croatia, Cyprus and Austria ranking in the top 4 on both indicators. The indicators help explain some of the variation observed in Fig. 3 but clearly the combined demand for tourism/leisure, business and visiting friends and relatives (VFR) traffics will be country specific.

The air traffic patterns in depopulating EU states were examined in more detail to ascertain the nature of the traffic and connectivity patterns as they have evolved with EU membership. A short summary for each member state is presented and then some general conclusions are drawn.

4.1 Lithuania

Lithuania experienced the largest decrease in population over the period 2006–2017 as illustrated in Fig. 4, recording a 13% decline from 3.29 million in 2006 to 2.85 million in 2017. The rate of decrease was greatest in the 2006–2011 period. The EU report on population change demonstrated that Lithuania's population decline was largely as a result of negative net migration, though supplemented by a relatively low negative rate of natural population change. According to the Lithuanian Statistics Office, the top 5 host countries for Lithuanian emigrants were the UK, Norway, Germany,

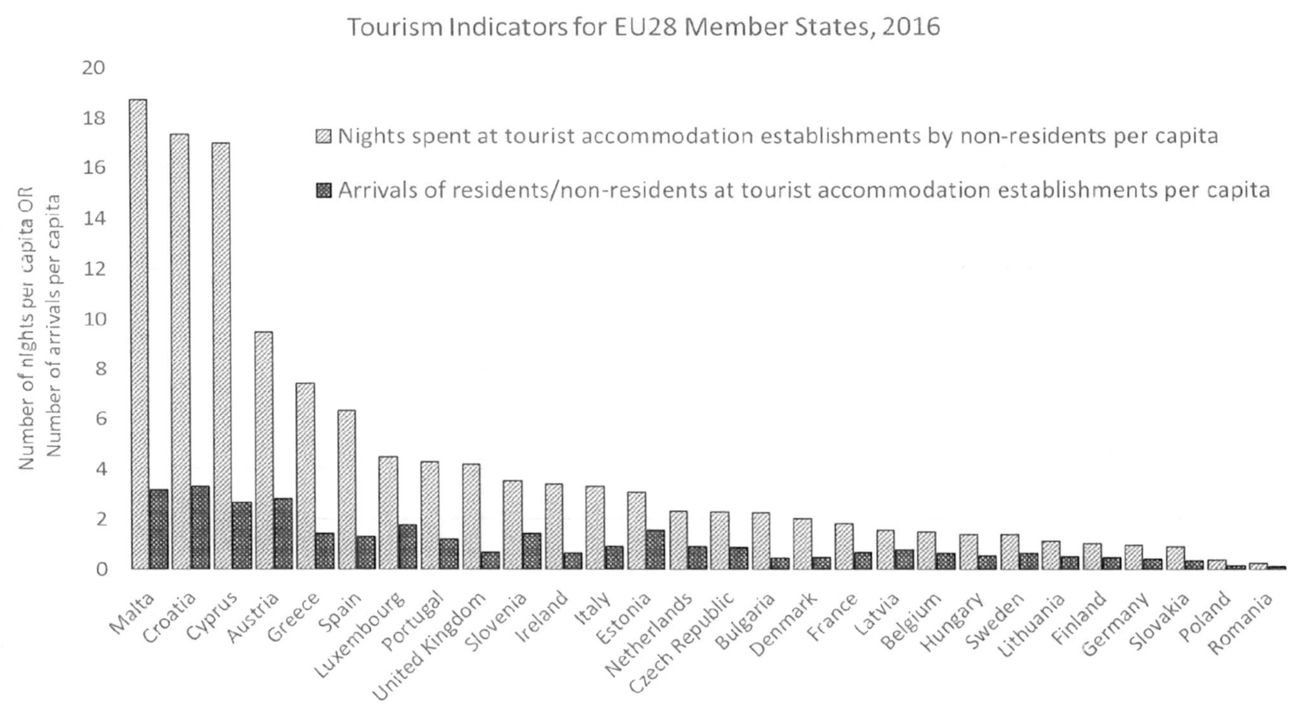

Fig. 6 Tourism indicators for EU Member states in 2016. *Source: Eurostat.*

Ireland and Denmark and this is reflected in the top air transport destinations. Air service routes operating to and from Lithuania in 2000 and in 2017 are illustrated in Fig. 7, along with data giving the share of seats and number of departure movements in 2017.

Lithuanian Airlines and Air Lithuania were the largest carriers in 1996 with 82% of all departures. These airlines expanded air services westwards after Lithuania's independence from the Soviet Union in 1991. Both of these state-owned airlines ceased operations during the 2000s as they had faced strong competition from non-Lithuanian carriers, particularly low-cost operators. In 2017, Ryanair (Irish) and Wizz Air (Hungarian) were the two largest carriers with 25% and 22% of traffic, respectively. No Lithuanian-registered carriers were among the 19 airlines operating in 2017. The reduction in the cost of travel is an important driver in air traffic growth and the dominance of low cost carriers in the Lithuanian market helps explain the 272% increase in available seating capacity between 2006 and 2017. Lithuania experienced a significant increase in per capita GDP over the period, rising from 55% of the European average in 2006 to 78% of the European average in 2017. The Lithuanian economy had experienced a sharp decline in GDP during the Great Recession, but real GDP has grown at roughly 3% per year since 2011.

The low costs carriers rely on identifying potential new traffics and can quickly respond to new opportunities to supply air services when they see demand. The new air services from Lithuania to the destination countries listed in the table accompanying Fig. 7 reflect demand generated from the migrant population, as well as links to the main western European capitals.

4.2 Latvia

Latvia experienced a 12% population decline between 2006 and 2017, falling from 2.2 million to 1.95 million, as with Lithuania, largely driven by negative net migration. Over this period, Latvia experienced a 35% increase in air traffic.

UN Population Division data indicate that the top 5 destination countries for Latvian emigrants are Russian Federation, UK, USA, Ireland and Ukraine. Fig. 8 shows the expansion of air transport services from Latvia between 2000 and 2017, along with summary data relating to the top destination countries. UK, Germany and Russia are the three largest destination countries, accounting for 52% of total available seating capacity.

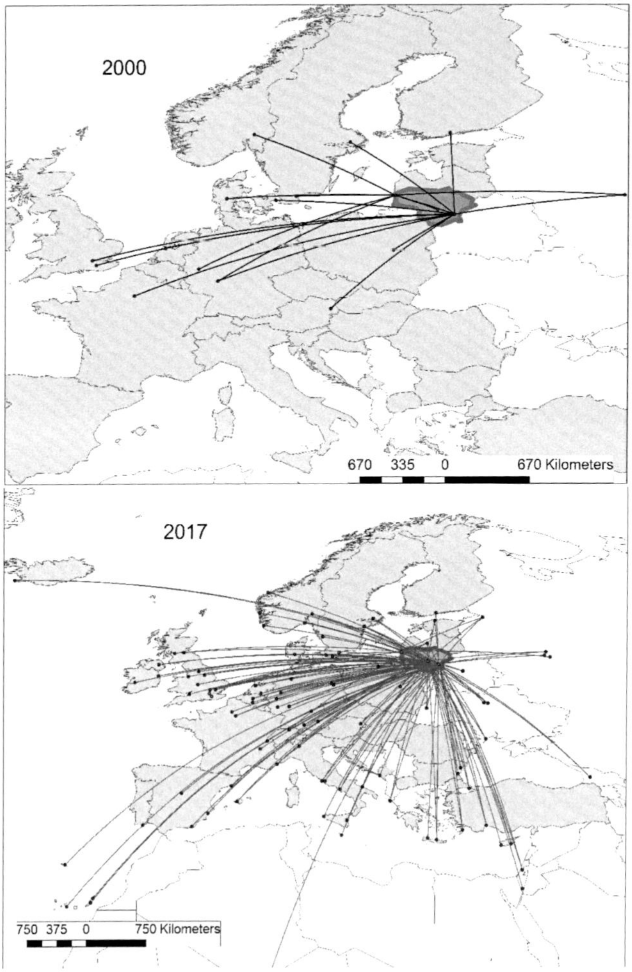

Destination Country from Lithuania in 2017	Share of total available non-stop departure seats	Non-stop departure movements
United Kingdom	21%	3073
Germany	11%	1782
Denmark	8%	1933
Norway	8%	1125
Italy	6%	952
Ukraine	5%	1027
Spain	5%	674

Fig. 7 Air service changes from Lithuania between 2000 and 2017, with top destination traffic shares.

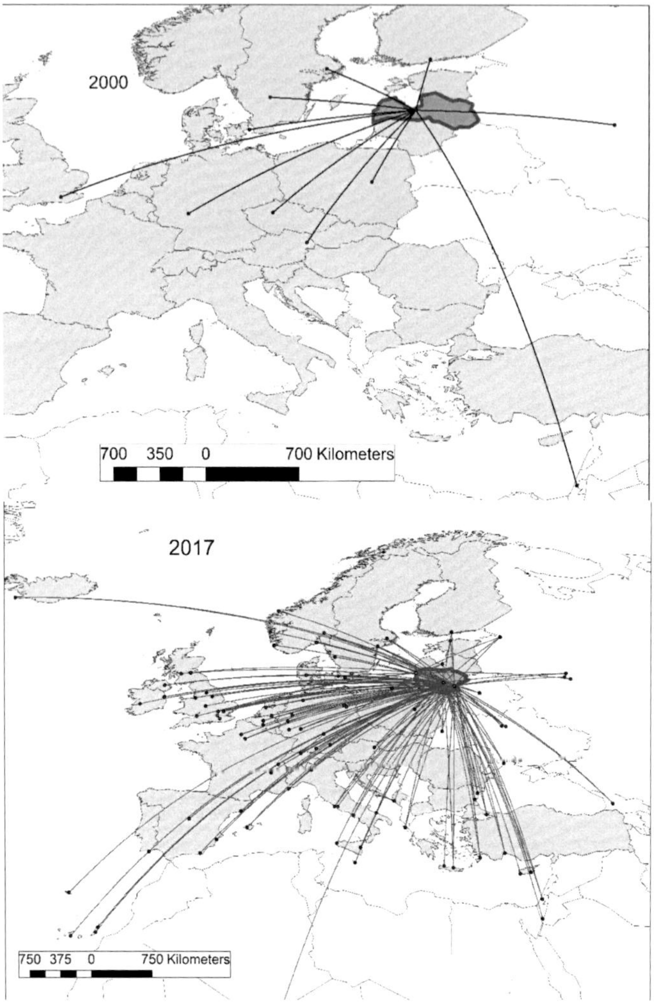

Destination Country from Latvia in 2017	Share of total available non-stop departure seats	Non-stop departure movements
Germany	18%	2503
United Kingdom	18%	2216
Russian Federation	16%	3021
Norway	7%	981
Italy	5%	642
Denmark	4%	717
Ireland Republic of	3%	317

Fig. 8 Air service changes from Latvia between 2000 and 2017, with top destination traffic shares.

The provision of air routes to the leading migrant destinations may be noted from the table accompanying the figure.

Latvian tourism has increased steadily since 2006 as has the country's per capita GDP, rising from 53% of the European average in 2006 to 67% of the European average in 2017.[8] The government-owned Air Baltic was established in the 1990s and has been the largest carrier operating from the state every year since 1996. In 2017, Air Baltic offered 31.7% of all departing seating capacity from Riga Airport (the only airport with commercial air services), with low cost competitors Ryanair and Wizz Air offering 23% and 14%, respectively. While the range of destinations has greatly expanded, service frequency levels are low.

4.3 Romania

Romania's population declined by 8% from 21.5 million in 2006 to 19.6 million in 2017. The population change was driven by a negative rate of natural increase supplemented by a low negative rate of net migration, though this outmigration was considerably higher in the 1990s. UN forecasts suggest that natural decrease will continue in the medium to long term. Romanian air traffic increased by 286% between 2006 and 2017, albeit from a very low base. The top destinations for migrants from Romania according to UN data were Italy, Spain, Germany, Hungary and USA.

The state-owned flag carriers dominated air traffic in the 1990s with the country having direct air services operating to the major European capital cities in 2000, as well as to the USA, Middle East and China (though the US and Chinese services ceased in the 2000s as they were loss-making). The Romanian air route networks in 2000 and in 2017 are illustrated in Fig. 9. With EU membership, air services have expanded and once again the low cost carriers have played a key role in driving this growth particularly westward. The largest carrier in 2017 was Wizz Air with 30% of departure movements, followed by two Romanian carriers Blue Air (22%) and Tarom (17%—state owned) and Ryanair (10.5%). There were 12 airport communities receiving commercial air services in 2017, the largest of which was Bucharest Henri Coandă International Airport (designated as a medium hub in Table 2). Domestic air services are relatively high in Romania, with internal services accounting for

[8] Latvia experienced a substantial drop in GDP during 2008/2009 (−14%), with consistent real GDP growth of 3.5% on average between 2011 and 2017.

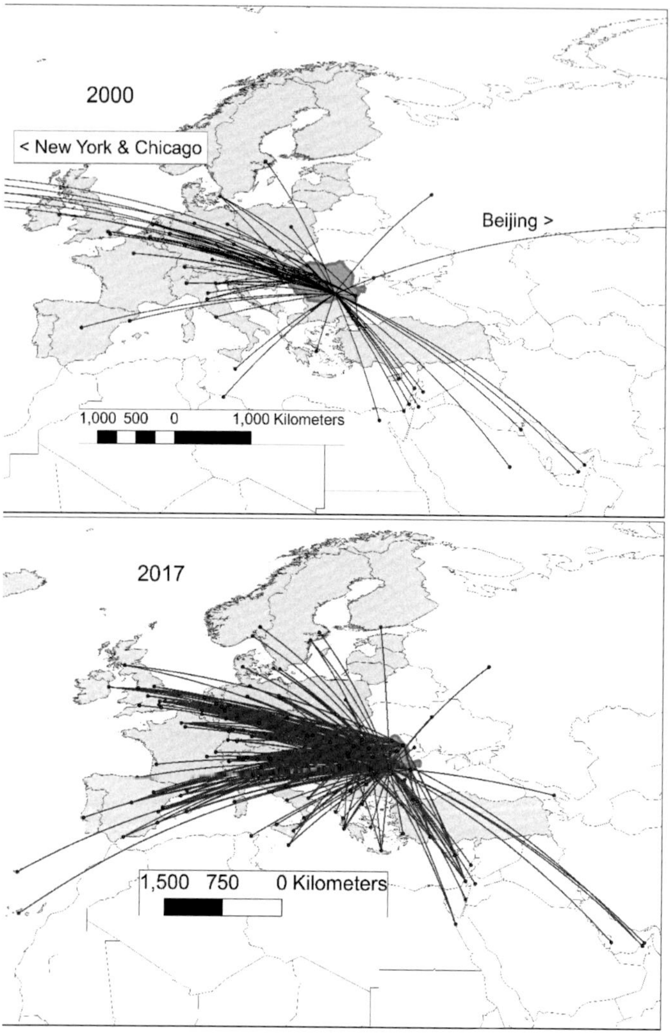

Destination Country from Romania in 2017	Share of total available non-stop departure seats	Non-stop departure movements
Italy	18%	12023
Germany	14%	11143
United Kingdom	14%	8755
Romania	13%	10449
Spain	8%	5518
France	5%	3455
Israel	3%	2433

Fig. 9 Air service changes from Romania between 2000 and 2017, with top destination traffic shares.

13% of total seating capacity in 2017. Romania is the ninth largest EU state by area, with an area of 5100 km^2.

Romania continues to have one of the lowest income levels in the EU: As Fig. 2 indicates, GDP per capita was 39% of the EU average in 2006 and has risen to 63% in 2017.[9] The state is ranked last in both tourism indicators in Fig. 6.

4.4 Bulgaria

Bulgaria suffered a 7% decline in population between 2006 and 2017 (7.63 million to 7.1 million). As with Romania, the population decrease was mainly attributable to negative natural increase, supplemented by negative net migration. The top destinations for migrants were Turkey, Spain, USA, Germany and UK. Surface transport links enable easy access on Bulgaria's southern border to Turkey. Bulgaria has a relatively high degree of urbanization at 74%, equivalent to the average for the European Union. The population density is low at 64 persons per square kilometer.

Between 2006 and 2017, there was a 185% increase in air traffic, with growth focused on Sofia, a medium hub in Table 2. Burgas and Varna, two small hubs, are both located on the Black Sea and 129 km apart (2 hours by road). Burgas had a small route network of five to seven (three to four countries) routes up to 2001 but then saw a substantial expansion after 2004 EU accession. Domestic air services accounted for 7% of total departure seating capacity in 2017, linking the three regional airports with Sofia which is located in the western part of the country. Tourism is important to the economy and Bulgaria's tourism indicators illustrated in Fig. 6 would lie in the mid-range among EU28 states. In terms of income, Bulgaria had the lowest GDP per capita among the EU 28 in 2017: GDP per capita was 37% of the European average in 2006 and had risen to 49% in 2017.

The air route networks for Bulgaria in 2000 and in 2017 are illustrated in Fig. 10, along with summary statistics on the principal destination countries and show a strong western European orientation. The airports in the UK and Germany account for 36% of seating capacity. The government-owned airline Balkan Air was the largest carrier operating in Bulgaria prior to its liquidation in 2002. In 2017, the largest carriers were Wizz Air (24.5% of seating capacity), Bulgaria Air (17%) and Ryanair (14.6%).

[9] Real GDP growth average 5.85% between 2011 and 2017 (Eurostat).

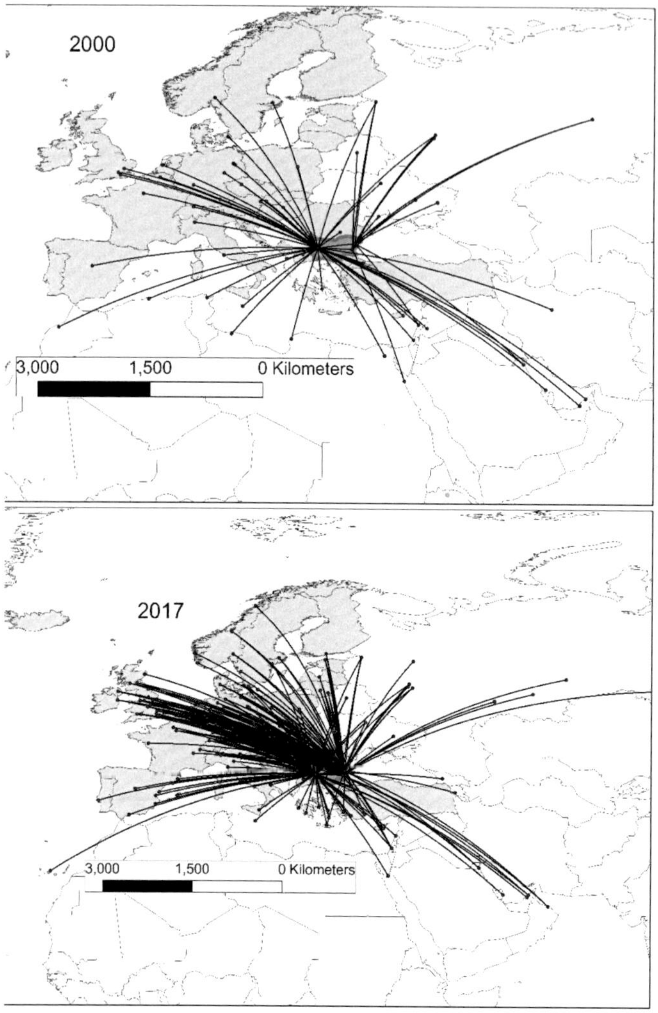

Destination Country from Bulgaria in 2017	Share of total available non-stop departure seats	Non-stop departure movements
United Kingdom	18%	5406
Germany	16%	5391
Italy	9%	2585
Russian Federation	7%	2437
Bulgaria	7%	2835
Spain	5%	1596
Austria	5%	2043

Fig. 10 Air service changes from Bulgaria between 2000 and 2017, with top destination traffic shares.

4.5 Estonia

Estonia experienced a population decline of 3% between 2006 and 2017 falling from 1.35 million to 1.31 million. Estonia has the third lowest population density among the EU28, with just 29 persons per square kilometers and 68% of the population living in urban areas (the EU average is 74%). Along with the other two Baltic nations, Estonia experienced a substantial increase in GDP per capita between 2006 and 2017, despite the great recession, rising from 64% to 77% of the EU28 average. The main destination countries for Estonian emigrants according to UN statistics were Russia, Finland, USA, Ukraine and Sweden, mostly near neighbor countries accessible by surface or maritime transport. The UN forecast is for population decline to continue for the medium to long term as natural change is the main driver of the depopulation rather than net migration.

Estonian air traffic increased by 72% from 2006 to 2017 with all of the traffic routed through the small hub of Tallinn, the state capital. Estonian tourism growth has been strong and steady over the past decade (43% increase in accommodated tourists between 2008 and 2017) and the country is middle-ranked in the tourist statistics presented in Fig. 6. Route network developments are illustrated in Fig. 11 along with summary data showing the main destination countries in 2017. There are a substantial number of direct routes to EU capital cities, Mediterranean resort locations as well as neighboring states.

Given Tallinn's coastal location in the Baltic Sea, ferry services to Finland, Russia and Sweden offer a low cost high frequency alterative to air transport. There are no direct intercontinental connections from Tallinn, so long haul air services are routed through the large hubs in Germany (Frankfurt) and Sweden, and to a lesser extent Amsterdam, London and Paris. The largest EU hubs draw connecting traffic from across many of the smaller EU states that do not have direct air links. During the 1990s and 2000s, the main carrier was the state-owned Estonian Air which ceased operations in 2015 after the EU Commission ruled that state aid given to the airline was illegal under EU competition rules and would need to be repaid.[10] In 2017, the largest carrier was LOT (Polish), offering 30% of seating capacity, followed by the Latvian carrier Air Baltic (11.3%), Lufthansa (11.2%) and low cost carrier Ryanair (9.6%).

[10] See EU case State aid SA.35956 (13/C) (ex 13/NN) (ex 12/N)—Rescue aid to Estonian Air, Official Journal of the European Commission, 29.5.2013 (https://eur-lex.europa.eu/legal-content/EN/TXT/?uri=uriserv:OJ.C_.2013.150.01.0003.01.ENG&toc=OJ:C:2013:150:TOC, accessed August 2018).

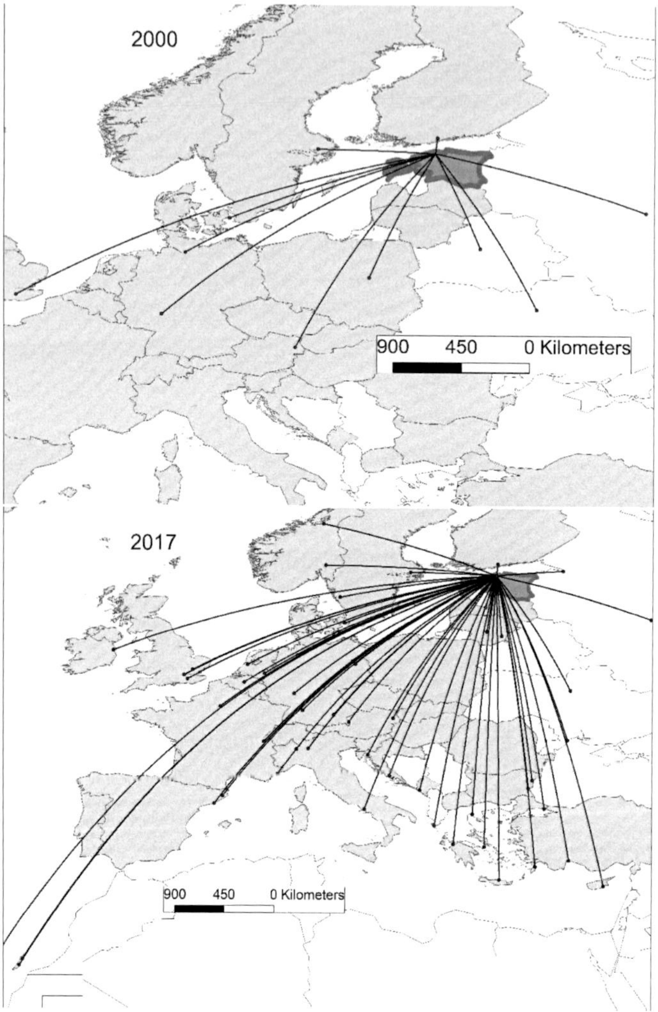

Destination Country from Estonia in 2017	Share of total available non-stop departure seats	Non-stop departure movements
Germany	20%	2110
Sweden	10%	1635
Russian Federation	9%	1298
Norway	7%	928
Netherlands	5%	729
United Kingdom	5%	406
Turkey	5%	391

Fig. 11 Air service changes from Estonia between 2000 and 2017, with top destination traffic shares.

4.6 Croatia

Croatia's population fell from 4.31 million in 2006 to 4.15 million in 2017, a 4% decline with net migration being the primary driver. The main destinations for Croatian migrants were Germany, Serbia, Australia, Slovenia and Canada. There was significant in-migration from Bosnia and Herzegovina up to 2013. Croatia has the second lowest per capita income of the EU28, though this has increased from 58% to 61% of the EU28 average from 2006 to 2017. Croatia has a relatively low population density (73 persons per square kilometer) and low degree of urbanization (59%). The country has an extensive coastline and relies heavily on tourism with over 40 habitable islands. This is reflected in the data displayed in Fig. 6 where Croatia lies first in terms of arrivals by residents and non-residents at tourist accommodations per capita and second after Malta in total nights spent at tourist accommodation by non-residents per capita.

Fig. 12 shows the air route developments between 2006 and 2017 for Croatia, along with summary data on the main destination countries. Air traffic (as measured by available seating capacity) increased by 119% over this period, with departure seating capacity per capita increasing from 0.48 in 2005 to 1.18 in 2017, the highest among the post-2004 new entrant Central European states (Fig. 5). The main airline operating air services to and from Croatia in 2017 continues to be the majority-state-owned Croatia Airlines (IATA Code "OU"), offering 23% of seating capacity. This is followed by several low cost carriers the three largest being Easyjet (10.6%), Eurowings (5.5%) and Ryanair (5.4%). The extensive network of routes shown in Fig. 12 for 2017 operates from eight airports, only three of which are small hubs (Table 2). Air services are highly seasonal with no services on many routes during the winter season. Domestic air services accounted for 9% of seating capacity in 2017.

4.7 Hungary

Hungary experienced a 4% decline in population between 2006 and 2017, with the population falling from 10.07 million to 9.79 million. Hungary is similar in size to Portugal, with a population density of 105 persons per square kilometer and a 71% urbanization rate. The state experienced an increase in per capita GDP from 61% to 68% of the EU28 average over the period 2006–2017, with 2.3% annual growth in GDP per year since 2011.

Hungary experienced a 34% growth rate in air traffic seating capacity between 2006 and 2017, one of the lowest among post-2004 EU accession

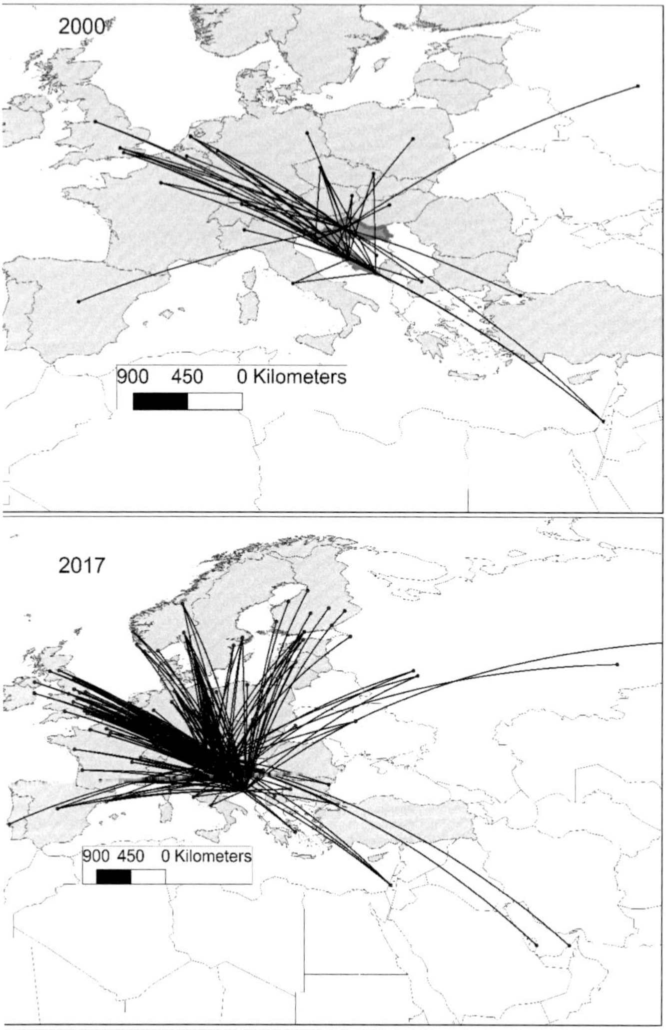

Destination Country from Croatia in 2017	Share of total available non-stop departure seats	Non-stop departure movements
Germany	23%	7717
United Kingdom	18%	5181
Croatia	9%	2932
France	7%	2095
Netherlands	4%	1300
Sweden	4%	993
Turkey	3%	956

Fig. 12 Air service changes from Croatia between 2000 and 2017, with top destination traffic shares.

Central European states. Despite the relatively large size of Hungary, it is served by three airports, the largest of which is Budapest designated as a medium hub in Table 2. Debrecen and Balaton were designated as a non-hub type A and non-hub type B, respectively, in 2017.

Hungary's seating capacity in 2017 was largely offered by low cost carriers, with the Hungarian-registered Wizz Air being the largest carrier (32%), followed by Ryanair (16%), Lufthansa (7%) and EasyJet (5%). Malév, the former state-owned carrier had been part-privatized during the 1990s, but was re-nationalized in 2010 as it faced bankruptcy. The Hungarian government injected state funds into the airline between 2007 and 2010, but these were found to be illegal by the European Commission as they breached state aid rules. The airline was declared bankrupt and ceased operations in February 2012 having been forced to repay the state aid.[11] Direct air services to the USA by American Airlines and to Beijing by Hainan Airlines were also withdrawn as the loss of Malev's feeder traffic through Budapest made the long haul services unsustainable financially.[12]

As a landlocked state, Hungary has extensive rail and road links to its neighbors and air transport services have driven important connections to western European centers, particularly in Germany and the UK. Hungarian depopulation has been driven by negative natural increase and the UN forecast this trend to continue in the medium term at least. The main destinations for Hungarian migrants, which amounted to a migrant stock of just over 331,000 in 2013 were Germany, USA, Canada, UK and Austria (UN Economic and Social Affairs Country Migration profiles, 2017[13]).

4.8 Synopsis

The post-2004 EU member states in Central Europe had very low levels of air accessibility when they became members and in almost all cases were served by a state-owned national airline. These states had significantly lower levels of economic activity with very low GDP per capita compared to existing member states. Prior to the 2000s, air traffic networks were oriented

[11] See (i) European Commission State Aid Case *SA.30584 Malév Hungarian Airlines*, Official Journal of The European Commission, 3rd April 2013 (available at https://eur-lex.europa.eu/legal-content/EN/TXT/PDF/?uri=OJ:L:2013:092:FULL&from=EN—accessed August 2018) and (ii) "Hungary's airline Malev grounded" Guardian Newspaper, February 3rd 2012 (https://www.theguardian.com/business/2012/feb/03/hungary-malev-bankruptcy-airline-grounded).

[12] See "Life after Malev," The Economist, May 31st 2013 (https://www.economist.com/gulliver/2013/05/31/life-after-malev, accessed August 2018).

[13] UN Department of Economic and Social Affairs Migration Profiles are available online at https://esa.un.org/miggmgprofiles/Indicators/indicators.HTM#europe (accessed August 2018).

toward the former USSR nations. Air transport accessibility has increased substantially in all of the new member states since joining and this has facilitated and enabled the economies of Central Europe to realize the overarching objectives of the European Union, namely freedom of movement of people, goods, services and capital. Air transport has enabled the mobility of the population and for many of the Central European states, this has led to net migration westwards and depopulation. The opportunities in Western European states of more favorable labor markets,[14] higher incomes and wage rates and greater flexibility, growth and capabilities in terms of economic wellbeing are strong pull factors for citizens of Central Europe to migrate. However the depopulation has been accompanied by significant increases in GDP per capita fuelled by strong local economic growth, EU investment strategies as well as transfers from abroad by the migrant populations.

Further research examining patterns of migration at the regional scale would help to better understand the timing and scales of air transport service development as new patterns of demand emerge.

Most of the depopulating states examined have seen the demise of their flag carrier and influx of low cost carriers who have driven growth and route developments. Few post-2004 member states have direct intercontinental air services and long haul travel takes place via indirect routing through the much larger western hubs in Germany, the UK, Netherlands and France, with Frankfurt being particularly important in this regard as the most connected global hub.[15]

Lufthansa, the German airline, has substantially expanded its long haul network in the period from 2006 to 2017 and used its short haul services to feed its Frankfurt, Munich and Hamburg hubs. Lufthansa is among the top 5 carriers serving all of the post-2004 Central European states and as Figs. 7–13 demonstrate, German destinations are typically ranked in the top 3 for air transport services from these states. Lufthansa's top 5 airports (in terms of total departures *and* available seating capacity) are all within Germany despite having had full access to the internal European market since 1997.

It is difficult for the depopulating Central European states to gain critical mass to develop direct long haul services and compete with the larger western European carriers. This is similar to the US experience for relatively large

[14] Western European states have consistently higher employment rates for men and women (see, for example, Eurostat's interactive map displays at http://ec.europa.eu/eurostat/statistics-explained/index.php/Employment_rates_and_Europe_2020_national_targets).

[15] Frankfurt has consistently had the largest number of direct air connections of any airport worldwide since 2000.

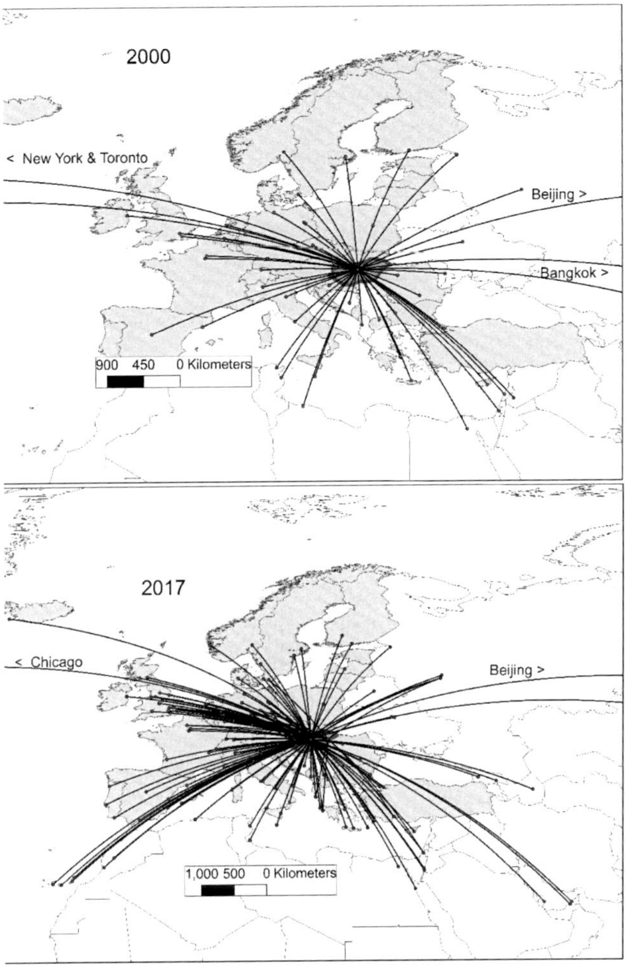

Destination Country from Hungary in 2017	Share of total available non-stop departure seats	Non-stop departure movements
Germany	17%	7822
United Kingdom	16%	6337
Italy	9%	3338
France	6%	2664
Netherlands	6%	2445
Spain	5%	1994
Belgium	4%	1868

Fig. 13 Air service changes from Hungary between 2000 and 2017, with top destination traffic shares.

communities that have not been selected as airline hubs, or have lost hub status because of airline reorganization, bankruptcies or mergers. Network economies have positive circular and cumulative effects: as these grow in significance for existing large hubs, they become increasingly difficult to counter or compete against for developing economies like the depopulating states examined. For long term economic growth and development, and to try to counter several of the factors that seem to drive depopulation, air accessibility and connectivity are important enabling factors. However, Central European states face enormous difficulties trying to generate positive circular and cumulative cycles.

The low cost carriers have been hugely important in driving short haul air traffic growth within the EU28 market as illustrated in Figs. 7–13. The relatively low cost of air transport infrastructure compared to surface transport provision means that access and connectivity at national and regional scales can be quickly developed, enhanced and re-oriented. However, low cost carrier traffic tends to be more seasonal, focused on secondary airports in the western European states and vulnerable to changes, reductions and service cancellations associated with fluctuations in the economic cycle.

4.9 Portugal and Greece

Both of these states experienced depopulation since 2010, mostly driven by a negative rate of natural population change and amplified by low negative net migration rates. The depopulation followed the great recession and dramatic economic crises and falls in living standards, employment prospects and quality of life indicators that ensued. Fig. 14 illustrates the trends in GDP per capita and total population for Greece and Portugal from 1996 to 2017, as well as the air traffic volumes as measured by available seating capacity. The population in both states had been increasing steadily up until 2010 and has fallen since then by 2% (in 2017). Greece became an EU member in 1981, with Portugal and Spain joining in 1986. Substantial EU investment through the EU's regional policy programs resulted in dramatic improvements in living standards up until the great recession of 2008–2010. Greek per capita GDP was at 96% of the EU average in 2006; Portugal's was at 83%. By 2017, Greek GDP per capita had fallen to 67% of the EU average, while Portugal's fell to 77%. Unemployment rose sharply and in 2017 stood at 23% in Greece and 8.5% in Portugal, having peaked at 27% and 16% in 2013 in Greece and Portugal, respectively.

Air traffic fell sharply in Greece from 2009, with 2014 being the first year of positive growth in the 2010s. In the most recent period, 2015–2017, strong air traffic growth has been recorded, with more than 27 million non-stop departure seats available in 2017. Portugal did not experience a decline in air traffic, though the growth rate declined following the great

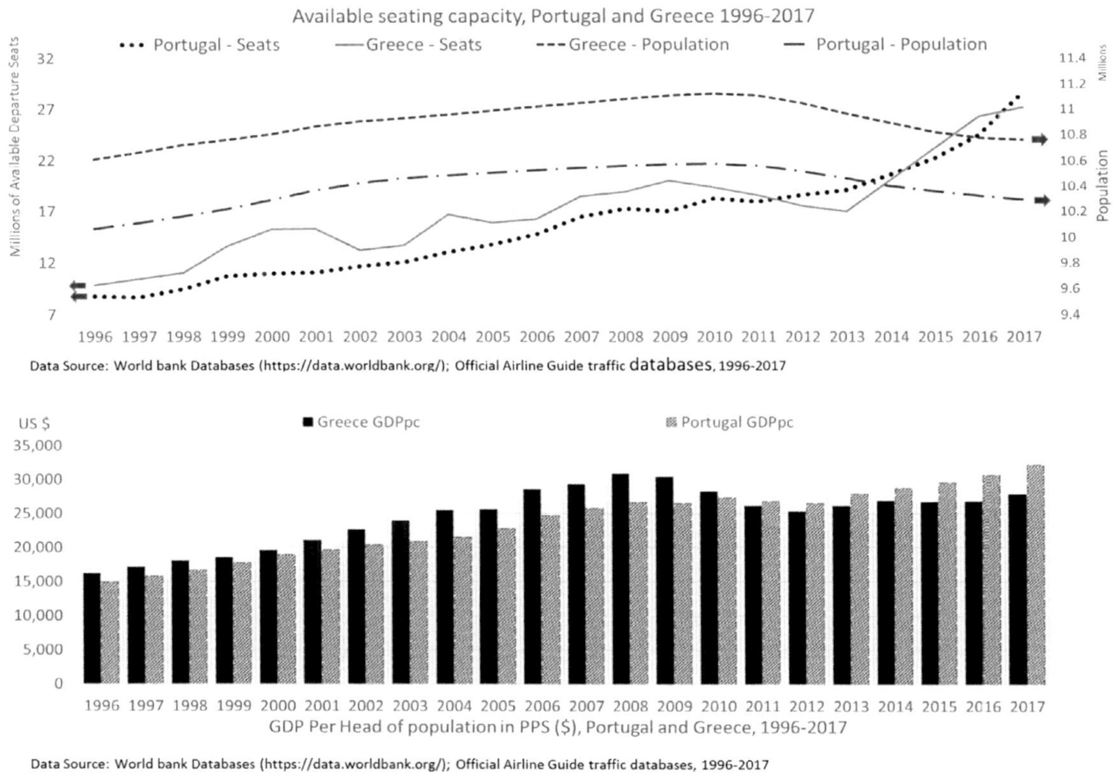

Fig. 14 Population, GDP per capita and departure seating capacity trends for Portugal and Greece, 1996–2017.

recession. Strong growth was recorded between 2015 and 2017, when more than 28.5 million non-stop departure seats were available. Greece and Portugal rely heavily on tourism and this is reflected in their high rankings in Fig. 6, indicating fifth and eighth highest number of nights per capita at tourist accommodation establishments by non-residents in 2016, respectively. Both countries have relatively high levels of air traffic per head of population as illustrated in Fig. 5 and this has risen rapidly since 2005 for both countries.

Greece had 25 air traffic communities handling commercial air traffic in 2017; 1 large hub (Athens with 42% of total seating capacity), 2 medium hubs (Thessaloniki (12.5%) and Heraklion (11.2%)), 7 small hubs and 15 non-hubs. The extensive airports network reflects the large number of islands in Greece and the role that air transport plays in providing connectivity within the state as well as between Greece and other countries. Many of the smaller airports do not receive year-round service and this accounts for the high degree of seasonality indicated by the Gini Index scores in Table 2. The largest airlines in Greece in 2017 were Olympic Airlines (18%) and Aegean Airlines (14%) (both of which are Greek and owned by Aegean Airlines[16]) followed by Ryanair (13%) and EasyJet (5%). Greece had 1038 non-stop air routes in 2017, 977 to European destinations, 51 to Asia and the Middle East, 5 each to Africa and North America. Many of these routes are seasonal, have low frequency, and/or may only operate for a few weeks during the year. Aegean Airlines is a member of the Star Alliance airline group, an alliance which facilitates code sharing and other agreements between the 27 member airlines.

Portugal had 10 air transport communities handling commercial air services in 2017, of which Lisbon, a large hub, was the largest with 52% of total Portuguese seating capacity. In addition there were two medium hubs (Porto and Faro), two small hubs and five non-hubs. TAP, the Portuguese national carrier, is now 50% owned by the Portuguese government[17] and was the largest operator, offered 33.4% of available seats in 2017. TAP is

[16] The European Commission had rejected the application by Aegean Airlines to merge with Olympic Airlines in 2010. Olympic Air was close to filing for bankruptcy in 2012 when Aegean Airlines made a second successful attempt to take over the ailing airline. This received European Commission approval in 2013.

[17] According to the TAP Annual Reports in 2015, 2016 and 2017, the airline was part-privatized initially in 2015 with the sale of 61% to the Atlantic Gateway consortium. In February 2016 a Memorandum of understanding between the Portuguese State and Atlantic Gateway SGPS was concluded whereby part of this share was transferred back to the State so that Atlantic Gateway would reduce its share to 45%, with 50% owned by the Portuguese state and 5% owned by the employees. This was approved by the European Council of Ministers in 2017. In July 2017, Hainan Airlines of China acquired 7% of Atlantic Gateway and this rose to 11% by November 2017.

a Star Alliance member since 2005. Ryanair (19% of seating capacity), EasyJet (11.8%) and the Portuguese-owned Azores Airlines (3.6%) were the next busiest airlines operating in 2017. Portugal has an extensive air route network: Lisbon had 140 and Porto had 92 direct services to Europe (95 from Lisbon/78 from Porto), Africa (19 from Lisbon/8 from Porto), South America (12 from Lisbon/2 from Porto) and North America (10 from Lisbon/3 from Porto). Faro had 93 direct air services mostly to other European countries with 2 African services and 1 North American service.

The high degree of air connectivity and accessibility has enabled both Portugal and Greece to stabilize their tourism sectors and see significant growth in tourist numbers since 2013. Portugal has seen its GDP per capita at 77% of the European average since 2013. Greece has continued to face a debt and economic crisis up to 2018, resulting in a continuous decline in GDP per capita since 2009.

5. Conclusions

The area of the European Union is relatively small compared to other major continental regions and trade blocs. Since 2006, the EU population has been declining in Central and Eastern states and increasingly shifting to the Western and North-western states. European depopulation has resulted from a combination of negative natural increase and negative net migration and this depopulation has characterized almost all of the post-2004 Central European member states since they joined the customs union.

Transport linkages facilitate the movement of people and surface transport networks have enabled the movement of migrant populations between neighboring or bordering states. Air transport growth has facilitated the mobility of the populations to more distant states or peripheral regions. There is a clear relationship between the development of new route structures and the location of migrants from the Central European states. Low cost carriers have dominated the air traffic development for all of the depopulated states and their air services are overwhelmingly point-to-point with little facility for connecting traffic. The low cost airlines have shown tremendous responsiveness to evolving patterns of demand and have facilitated the maintenance by migrants of family and social linkages with their countries of origin. This has also generated new tourism traffic, in varying degrees, to the depopulated member states. A feature of the air traffic is that it has relatively low seasonality which is attractive for short break sustainable tourism development. Modeling of Central and Eastern European air transport development at the sub-national scale could provide valuable insights into the relationships and causality between economic forces and changes in air transport system developments in the context of declining population. As connectivity between regions improves, this may lead to further waves of migration. The long run and short run effects could help shed light on the family dynamics and strength of ties evolving between regions and nations over time.

Most of the depopulated post-2004 entrant states have seen the demise of their national flag carriers. These states have few if any direct long-haul intercontinental air links. Hungary is a notable exception, having two non-stop long-haul routes to North America and one to China, although it has lost services since the demise of the state-owned flag carrier Malev. Among the European network carriers, the German airline Lufthansa has most successfully established air services to all of the post-2004 member states and features in the top 5 carriers to all of the depopulating states. This has provided for substantial traffic feed into the main Lufthansa hubs and enabled the development and expansion of long haul services through the carrier's main airports (all of which are located in Germany). As seen in the US market, the circular and cumulative effects of airline network economies make their large hubs very difficult to counter once they become established. There are significant benefits associated with high degrees of global accessibility via air transport services, including trade, the attraction of inward investment and the diffusion of innovations.[18] It is unlikely that the depopulating European states will develop direct long-haul air transport networks in the future.

Europe's depopulating states have seen substantial increases in GDP per capita, though Portugal and Greece have seen declines resulting from the Great Recession of 2008–2010. The process of developing the economic potential of the new member states is long term and will take many years of investment in infrastructure, education and business development. Air transport can very quickly change patterns of access and mobility and enable short term opportunities: this was demonstrated in relation to the depopulating states. The liberalization of the European air transport market was crucial in fundamentally changing the ability of private carriers to operate and develop services in the European space and is helping to realize the long term goals of the "four freedoms."

[18] See, for example, Oxford Economics (2011) "Economic Benefits from Air Transport in Germany," commissioned report by IATA and available online at https://www.iata.org/policy/Documents/Benefits-of-Aviation-Germany-2011.pdf (accessed August 2018).

Acknowledgments

Comments from Kieran Feighan and two anonymous referees are gratefully acknowledged. Any errors are the author's.

References

Airbus, 2018. Global Market Forecast 2018–2037. online presentation of data and forecasts. available at https://www.airbus.com/aircraft/market/global-market-forecast.html. Airbus SAS. Accessed September 2018.

Airbus Industries (2016), 'Global Market Forecast: Mapping Demand: 2016–2035', Airbus SAS, 2016 accessed August 2018 at http://www.airbus.com/company/market/global-market-forecast-2016-2035/.

Bachtler, J., Mendez, C., Wishlade, F., 2016. EU Cohesion Policy and European Integration: The Dynamics of EU Budget and Regional Policy Reform. Routledge, New York.

Benton, M., Petrovic, M., 2013. How Free is Free Movement? Dynamics and Drivers of Mobility Within the European Union. Migration Policy Institute Europe, Brussels. Available online at https://emnbelgium.be/sites/default/files/publications/mpieurope-freemovement-drivers.pdf.

Button, K.J., Yuan, J., 2013. Airfreight transport and economic development: an examination of causality. Urban Stud. 50 (2), 329–340.

Button, K., Lall, S., Stough, R., Trice, M., 1999. High-technology employment and hub airports. J. Air Trans. Manag. 5 (1), 53–59.

Castro-Martín, T., Cortina, C., 2015. Demographic issues of intra-European migration: destinations, family and settlement. Eur. J. Popul. 31 (2), 109–125.

Chevallier, J., Chèze, B., Gastineau, P., 2011. Forecasting world and regional air traffic in the mid-term (2025): an econometric analysis of air traffic determinants using dynamic panel-data models. In: 60e Congrès AFSE, Open Access Publications From Universitè Paris Dauphine. https://core.ac.uk/download/pdf/6279333.pdf.

Giordano, B., Dubois, A., 2018. Combining territory and competitiveness in EU regional policy? Analyzing ERDF investment profiles in regions with specific geographical features. Reg. Stud. https://doi.org/10.1080/00343404.2018.1495323, (publish online Aug 1st 2018).

Hakim, M.M., Merkert, R., 2016. The causal relationship between air transport and economic growth: empirical evidence from South Asia. J. Transp. Geogr. 56 (10), 120–127.

Ishutkina, M., Hansman, R.J., 2009. Analysis of the Interaction Between Air Transportation and Economic Activity: A Worldwide Perspective. Report No. ICAT-2009-2, MIT, Cambridge, Mass.

McMillan, R., 2016. Policy responses to depopulation. N. Z. Popul. Rev. 42, 65–101.

Mukkala, K., Tervo, H., 2013. Air transportation and regional growth: which way does the causality run? Environ. Plan. A 45, 1508–1520.

Reynolds-Feighan, A.J., 2017. Small community impacts of liberalization and the provision of social air services. (Chapter 11). In: Finger, M., Button, K. (Eds.), Air Transport Liberalization: A Critical Assessment. 2017. Edward Elgar.

United Nations, 2015. World Population Prospects: The 2015 Revision, Key Findings and Advanced Tables. United Nations Department of Economic and Social Affairs, Population Division, New York, NY.

Further reading

Boeing, 2016. Current Market Outlook. Boeing. 2016. at http://www.boeing.com/resources/boeingdotcom/commercial/about-our-market/assets/downloads/cmo_print_2016_final_updated.pdf. Accessed August 2018.

CHAPTER THREE

The potential of a Mobility-as-a-Service platform in a depopulating area in The Netherlands: An exploration of small and big data

Karst T. Geurs[a,*], Konstantinos Gkiotsalitis[a], Tiago Fioreze[a], Gideon Visser[b], Mettina Veenstra[c]
[a]University of Twente, Enschede, The Netherlands
[b]HAN University of Applied Sciences, Arnhem, The Netherlands
[c]Saxion University of Applied Sciences, Enschede, The Netherlands
*Corresponding author: e-mail address: k.t.geurs@utwente.nl

Contents

Abstract

This chapter describes a case study examining the potential of a community-driven Mobility-as-a-Service (MaaS) platform in a rural and depopulating area in the Netherlands. The aim of the 5-year project is to examine if a MaaS platform can be an effective and efficient solution to improve accessibility and liveability of rural areas. The potential for a MaaS is examined by addressing the current mobility patterns and mobility and accessibility barriers. We use a mixed method approach using a combination of small data (primary data) and big data (secondary data).

Keywords: Mobility-as-a-Service, Rural area

Advances in Transport Policy and Planning, Volume 2
ISSN 2543-0009
https://doi.org/10.1016/bs.atpp.2018.09.001

1. Introduction

International experiences on providing public transport services for rural and sparsely populated areas are similar around the world. An ageing population in low-density and dispersed areas, combined with strong competition from private cars, make it difficult to operate profitable commercial public transport services which also meet the accessibility needs of different user groups (ITF, 2015). The need for public transport services to tackle problems related to accessibility and mobility is undisputable (Currie, 2010). In the Netherlands, in particular in rural areas, public transport has become more expensive and increasingly unprofitable due to demographic changes (i.e., aging), higher fuel costs and the increasing use of cars and e-bikes, leading to the need for high(er) subsidies (Dutch Ministry of Transport, 2010). Providing efficient and high-quality public transport alternatives at a fair price is a major challenge for the government and is often hampered by financial pressure. According to Brake and Nelson (2007), in an ideal world, public transport would be as convenient and flexible as private transport, suggesting that public transport services would be completely demand responsive and that travelers could use a service whenever desired. Such level of flexibility or convenience is infrequently achieved by conventional public transport services. Cervero (1997) states that conventional public transport cannot compete with the private car, because it is, among other things, unable to serve spontaneous travel. What stands out is that it is not so much the travel speed that is considered important, but the ability to travel spontaneously; when, where and as often as desired (Daniels and Mulley, 2010).

To tackle the problem of the inflexibility of conventional public transport, a myriad of alternative transport services have been developed where service provision is influenced by the demand and needs of the users, for example, through flexible routing or demand responsive scheduling (Mageean et al., 2013; Nelson and Phonphitakchai, 2012). The development of ICT has given opportunities to develop new mobility solutions in rural areas, including ride sharing platforms, demand responsive public transport systems, and combinations of public and private transport and with personalized flexible routes and schedules. More recently, Mobility as a Service (MaaS) has been presented a new and more comprehensive mobility concept, delivering users' transport needs through a single interface of a service provider. In several cities around the globe MaaS systems have been piloted since 2012.

This chapter aims to examine the potential demand for a MaaS deployment in a rural and depopulating area in the Netherlands by using multiple data sources. First, a survey is conducted to examine user preferences, satisfaction with the degree to which existing transport modes offer a sufficient level of access to important destinations and the willingness of car travelers to share a ride. Second, smart card and cellular data are used to examine the spatial and temporal variation in travel patterns. To the authors' knowledge, this is the first study to examine the potential demand of a MaaS platform in a rural area prior to its implementation using small and big data. The study is part of the 5-year research project Netmobil in which a community-driven MaaS platform is developed, tested and implemented. The aim of the Netmobil project is to examine if a MaaS platform can be an effective and efficient solution to improve the accessibility and liveability of rural areas.

The remainder of the chapter is structured as follows. Section 2 presents a literature review on mobility solutions in rural areas. Section 3 describes the case study area. Section 4 describes the results of the survey and analysis of smart card and mobile phone data. Section 5 presents the conclusions and describes the next steps to be taken within the framework of the Netmobil project.

2. Mobility solutions for rural areas: Literature review

The problems of insufficient public transport supply and high car dependency in rural areas are not new. Many different demand responsive mobility services have been developed and applied in practice around the globe. Early solutions in the Netherlands involve community-based public transport, in which local citizens collaborate with public transport operators in providing mini-bus transport services on fixed routes and timetables. In some regions in the Netherlands, some of these systems have existed for over 30 years. The provision of these traditional forms of neighborhood-based bus services is however becoming increasingly problematic. Budgets for public transport are decreasing and will decrease further in the coming years, costs are increasing and the operations are inefficient (demand is high during peak-hours and very low in off-peak hours). In short, this form of community-driven public transport with fixed routes and schedules is likely to prove not to be viable. Also, other public transport services in rural areas such as taxi systems are expensive (de Jong et al., 2011) and demand responsive transport (DRT) services are not, in most cases, financially viable (e.g., see Papanikolaou et al., 2017; Ryley et al., 2014; Wang et al., 2015).

In recent years, ICT developments have stimulated the development of ride-sharing platforms. Many of these platforms are small scale. All modern ride-sharing tools use some kind of information technology (internet site, an app, sms, email or a combination of these) but differ in the degree of automatic matching, payment solutions and target groups. Currently, there seem to be many operational ride sharing platforms in rural communities in developed countries. However, not all ride sharing platforms are successful. An evaluation of six trials of ride sharing platforms in rural areas in Sweden and Germany showed that throughout the 6 months implementation phase all platforms struggled with a low number of participants (50 active users or less) and consequently few shared rides (Alvanger, 2014). Issues that need to be addressed are a lack of user involvement and incentives for joining a ride-sharing initiative and the balance between the price a passenger pays and what the driver gets.

Recently, the concept of Mobility-as-a-Service (MaaS) is receiving increasing attention both in academic literature and in policy making. Jittrapirom et al. (2017) describe the main elements of a MaaS platform in their review paper. To summarize, a MaaS platform offers several transport options (public transport, taxi, car-sharing, ride-sharing, bike-sharing, car-rental) in one platform with integrated ticket and payment in monthly payments and/or "pay-as-you-go." A MaaS ecosystem is built on interactions between different groups of actors through a digital platform: users (e.g., private customer or business customer), suppliers of transport services and platform owners. MaaS is a user-centric paradigm as it seeks to offer a transport solution that is best from the customer's perspective via a multimodal trip planning feature. It also involves customization to modify the offered service option in accordance to the customer's preferences.

Jittrapirom et al. (2017) and Kamargianni et al. (2016) give an overview of operational MaaS systems and pilot projects in Europe (Austria, Finland, Sweden, Germany, France and the Netherlands) and the United States. These overviews show that current operational platforms focus on integrating car sharing, bike sharing and public transport and none of these systems target rural areas. In rural areas, the business case for MaaS will differ from urban areas, with a stronger focus on ride sharing and car sharing and less on public transport services. In the Netherlands, advanced integration schemes are designed for business travelers (such as Mobility Mixx, NS-Business Card) which provide a smart card to access a variety of modes across the country including shared modes, public transport and taxis. To date, however, these systems do not include ride sharing as a mobility option. In the

Netherlands several MaaS pilots are currently being planned. MaaS is a main transport policy focus at the national and regional level. For example, the Dutch Ministry of Infrastructure and Water management plans to experiment with seven MaaS pilots in 2019. One of these pilots is to be conducted in a rural area, aiming to contribute to more efficient transport in rural areas.

This overview shows that there is little experience with MaaS applications in rural areas. From the literature it is clear that many ride sharing platforms in rural areas struggle to capture a sufficient number of participants in rural and scarcely populated areas. Issues are a lack of community involvement, incentives for joining a ride-sharing initiative and the financial and non-financial benefits for passengers and drivers. Currently there is no evidence from the literature showing how much potential a MaaS platform, offering a variety of transport options in a single platform, has to overcome the issues and barriers that many ride sharing platforms have experienced.

3. Case study area

The study area for the development and implementation of the Netmobil MaaS platform is the "Achterhoek" region, in the eastern part of the Netherlands belonging to the Province of Gelderland. The Netmobil MaaS platform is being designed as a community-driven platform and integrates bike sharing, car sharing, ride sharing, taxi and public transport services in a single platform. The Netmobil project started early 2018 and will finish in 2021.

The Achterhoek region is a predominantly rural region, with much open space, forests and farms, with approximately 400,000 inhabitants. It is one of the regions in the Netherlands with a projected population decline in the next decades. In comparison with 2018, the population in that region is projected to decline by 5% in 2030 and by 9% in 2040 (PBL/CBS, 2016). Moreover, the population structure is also changing. Young, highly educated people and families are leaving so that the remaining population consists of relatively many elderly people. Facilities such as shops, sports clubs, schools and care facilities are becoming increasingly difficult to maintain. On the other hand, social capital is high within villages and the region is moving from a traditional rural and industrial region toward a region with new innovative industries, making it a dynamic region. Therefore, the Achterhoek should not be looked at as just a region in decline (Atzema et al., 2017).

The first application of the Netmobil MaaS platform will be conducted in one of the municipalities in the Achterhoek called Oost-Gelre (see Fig. 1),

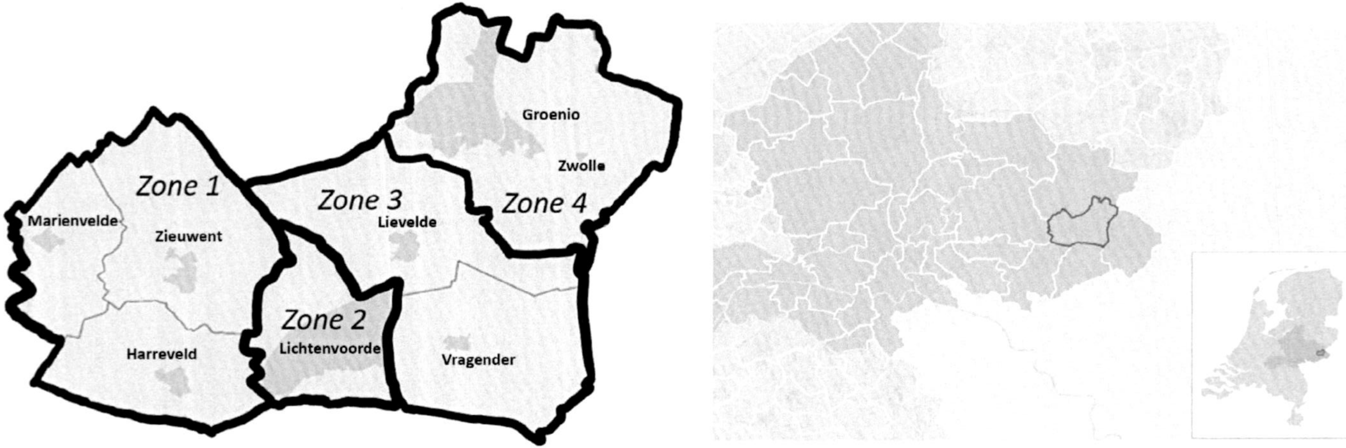

Fig. 1 The case study area in the Netherlands, location of towns and villages and zoning Source municipality boundaries: Statistics Netherlands/Topografische Dienst Kadaster, 2015.

in 2019. The municipality of Oost-Gelre has about 30,000 inhabitants and consists of two main cores: Groenlo (around 10,000 inhabitants) and Lichtenvoorde (about 13,000 inhabitants) and six villages of around 1000–2000 inhabitants (Harreveld, Lievelde, Mariënvelde, Vragender, Zieuwent and Zwolle). For the analysis in this chapter, the study area has been divided into four zones as shown in Fig. 1. The zoning is based on the spatial resolution of the mobile phone data used in the analysis (see Section 4). Zone 1 consists of the villages Harreveld, Mariënvelde, Zieuwent and its rural surroundings, about 4350 inhabitants altogether. Zone 2 consists of the city of Lichtenvoorde. Zone 3 consists of the villages Lievelde and Vragender, about 2500 inhabitants altogether. At last, zone 4 consists of the city of Groenlo and the small village of Zwolle.

The population in the municipality of Oost-Gelre is forecasted to decline by 6% by 2030 and 10% by 2040 (PBL/CBS, 2016). Public transport in the areas consists of one train station (located in a small village Lievelde in between Groenlo and Lichtenvoorde) connected to the network of traditional bus lines and scheduled minibuses ("buurtbus"). The minibuses are driven by volunteers and operate during working days with fixed routes and schedules between 7 am and 7 pm (and flexible stops) and in evenings and weekends with on-demand services (reservation 1 h in advance). In addition, a taxi-based public transport service is in operation, as in many low-density areas in the Netherlands, targeting residents such as school children who are not capable of traveling by regular public transport.

The municipality of Oost-Gelre was selected for several reasons. First, there was a local sense of urgency considering mobility and accessibility. Second, the local authority as the local community organized in a network active in six villages within the municipality considers the development of a MaaS platform an addition to local mobility and projects. Participation of the municipality and local communities is absolutely necessary to conduct a successful pilot. Both the municipality and local communities (especially a network of six small villages) showed their interest in the Netmobil project. Third, the municipality has a varied population and a variety of medium sized and small sized settlements which is suited for a Maas application.

4. Evaluating the potential for a mobility as a service

4.1 Survey setup and results

A revealed preference survey is conducted among residents over the age of 18 of the municipality using a mixed mode recruitment method. First, a pen-and-paper survey was distributed to 2000 residents, based on a random draw of the population. Second, participants were recruited for an online survey by using adds and Facebook posts. Third, fieldworkers have recruited respondents, focusing particularly on elderly people and younger people (in between 15 and 25 years of age). Responses were collected for 7 weeks from May 1st till June 17th, 2018. All responses were automatically recorded via the survey platform. Of the 1014 survey entries recorded, 862 were entitled to be further analyzed. The remaining 152 entries were discarded either because the participant did not answer any question or he or she reported to live outside the municipality of Oost-Gelre. The mixed mode recruitment method resulted in a good distribution of respondents by gender, age, household composition and education level compared to the population. More importantly, the survey sample is representative of the population of the municipality of Oost-Gelre, as illustrated in Fig. 2.

The survey comprised revealed preference questions on existing travel patterns (such as frequently visited locations), attitudes toward different transport modes (including ride sharing), satisfaction with the level of access specific destinations and level of capability to travel independently and use smartphone and internet. In addition to the survey, respondents were asked to download and use a smartphone app to allow a detailed analysis of travel

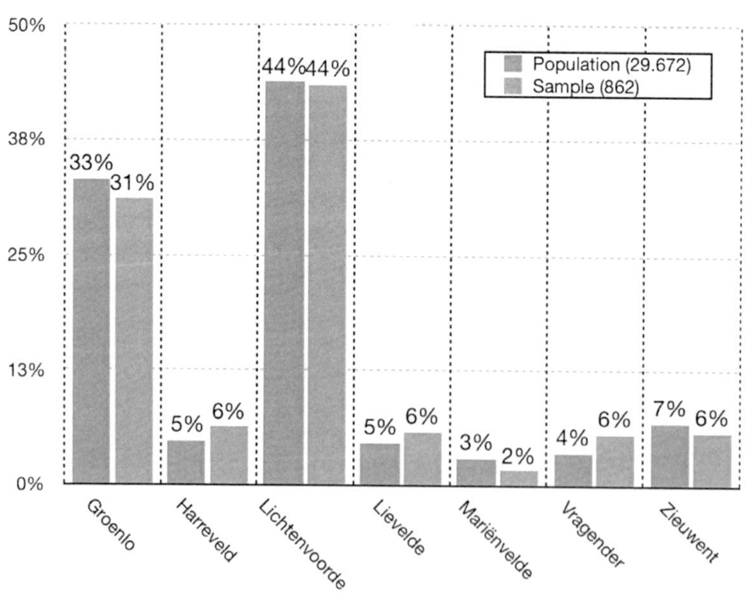

Fig. 2 Frequency distribution of survey respondents in comparison with the distribution of inhabitants in the municipality of Oost-Gelre.

patterns over a multi-week period. About 130 respondents participated and provided useful data.

The survey data are analyzed with SPSS Statistics (version 24) by using descriptive and inferential statistics techniques. The statistical approach is based on the distribution of responses with a margin of error of plus or minus 3 percentage points and a confidence interval of 95%. Moreover, we are particularly interested in finding out whether there is any association between some categorical variables of interest, such as the satisfaction of inhabitants of different zones with the level of accessibility and the current mobility services. In order to evaluate whether any relation exists, we use the Chi-square independence test (denoted by χ^2). If associated (using a significance level of 0.05), we subsequently employ Cramer's V (denoted by φ_c) to quantify how strong the relation is, i.e., how strong the two categorical variables are associated.

First, we examine how satisfied are the inhabitants of the considered zones based on the purpose of their travel. In general, the inhabitants of the municipality of Oost-Gelre are mostly satisfied with the accessibility of their destinations when performing fixed trips, but less satisfied when performing trips with low recurrency. In more detail, when analyzing the levels of satisfaction in the different zones of interest (see Fig. 3), significative differences are observed for some travel motives that do not have a fixed pattern.

We observed very weak ($\varphi_c < 0.15$) levels of significative association ($P < 0.05$) with respect to the zones of interest and how satisfied inhabitants are concerning accessibility for the following travel motives: *doing the daily grocery shopping, going out socially, and making a day trip*. The remaining travel motives did not show a significant association.

Residents in the rural areas (zones 1 and 3) are slightly more prone to be dissatisfied when doing groceries than the residents in the city areas (zones 2 and 4). Moreover, residents in zone 2 (Lichtenvoorde) are slightly more satisfied when going out socially than the rest. Finally, residents in zone 1 are more likely to be dissatisfied when making a day trip, whereas residents in zone 2 are more likely to be satisfied when doing so.

Independent of the zone of interest, the residents' level of dissatisfaction when traveling to school or other study locations is considerably higher when compared to the other travel destinations. Residents were not asked about which modes of transport they use for each travel motive, but it is very likely that most of them (especially students) use public transport (mostly bus) for that. Interestingly enough, students are entitled to travel for free

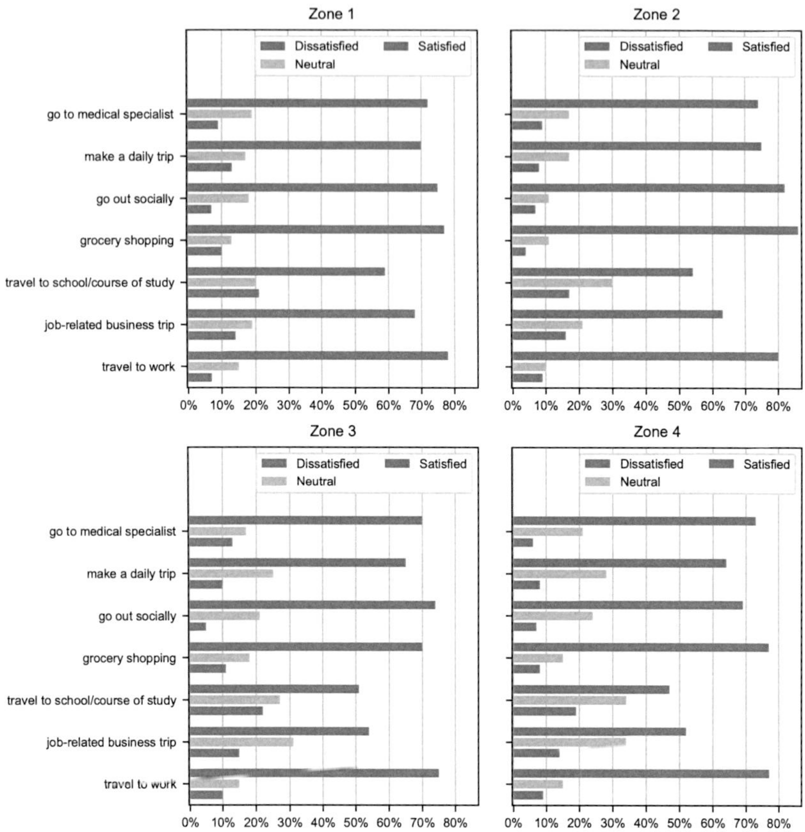

Fig. 3 The levels of satisfaction per travel motive in the four zones of interest.

(or with discount) on public transport to and from their school/course and, even so, their level of dissatisfaction is the highest.

After establishing a connection between the satisfaction of travelers and the trip destinations, we note that non-recurrent (infrequent) trips such as making a job-related business trip or a day trip exhibit the lowest satisfaction levels in all zones (after the education-related trips). These trips can potentially be accommodated by a MaaS platform; thus, later on, we will investigate the origin-destination pairs of infrequent trips with the use of detailed mobile phone data.

Except the activity type at the destination, another factor that can affect the satisfaction level of travelers is the mobility supply. For this, we analyze the modal split in the zones of interest to investigate if the mobility supply affects the level of dissatisfaction associated with the less frequent trips (such as grocery shopping, business trips and others that do not have a fixed destination like the home-to-work trips). In general, the frequency of car and bicycle use in the municipality of Oost-Gelre is higher than the other modes of transport, whereas taking the public transport occurs sporadically, at best (see Fig. 4 that presents the responses of the surveyed population).

As one might have expected, Fig. 4, which is based on the responses of the survey data, demonstrates a significantly higher frequency of almost daily use of car (as driver) in the sparcely populated areas (zones 1 and 3) when compared to the city areas (zones 2 and 4). Moreover, zone 3 has not only the highest frequency of almost daily use of car (as driver) but also the highest frequency of weekly ride sharing (i.e., use of car as passenger). This can be linked with another observation in our study. We observe that the frequency of sole car use goes hand in hand with the frequency of ride sharing, as seen in the weak level of association between frequency of car use (as driver) and frequency of car use (as passenger), $\chi^2(9) = 78.69$, $P = 0.000$ and $\varphi_c = 0.176$ (Table 1).

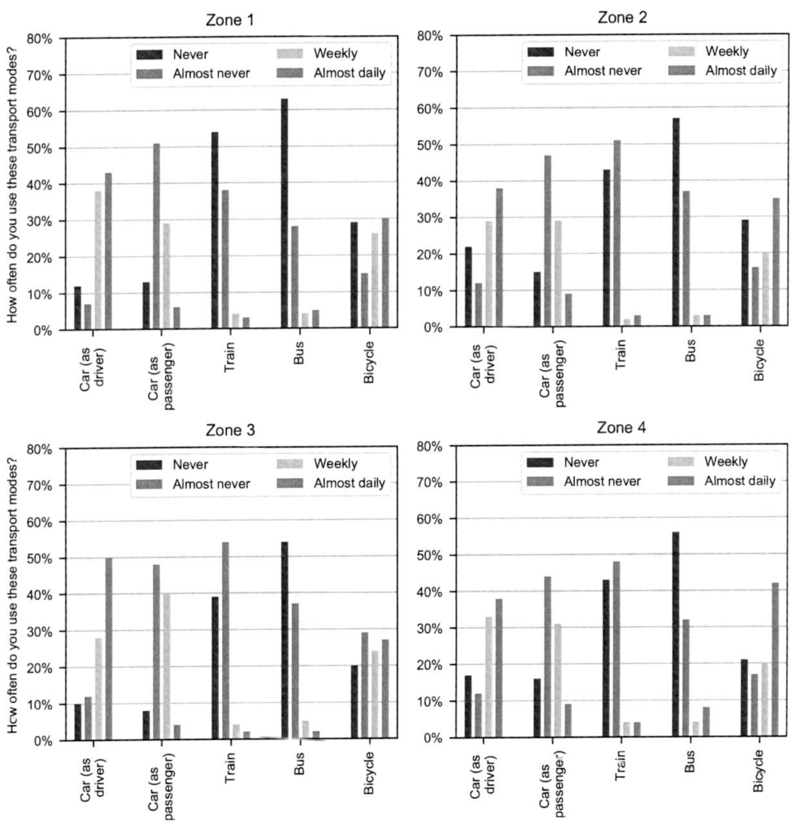

Fig. 4 Frequency of transport mode use per different zone of interest.

Table 1 Crosstabulation frequency of sole car use and ride sharing.

Ride sharing

	Never		Almost never		Weekly		Almost daily		Total	
Car (as driver)	Count	% Within car as driver	Count	% Within car as driver	Count	% Within car as driver	Count	% Within car as driver	Count	% Within car as driver
Never	22	13.7	76	47.2	51	31.7	12	7.5	161	100.0
Almost never	19	20.0	64	67.4	10	10.5	2	2.1	95	100.0
Weekly	41	15.8	111	42.9	104	40.2	3	1.2	259	100.0
Almost daily	34	10.3	138	41.9	106	32.2	51	15.5	329	100.0
Total	116	13.7	389	46.1	271	32.1	68	8.1	844	100.0

From the analysis of the survey data, one can observe a link between (a) the dissatisfaction of the mobility options of inhabitants of sparsely populated areas when conducting flexible trips with low recurrency and (b) the high levels of car use and ride sharing in those areas (zones 1 and 3). This topic requires further examination since it is interesting to see how the non-recurrent trips vary within the day and investigate whether they can justify the use of a MaaS by analyzing the more detailed data sets of the mobile phone data which provide information about the variation of infrequent trips in time and space.

Before proceeding to this analysis though, we examine the level of willingness to share a ride for inhabitants that are frequent car drivers and frequent car passengers using the responses of the survey data. Even if one would expect that car drivers and car passengers share the same thoughts on MaaS solutions, this is not the case.

The crosstabulation of Table 2 shows a very weak level of association between frequency of car use (as driver) and standing toward sharing a ride with strangers, $\chi^2(6)=20.75$, $P=0.002$ and $\varphi_c=0.111$. This crosstabulation shows that if somebody drives a car almost daily, it is more probable that he or she will have a negative standing toward sharing a ride (with strangers).

However, when raising the same question to car passengers, we see the opposite answer. Indeed, a very weak level of association between frequency of car use (as passenger) and standing toward sharing a ride with strangers was

Table 2 Crosstabulation frequency of sole car use and sharing a ride with strangers.
Standing on sharing a ride with strangers

	(Very) negative		Neutral		(Very) positive		Total	
Car (as driver)	**Count**	**% Within car as driver**	**Count**	**% Within car as driver**	**Count**	**% Within car as driver**	**Count**	**% Within car as driver**
Never	73	47.7	61	39.9	19	12.4	153	100.0
Almost never	30	31.3	49	51.0	17	17.7	96	100.0
Weekly	115	44.1	89	34.1	57	21.8	261	100.0
Almost daily	158	48.2	99	30.2	71	21.6	328	100.0
Total	376	44.9	298	35.6	164	19.6	828	100.0

Table 3 Crosstabulation frequency of car users as passengers and sharing a ride with strangers.
Standing on sharing a ride with strangers

	(Very) negative		Neutral		(Very) positive		Total	
Car (as passenger)	Count	% Within car as driver	Count	% Within car as driver	Count	% Within car as driver	Count	% Within car as driver
Never	52	46.8	38	34.2	21	18.9	111	100.0
Almost never	186	48.1	135	34.9	66	17.1	387	100.0
Weekly	110	41.0	107	39.9	51	19.0	268	100.0
Almost daily	28	41.2	15	22.1	25	36.8	68	100.0
Total	376	45.1	295	35.4	163	19.5	834	100.0

observed, $\chi^2(6)=18.69$, $P=0.005$ and $\varphi_c=0.106$ (Table 3). The contingency table shows that if somebody uses the car as passenger almost daily, it is more probable that he or she will have a positive attitude toward sharing a ride (with strangers).

The conclusion here is that frequent car drivers could potentially share a ride, but they are more likely not willing to do so. This conclusion comes as no surprise since offering a ride can be more complicated than taking one. Most likely the driver has to take another route that he is used to in order to pick up someone, which results in longer travel times.

4.2 Spatio-temporal variations of infrequent trips and public transport use

This section examines the spatio-temporal variation of trips in the study areas based on big data from smart cards and mobile phones to help us understand which origin-destination pairs and times of day have the highest potential for a MaaS service in Oost-Gelre.

For this, we use cellular data from mobile phones in combination with smart card data from buses and trains. Mobile phone data have the advantage that sampling bias is relatively low (because of large geographic coverage and high penetration of mobile phones) but have the disadvantage that the spatial resolution is fairly low; thus we had to merge a number of villages into the four larger zones. To perform a comparative analysis, we aggregate the national public transport smart card (OV chipkaart) data on the level of the four zones depicted in Fig. 1 to ensure that the public transport and the mobile phone data cover the same zones.

Detailed and anonymized smart card data have been made available by the Province of Gelderland, the regional public transport authority for the year 2016. The smart card data contain information of all tap-ins/tap-outs of passengers at the Achterhoek region, enabling the identification of the origin and destination stop for each trip. The total amount of analyzed smart card trips is 4,553,777 (on average, 12,476 trips per day).

From the public transport trips made in the Achterhoek region in 2016, 629,461 were performed[1] at the Oost-Gelre municipality (~13.82%). It should be noted here that two out of the six villages in Oost-Gelre (namely, Vragender and Zwolle) do not have any public transport stops. Table 4 and Fig. 5 present the origin-destination matrix of the smart card trips in Oost-Gelre (including the incoming and outgoing trips from the Achterhoek region) for March (note that we select March as the month of reference because we have mobile phone data from the same month). The key observations from Table 4 and Fig. 4 are:

1. The incoming and outgoing trips from other areas outside the Oost-Gelre municipality to the cities of Groenlo (zone 4) and Lichtenvoorde (zone 2) account for 62.5% of all public transport trips in Oost-Gelre. This indicates that public transport is not commonly used for trips inside Oost-Gelre;
2. Zone 1 has low interaction with the other three zones in Oost-Gelre and most public transport trips from zone 1 are from/to other areas in the Achterhoek region.

Table 4 Oost-Gelre's origin-destination matrix of all smart card trips in march (including the incoming and outgoing trips from other areas in the achterhoek region).

	Zone 1	Zone 2	Zone 3	Zone 4	Outside Oost-Gelre
Zone 1	0	65	75	63	763
Zone 2	87	98	3100	1554	6984
Zone 3	100	3526	36	3128	2085
Zone 4	80	1591	2735	448	12,074
Outside Oost-Gelre	844	6261	2155	12,199	0

[1] We assume that a trip is performed in Oost-Gelre if it is originated or attracted by a public transport stop in Oost-Gelre.

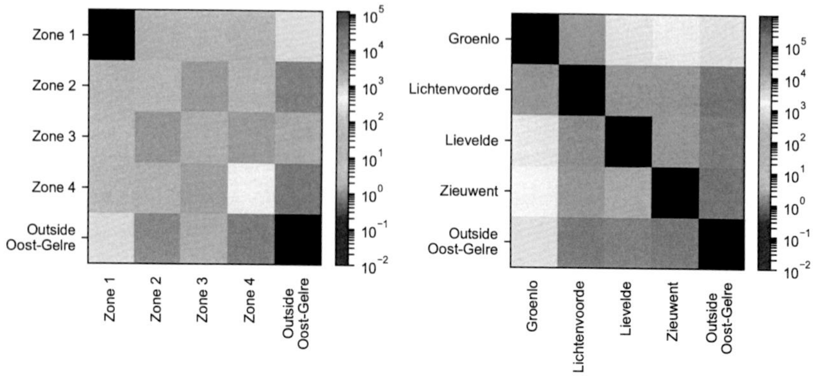

Fig. 5 Visualization of the origin-destination matrix of public transport trips (left) and the origin-destination matrix of mobile phone data trips (right).

Note also that the sum of all trips in Table 4 gives us the total number of public transport trips generated by and attracted from the four zones in Oost-Gelre. This sum is equal to 60,051 trips and is a reasonable number since the yearly number of trips in Oost-Gelre is 629,461 dictating that almost a 10th of the yearly trips are performed in March.

In addition to the smart card data, we analyze an anonymized and preprocessed origin-destination matrix of mobile phone data derived from Vodafone users, one of the largest mobile phone operators with a market share of about 30–40% in the Netherlands. The mobile phone data cover 1 month of data from March 1st to March 31st, 2018. Note that trips with an origin and destination at the same zone are not provided because of privacy reasons. When mobile phones are used to make calls, text messages or to send or receive data, signals are transmitted to a central computer. The Call Detail Records (CDR) have been preprocessed by a company to determine where mobile phones are located and how they move and translated into Origin-Destination data based on several decision rules (see Wismans et al., 2018 for a description of the methodology).

Using the origins and destinations[2] of all mobile phone trips in March, the origin-destination matrix of the trips in Oost-Gelre (including the incoming and outgoing trips from/to the Achterhoek region) is presented in Table 5 and Fig. 5. Given that the retrieved mobile phone trips do not represent the entirety of the trips in the region, the number of observed trips

[2] The mobile phone data indicate as a trip origin the area from which a traveler starts his/her journey and a trip destination the a place where someone stays for at least 30 min. OD-pairs with less than 16 trips per day are excluded from the data for privacy reasons.

Table 5 Oost-Gelre's origin-destination matrix of all trips derived from mobile phone data in March (including the incoming and outgoing trips from/to other areas in the Achterhoek region).

	Zone 1	Zone 2	Zone 3	Zone 4	Outside Oost-Gelre
Zone 1	0	17,404	1178	1581	2433
Zone 2	17,758	0	16,991	17,741	80,558
Zone 3	1271	20,881	0	13,298	40,318
Zone 4	1674	17,313	9168	0	71,772
Outside Oost-Gelre	2961	80,804	41,971	72,954	0

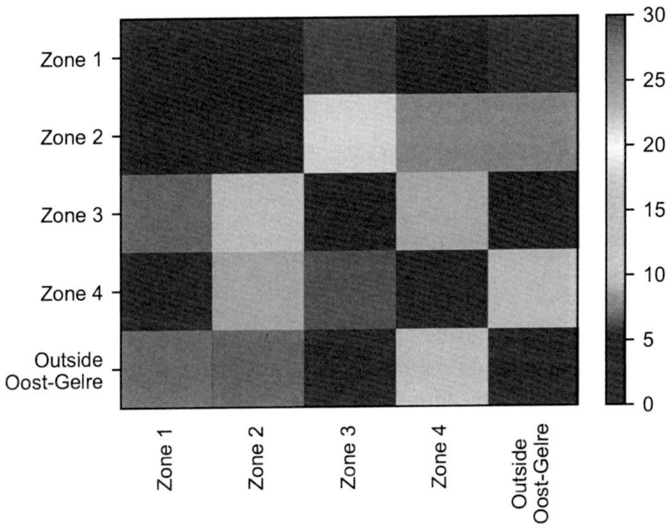

Fig. 6 Percentage (%) of public transport trips per origin-destination pair in Oost-Gelre.

has been expanded (using the Vodafone market share) to achieve the total amount of trips in the study area.

Investigating further the public transport use in different zones, we calculate the portion of public transport trips at each zone and present the results in Fig. 6. Note that the diagonal of the figure is always 0% because there is no mobile phone data availability for the intra-zonal trips. Notably, the percentage of public transport trips for each origin-destination pair is below 15% except the case of trips from zone 1 to other areas outside Oost-Gelre. Zone 1 is an interesting case because its inhabitants use public transport for traveling from and to other areas outside Oost-Gelre, but they do not use it for trips within the municipality. In contrast, inhabitants of zone 3 use public transport frequently to travel to zone 4 and vice versa. In summary, the public transport use for trips within the municipality is limited with percentages in the range of 0–10% (this is in line with the responses of the surveyed population which were presented in Fig. 4).

Continuing the analysis, we examine the spatio-temporal variations of the infrequent trips to explore the potential of a MaaS service that targets infrequent trips for which the survey respondents indicated a lower level of satisfaction. In the mobile phone data, there are two trip categorizations: (i) *infrequent trips* which are origin-destination trips that are conducted by a specific individual nine times or less per month and (ii) *frequent (regular) trips* which are trips performed more than 10 times per month by an individual. In addition, the temporal resolution of the mobile phone data is hourly (an origin-destination matrix can be provided for each hour of the day).

Let us consider two 1-h periods of the day, $I_j \neq I_k$, where each period I_j starts at hour $j \in \{0, 1, 2, \ldots, 23\}$ and ends 60 min later. Using the mobile phone data, for each hourly period I_j we can compute the origin-destination (OD) matrix of the infrequent trips, $\mathbf{O}^{I_j} = \{O_{rq}^{Ij}\}$, where r and q are the origin and destination zones of each OD pair and can take any value from the set Q = {zone 1, zone 2, zone 3, zone 4}. From this OD matrix, one can derive the probability of having an infrequent trip from origin r to destination $q \in Q$ within the time period I_j as:

$$P_{rq}^{I_j} = \frac{O_{rq}^{Ij}}{\sum_{r \in Q} \sum_{q \in Q} O_{rq}^{Ij}} \tag{1}$$

Computing this probability for all OD pairs indicates the spatial variation of infrequent trips within the time period I_j. This hourly matrix with the trip probabilities between all OD pairs, $\mathbf{P}^{I_j} = \{P_{rq}^{Ij}\}$, can be used for comparing the spatial distribution of trips for different time periods of the day, $I_j \neq I_k$. For this, one can employ a modified version of the Kullback-Leibler (KL) divergence (Kullback and Leibler, 1951) that indicates the difference between probability distributions. KL divergence is an asymmetric measure of the difference between two probability distributions and several modifications (i.e., Briët and Harremoës, 2009; Gkiotsalitis and Stathopoulos, 2016) can be used for transforming it into a symmetric one.

For ensuring a symmetric KL probability distance, where $\mathrm{KL}_{I_j,Ik} = \mathrm{KL}_{I_k,Ij}$, $\forall k, j \in \{0, 1, \ldots, 23\}$, we introduce the following formulation:

$$KL_{I_j,I_k} = \frac{1}{|Q|^2} \sum_{r \in Q} \sum_{q \in Q} \left| P_{rq}^{I_j} - P_{rq}^{I_k} \right|^2 \tag{2}$$

where $P_{rq}^{I_j}$ and $P_{rq}^{I_k}$ indicate the trip probabilities between all OD pairs for the time intervals I_j and I_k, respectively. The KL divergence matrix can be constructed by comparing the probability distance of the spatial distributions of trips for all hourly time periods of the day following Eq. (2). Obviously, this is a 24×24 symmetric matrix. For comparing the spatio-temporal variations of frequent and infrequent trips, we compute the KL divergence matrices for both the frequent and the infrequent trips in the mobile phone data and we present the results for a typical weekday in Fig. 7.

In Fig. 7, the symmetric KL divergence matrix starts from 6 am because there are no data for the first hours of the day. The figure shows that the spatial distribution of *infrequent* trips varies significantly from hour to hour. This demand cannot be easily accommodated by a fixed public transport service that operates in a schedule-basis.

Compared to the infrequent trips, the spatial variation of frequent trips exhibits a more stable behavior and there is a clear area (indicated with blue color) where the KL divergence is very small and the spatial distribution of trips remains almost unchanged. The time period of the day with the most similarities in terms of the spatial distribution of fixed trips is 1–4 pm. The spatial distribution of trips from 6 am until 10 am appears to be quite random and does not match the distribution of trips in other periods of the day. The same applies for trips after 4 pm.

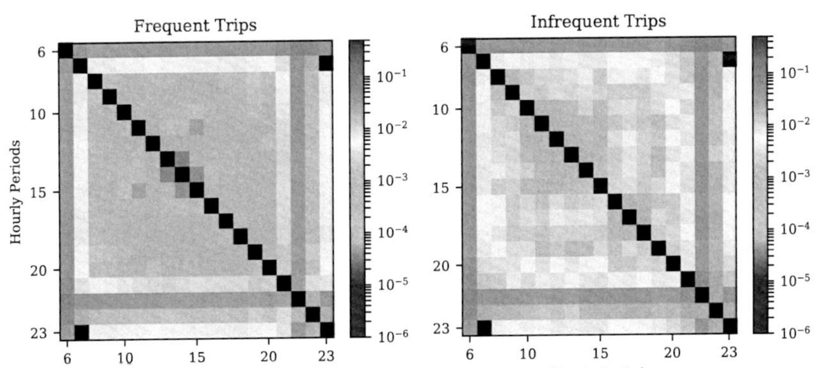

Fig. 7 Symmetric KL divergence matrices for both the frequent and infrequent trips for a typical weekday in March in the form of a 2D contour (plotted in logarithmic scale).

Table 6 Oost-Gelre's origin-destination matrix of all infrequent trips from 10 am to 9 pm for a typical weekday in March.

	Zone 1	Zone 2	Zone 3	Zone 4
Zone 1	0	273	0	0
Zone 2	297	0	296	318
Zone 3	30	409	0	281
Zone 4	38	332	149	0

Derived from the mobile phone data.

In contrast to the stability of frequent trips, the lack of (substantially) long time periods with mild spatial variations for the infrequent trips impedes the introduction of a fixed-schedule service (i.e., bus or train service) for accommodating them and reinforces the need to introduce more flexible mobility solutions. Focusing on infrequent trips, we examine the potential infrequent trip demand at each OD pair and we present the results for all infrequent trips from 10 am until 9 pm in Table 6.

Especially in zones 1 and 3 (which rely heavily on car use for trips within the municipality), there are 993 infrequent daily trips within Oost-Gelre that have a potential to be accommodated by a MaaS service.

5. Conclusions and further steps

In this chapter we used multiple data sources spanning from household surveys to smart card and cellular data to examine the potential of a MaaS platform in the municipality of Oost-Gelre, a rural and depopulating area in the Netherlands.

From the statistical analysis of the survey it can be concluded that inhabitants are generally satisfied with their accessibility and mobility options when conducting fixed, re-current trips (i.e., trips to/from work, etc.) even in sparsely populated areas with no public transport connections. This might be the result of residential self-selection processes where residents typically have access to a car and have a preference for car use and/or are capable of finding alternative mobility solutions for conducting their most common trips. Residents do show relatively high dissatisfaction levels for infrequent trips to varying destinations which are not fixed and study-related trips (i.e., trips to school). Infrequent trips with varying destinations (i.e., groceries, etc.) lead to a higher level of dissatisfaction in sparsely populated areas with less mobility options because, even if inhabitants of sparsely populated areas are able to organize well their fixed trips, the lack of alternative mobility options probably impacts the efficient planning of trips with no fixed destinations.

Furthermore, car drivers in the study area do not seem to be very willing to share rides. Frequent car passengers are more willing to adopt new mobility solutions. This is in line with the literature on ride sharing platforms in rural areas showing issues such as the need for community involvement, incentives for joining a ride-sharing initiative and financial and non-financial benefits for passengers and drivers.

Analysis of smart card and mobile phone data revealed that less than 5% of the respondents use public transport on a daily basis, and most of the public transport trips are to and from other areas in the Achterhoek region. The analysis of the spatio-temporal trip variation shows that infrequent trips exhibit a significant variation on the spatial distribution of trips across different times of the day (something that hampers the introduction of fixed-schedule services for accommodating infrequent trips).

The combination of analyses conducted in this chapter indicates that a MaaS platform in the study areas should target students and travelers who perform infrequent trips with activity types at the destination that span from making a day trip to business trips.

The study presented in this chapter is part of the Netmobil project which aims to iteratively develop and evaluate a MaaS system in the Achterhoek region. The outcomes of this study are used to identify the mobility challenges and problems different target groups in the Achterhoek experience. The next step is to evaluate these quantitative results by collecting additional qualitative data from citizens in the Achterhoek, as a starting point for an iterative co-design process of a MaaS system for the Achterhoek with potential end-users. With an emphasis on the involvement of the community in the development of a MaaS solution, we aim to address issues identified in the literature review such as lack of user involvement and lack of financial and non-financial benefits for participants.

A first pilot with the MaaS system in the municipality of Oost-Gelre will be conducted in 2019 and will allow us to study if the demand potential as indicated in this ex ante evaluation can be realized. A second pilot is planned for part of the years 2020 and 2021 with a version of the MaaS system that is improved based on the outcomes of the first pilot. In the final phase of the project, not only the quality of the mobility system will be assessed but also the usability of the system for the inhabitants of the municipality where the pilots have taken place. At the same time, final conclusions will be drawn on whether and how the system could be used permanently at the pilot location and possibly beyond.

References

Alvanger, K., 2014. Implementation of Ride Sharing. Final Report Project Mobile Together. Energy Agency for the Southeast Sweden.

Atzema, O., Hospers, G.J., Van Oort, P., Renooij, P., Teisman, G. & Tordoir, P. 2017. De Kracht van Oost Nederland. Een economisch-geografische analyse. Werkdocument. Regioplan/ESD/IHS/Atelier Tordoir: Amsterdam/Den Haag/Enschede/Nijmegen/Rotterdam. Available at: https://www.gelderland.nl/De-Kracht-van-Oost-Nederland-werkdocument

Brake, J., Nelson, J.D., 2007. A case study of flexible solutions to transport demand in a deregulated environment. J. Transp. Geogr. 15 (4), 262–273.

Briët, J., Harremoës, P., 2009. Properties of classical and quantum Jensen-Shannon divergence. Phys. Rev. A 79 (5), 052311.

Cervero, R., 1997. Paratransit in America: Redefining Mass Transportation. Praeger, Westport, USA.

Currie, G., 2010. Quantifying spatial gaps in public transport supply based on social needs. J. Transp. Geogr. 18, 31–41.

Daniels, R., Mulley, C., 2010. Overcoming barriers to implementing Flexible Transport Services in NSW. In: 33rd Australasian Transport Research Forum Conference. Institute of Transport Studies, Monash University, Canberra, Australia.

de Jong, W., Vogels, J., van Wijk, K., Cazemier, O., 2011. The key factors for providing successful public transport in low-density areas in the Netherlands. Res. Transp. Bus. Manag. 2 (0), 65–73.

Dutch Ministry of Transport, Public Works and Water Management, 2010. Public Transport in the Netherlands. Ministry of Transport, Public Works and Water Management, The Hague, the Netherlands.

Gkiotsalitis, K., Stathopoulos, A., 2016. Joint leisure travel optimization with user-generated data via perceived utility maximization. Trans. Res. C Emerg. Technol. 68, 532–548.

ITF, 2015. International Experiences on Public Transport Provision in Rural Areas. ITF, Paris.

Jittrapirom, P., Caiati, V., Feneri, A.-M., Ebrahimigharehbaghi, S., Alonso-González, M.J., Narayan, J., 2017. Mobility as a Service: a critical review of definitions, assessments of schemes, and key challenges. Urban Plan. 2 (2), 13–25.

Kamargianni, M., Li, W., Matyas, M., Schäfer, A., 2016. A critical review of new mobility services for urban transport. Trans. Res. Proc. 14, 3294–3303.

Kullback, S., Leibler, R.A., 1951. On information and sufficiency. Ann. Math. Statist. 22 (1), 79–86.

Mageean, J., Nelson, J.D., Wright, S., 2013. In: T. O. R. Group, (Ed.), Demand Responsive Transport: Responding to the Urban Bus Challenge. University of Newcastle upon Tyne, Newcastle upon Tyne, UK.

Nelson, J.D., Phonphitakchai, T., 2012. An evaluation of the user characteristics of an open access DRT service. Res. Transp. Econ. 34 (1), 54–65.

Papanikolaou, A., Basbas, S., Mintsis, G., Taxiltaris, C., 2017. A methodological framework for assessing the success of Demand Responsive Transport (DRT) services. Trans. Res. Proc. 24, 393–400.

PBL/CBS, 2016. Regionale bevolkings- en huishoudensprognose 2016–2040 [Regional Forecast of Population and Household Developments 2016–2040]. Netherlands Environmental Assessment Agency/Statistics Netherlands, The Hague.

Ryley, T.J., Stanley, P.A., Enoch, M.P., Zanni, A.M., Quddus, M.A., 2014. Investigating the contribution of Demand Responsive Transport to a sustainable local public transport system. Res. Transp. Econ. 48, 364–372.

Wang, C., Quddus, M., Enoch, M., Ryley, T., Davison, L., 2015. Exploring the propensity to travel by demand responsive transport in the rural area of Lincolnshire in England. Case Stud. Transp. Policy 3 (2), 129–136.

Wismans, L.J.J., Friso, K., Rijsdijk, J., de Graaf, S.W., Keij, J., 2018. Improving a priori demand estimates transport models using mobile phone data: a Rotterdam-region case. J. Urban Technol. 25 (2), 63–83.

Further reading

Geurs, K.T., Thomas, T., Bijlsma, M., Douhou, S., 2015. Automatic trip and mode detection with MoveSmarter: first results from the Dutch Mobile Mobility Panel. In: Procedia of the 10th International Conference on Survey Methods in Transport, pp. 247–262.

CHAPTER FOUR

Evaluating relative accessibility to retail in depopulated areas: Case study of the Maestrazgo region in Spain

Julio A. Soria-Lara[a,*], Aldo Arranz-López[b], Ricardo Badía-Lázaro[b]
[a]Transport Research Centre (TRANSyT), Universidad Politécnica de Madrid, Madrid, Spain
[b]Department of Geography and Spatial Planning, Universidad de Zaragoza, Zaragoza, Spain
*Corresponding author: e-mail address: julio.soria-lara@upm.es

Contents

Abstract

While there is a vast body of literature on how to maximize accessibility to basic needs in urban areas, less attention has been paid to the effects of accessibility variations in rural, isolated, and depopulated places. This chapter aims to address this challenge by studying how accessibility to retail in depopulated areas can vary depending on socio-economic characteristics and transport mode preferences of the population. The empirical focus is on "the Maestrazgo," a Spanish region with a depopulation rate of 84% between 1900 and 2017. First, a face-to-face survey examined the population's willingness to cover distances to daily and non-daily retail via different transport modes (car, public transport, and walking). Second, a clustering process was used to identify three socio-economic groups: the young, adults, and seniors. Third, multimodal

Advances in Transport Policy and Planning, Volume 2
ISSN 2543-0009
https://doi.org/10.1016/bs.atpp.2018.09.004

accessibility between the three population groups was evaluated and compared by using a benchmarking accessibility cube. The results show very low accessibility levels to daily and non-daily retail and high car dependency, underlining that accessibility for seniors is significantly different than for the other groups. The chapter closes with concluding remarks on the policy implications of the obtained results.

Keywords: Depopulation, Rural, Transport, Walking, Seniors

1. Introduction

While maximizing accessibility to major daily activities has become an intrinsic component of everyday life in contemporary urban societies (Bertolini, 2017), residents of depopulated areas often have to make additional efforts to access basic need services (e.g., groceries and health care) (Escalona-Orcao and Díez-Cornago, 2007; McGrail and Humphreys, 2009; Nemet and Bailey, 2000; Shah et al., 2017; van Leeuwen and Rietveld, 2011). Each day in any urban area, mobility routines triggered by high accessibility levels are translated into multiples individual and collective travels to work, shop, spend leisure time, meet family and friends. However, carrying out similar activities in depopulated areas can be extremely difficult, due to the drastically reduced offer of activities, very limited (or absent) public transportation services, poor car infrastructure, and populations that are widely dispersed across large areas (Arcury et al., 2005; Gray et al., 2006; Jordan et al., 2004; Yeager and Gatrell, 2014). For those reasons, particular groups (usually the elderly, low-income, and disabled populations) often must rely on transportation services provided by friends and family.

Although the possibility to meet some of the abovementioned needs via information and communication technologies (ICTs) (e.g., online shopping) is growing, and this can be seen as part of the potential solutions, most residents will require some form of physical accessibility. But even recognizing the high potential of ITCs, depopulated areas also lag behind urban areas in the implementation of internet facilities, precipitating a growing digital divide. In sum, a frequent picture is to see how people in depopulated areas are constrained by poor accessibility levels to basic needs, which partially contributes to further depopulation of these underserved areas. The exploration, development, and implementation of policy actions in both the short- and long-term are urgent, and that should be done through a high level of consensus between administrations, citizens, and the private sector.

Based on these important considerations, this chapter aims to provide new insights into the academic debate on the accessibility to basic services in depopulated areas, by evaluating multimodal relative accessibility to retail.[1] The research question is structured as follows: *Is multimodal accessibility to retail similar for different socio-economic groups in the context of a depopulated area, which are the most disadvantageous groups, and which are potential policy actions to address that issue?* To answer those questions, the region of the Maestrazgo (Aragón, Spain) serves as a study case. It is one of the most depopulated areas in Spain, and its population is under severe risk of social exclusion due to its limited capacity to participate in the social, cultural, and economic life of the country due to the very low accessibility levels to basic needs retail and other services. First, the population's willingness to cover distances to retail by using different transport modes (car, public transport, and walking) was examined via a face-to-face questionnaire. Second, a K-modes clustering method was employed to identify three distinct socio-economic population groups (the young, adults, and seniors). Third, multimodal accessibility for each socio-economic group was estimated via a gravity-based model, and comparisons between the accessibility values of the mentioned population groups were made through both the application of Kruskal–Wallis and Mann–Whitney *U* tests and the use of a multimodal accessibility benchmarking cube. Fourth, a discussion on policy actions is carried out, describing potential solutions, implementability, and acceptability issues.

The remainder of the chapter is structured as follows: Section 2 presents the main characteristics of the case study, while Section 3 details the research design. Section 4 shows the obtained results and Section 5 discusses the implications of these results for policymaking. Finally, Section 6 concludes with some closing remarks.

2. Relative accessibility to basic need services

One predominant element in accessibility discussions—also employed in the context of depopulated and rural areas—is the notion of physical accessibility as an absolute concept that affects the full range of the population equally (Bocarejo and Oviedo, 2012; Yeager and Gatrell, 2014). However, accessibility is profoundly shaped by issues such as cultural norms,

[1] In the context of this research, retail activity refers to two types of retail: daily retail which includes food stores (e.g., supermarkets, groceries); and non-daily retail which includes health and body care (e.g., pharmacy, gym, hairdresser), fashion (e.g., clothes, accessories), and other retail (e.g., furniture, car dealership).

habits, and individual preferences. Based on these factors, people have different willingness to cover distances to destinations by different transport modes (Arranz-López et al., 2018; Morency et al., 2011; Páez et al., 2013). Accessibility should be seen as a relative concept that depends on people, on habits, and on cultural contexts. The recognition of accessibility as a relative issue is key to progress in the identification of socio-economic groups under risk of social exclusion, as well as to design customized and effective solutions in policy formulation processes. Inspired by Páez et al. (2010, p3), we view relative accessibility as the proportion of opportunities available to and reachable by an individual with defined characteristics at a selected location in the context of a depopulated area, relative to an individual from a reference group at the same location.

While a growing number of studies of depopulated areas has focused on analyzing the effects of accessibility to basic needs (e.g., healthy food, health care services) on certain population groups (mostly the aging population) (Abdullah et al., 2018; Shergold et al., 2014), limited attention has traditionally been paid to simultaneously comparing accessibility values between several socio-economic groups. Another missing aspect in studies on accessibility in depopulated contexts is related to the lack of multimodal accessibility approaches (Shergold et al., 2014; Yeager and Gatrell, 2014). Most focus on car accessibility, which diverges from the idea that accessibility to basic needs is provided by multiples modes, with different effects on specific population groups. For example, in the context of depopulated areas, accessibility to basic needs in bigger towns with a richer establishment of basic needs opportunities can include a combination of non-motorized modes (walking and cycling) with private vehicles for some socio-economic groups. However, the population of smaller towns would be more dependent on public transport and private cars to meet their basic needs. The palette of accessibility options can vary depending on the size of the town, the transport infrastructures, socio-economic issues, and individual habits. In the view of this research, multimodal accessibility should be considered as a key factor for obtaining a more in-depth understanding of the social effects of accessibility issues, facilitating more detailed insights (e.g., identifying which socio-economic groups are more car dependent or which are more likely to become public transport users).

3. Case of study: The Maestrazgo (Aragón, Spain)

The Maestrazgo is located in Aragón, Spain. It consists of 15 municipalities covering 1204 km^2, and its population has decreased from 20,600 inhabitants in the beginning of the 20th century to 3209 inhabitants today, with a resulting extremely low population density (2.66 inhabitants/km^2).

Both the geographical location of the Maestrazgo (far away from the main Spanish transport corridors) and its mountainous topography—along with the related economic factors—have profoundly influenced the high depopulation rate. The existing road network divides the Maestrazgo into three main zones (Fig. 1). The southern area is structured by secondary roads (A226 and A227) that cross several municipalities, with Cantavieja as the most populous with a total of 717 inhabitants. The north-eastern zone is also structured by another secondary road (A226), where the municipality of Castellote is the most populous with 688 inhabitants. It is worth to mention that Cantavieja and Castellote are the only municipalities with over 500 inhabitants in the region. Finally, the north-western part is structured by a local winding road (A1702), and its most populous municipality has only 169 inhabitants.

The Maestrazgo is not only one of the most depopulated regions in Spain but also one of the poorest. Recently, rural tourism has significantly increased in the region, and it generates the highest number of jobs (48%) (IAEST, 2017). On the other hand, the agricultural sector provides a total of 31% of all jobs, a rate particularly high compared to the Spanish average of 4.4% (INE, 2018a). The weak economic base and the poor connections to the Spanish transport system are the main drivers of depopulation. During the first half of the 20th century, the region lost nearly 7000 inhabitants. In the next 20 years (1950–1970) the depopulation process further intensified to 9000 departures. As a result, the population totaled 4900 inhabitants in 1981. Since then, the depopulation rate has decreased, but the region is still losing population. Additionally, the percentage of residents over 65 years old is very high (29%) (INE, 2018b).

Public transport services are very limited—even non-existent in most municipalities. There are only three regular bus routes. The first route, from Monday to Friday, from La Iglesuela del Cid to Teruel (capital of the province where the Maestrazgo is located), with one stop in Miravete de la Sierra (but only on Thursdays). The second route, from Monday to Friday, starts in Cantavieja and ends in Alcorisa with one stop in Montoro de Mezquita on Tuesdays and Fridays. Finally, the third route from La Iglesuela del Cid to Alcañiz (municipality not included in the Maestrazgo) is only available on Tuesdays and Wednesdays.

The number and type of retail opportunities in the Maestrazgo region is rather limited, with in total 34 daily shops and 23 non-daily shops. In 13 of 15 municipalities daily retail activity can be found, while only 5 municipalities

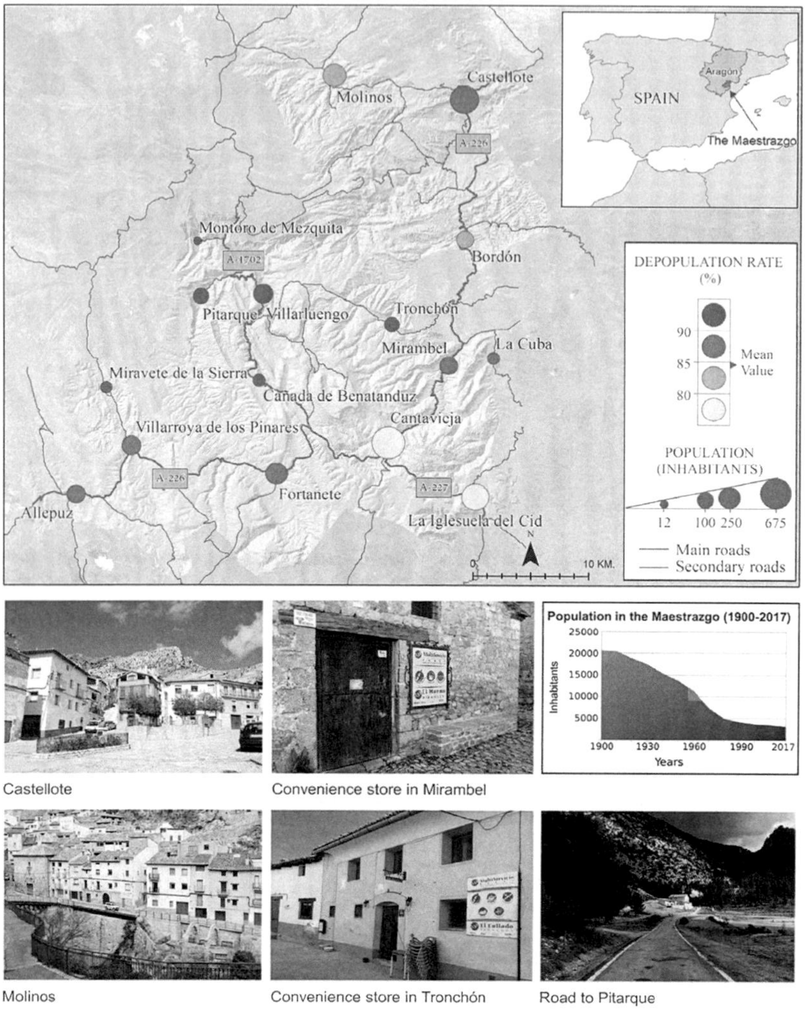

Fig. 1 Case study location.

have non-daily retail stores. The biggest municipalities such as Cantavieja, Castellote, and La Iglesuela del Cid have both daily and non-daily retail. The most representative example is Cantavieja with seven stores classified as daily retail, and seven stores classified as non-daily retail. In the other two municipalities, Villarroya de los Pinares and Molinos, non-daily retail is less commonly found. For example, Villarroya de los Pinares only has one store classified as non-daily retail. Finally, the smallest municipalities such as Allepuz and Miravete de la Sierra do not have both daily and non-daily retail activity.

4. Research design

To address the research questions of this chapter, analyzing if multimodal accessibility to retail is similar (or not) for different socio-economic groups of the population and its implications for policy-making, we followed a three-stage methodological approach (Fig. 2): (i) data collection; (ii) clustering techniques and distance-decay functions analysis; (iii) calculating and mapping relative multimodal accessibility.

4.1 Data collection

The main data source was a questionnaire regarding the willingness of respondents to reach daily and non-daily retail locations by three different

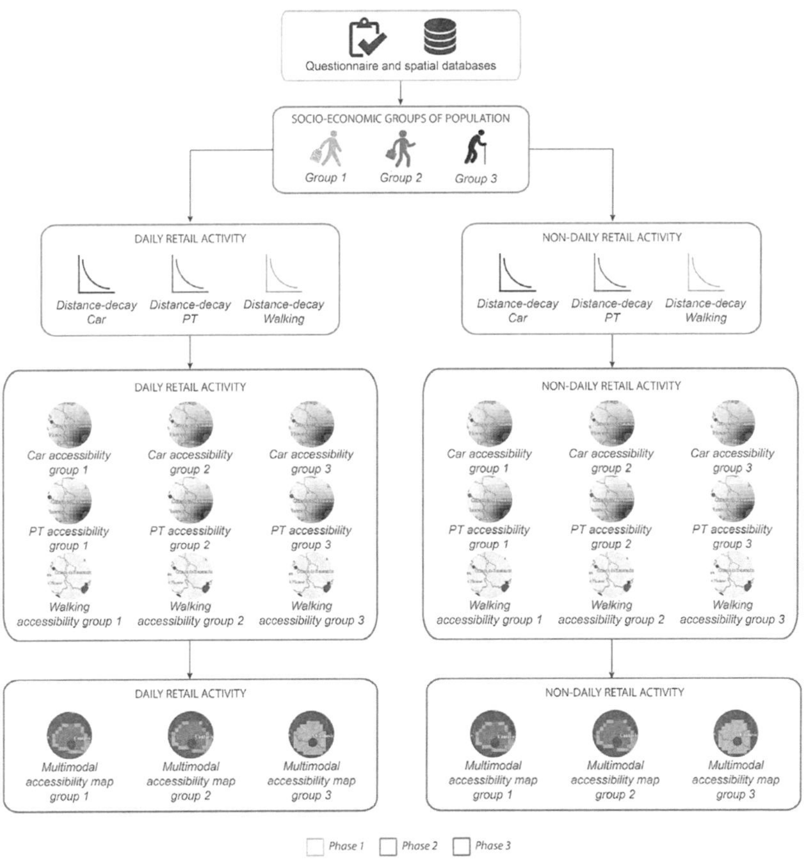

Fig. 2 Methodological scheme.

transport options: (i) car, (ii) public transport, and (iii) walking. A total of 96 people filled in the questionnaire, mostly face-to-face and occasionally online (only for the biggest municipalities with good internet facilities). Face-to-face surveys were crucial to obtain data, since the Maestrazgo has a high percentage of aging population with limited access to the internet. The selection of the participants was made in several fieldwork periods during March 2018. All municipalities and retail stores of the region were visited by the research team, asking people to fill in the questionnaire in the main entrance of those retail stores. That ensured that the selected participants usually were the people in-charge to access to retail activity from their respective households. The confidence interval for the sample was a 90%, with a 5% bias. The questionnaire served as input for clustering individuals and assessing distance-decay functions to retail activity, which was further used to estimate multimodal accessibility levels by using a gravity-based model.

The 30-question questionnaire was structured in two parts. The first part consisted of eight questions related to the socio-economic and demographic attributes of respondents, such as age, gender, home municipality, education level, employment status, monthly household income, and availability of both a driver's license and car. Responses based on gender, employment status, and the availability of a driver's license and car were coded as binary variables. Responses based on education level and monthly household income were classified into intervals. Levels of education were coded as follows: no formal education, low (primary school), medium (secondary school), and high (undergraduate studies and above). Monthly household income options were set as low (<€1000), medium (€1000–€1999), and high (>€2000).

The second part of the questionnaire consisted of nine questions related to willingness to reach daily and non-daily retail activities by car, public transport, and on foot. Responses were codified in intervals of 15, 30, 45, 60, 90, 120, 150, and 180 min for car and public transport, and 5, 10, 15, 30, 45, 60 min for walking. An example of such a question was: how much time are you willing to spend to reach daily retail stores by car/bus/walking?

Additionally, spatial databases were used including a 1 km × 1 km grid, from the European Environment Agency. Retail locations were manually digitized during the fieldwork campaign in the region. For accessibility calculations, both road and street networks from the Spanish National Centre of Geographic Information were used.

4.2 Clustering techniques and distance-decay functions analysis

In this methodological step, homogeneous socio-economic groups were identified according to key variables. These socio-economic groups form the basis for the estimation of distance-decay functions, which in turn lead to relative accessibility analysis by using gravity-based models. A K-modes algorithm was chosen due to the categorical nature of the data involved (Chaturvedi et al., 2001). A total of seven variables were taken into account for the clustering analysis: gender, age, education level, employment status, monthly household income, and availability of both driver's license and car.

First, a multiple correspondence analysis (MCA) was run in the Statistical Package for Social Sciences (SPSS 21), to explore the relationships between the socio-economic attributes collected in the questionnaire. This process revealed that age, monthly household income, employment status, and car availability were the less closely related variables, and they were used for the clustering analysis. The K-modes algorithm was run in the *klaR* package of the *RStudio* statistical computing environment, obtaining three different socio-economic population clusters (Section 4). The number of clusters was determined by using the *fviz_nbclust* function in *RStudio*, which determined the optimal number of clusters based on the silhouette width method.

Finally, distance-decay functions for each socio-economic cluster of the population were analyzed, based on the willingness to cover distances to retail by car, by public transport, and on foot. These functions provided the basis to calculate accessibility to daily and non-daily retail activities. Distance-decay functions were based on a negative exponential form, commonly used in transport studies (Handy and Niemeier, 1997; Iacono et al., 2010; Vega, 2012).

4.3 Calculating and mapping relative multimodal accessibility

A gravity-based model was used to calculate and map multimodal accessibility for the socio-economic clusters (Section 3.2). Accessibility indicators were designed according to three main components: (i) the number of retail stores at destinations; (ii) the distance between origins and destinations; (iii) distance-decay function that represents the willingness of each population cluster to reach daily and non-daily retail by car, by public transport, and on foot. The following formula was employed:

$$A_i = \sum E_{i \neq j} e^{\beta X_{ij}}$$

where A_i is the accessibility for zone i; E_j is the number of retail stores at destinations j; x_{ij} is the distance between origin and destination, and β is the parameter of the distance-decay function.

The distance between origins and destinations was assessed in minutes by calculating an Origin–Distance Matrix (ODM). The estimation of appropriate speeds per each transport mode was based on the maximum speed limits on the road network for car and public transport, while an average speed of 4 km/h was taken to travel on foot (Marquet and Miralles-Guasch, 2014). For car ODM, each cell of the study area was included as origin and destination, while the public transport ODM was based on the distance between cells that had a bus stop. Finally, walking ODM was obtained by calculating the travel time from each cell to the closest municipality by applying a location-allocation analysis.

Since accessibility values were only obtained for cells with retail opportunities, a natural neighbor interpolation analysis was carried out for car and public transport modes, in order to obtain continuous surface maps. In the case of walking accessibility, this step was not made, as it is assumed that people only walk inside town boundaries. Natural neighbor interpolation can be used for both interpolation and extrapolation, and the basic equation works as the Inverse Distance Weighted (IDW) method. Although natural neighbor can efficiently handle large datasets, variations of this method have also been used with small datasets (Boissonnat and Cazals, 2002). In order to facilitate the comparison of accessibility results for each transport mode, the obtained accessibility values were normalized between 0 and 1. The obtained accessibility results for each transport mode were then compared between socio-economic clusters by using Kruskal–Wallis and Mann–Whitney U tests. The non-parametric Kruskal–Wallis test was used to compare accessibility between the three socio-economic clusters simultaneously. Significant differences at P-level 0.05 would indicate that at least one socio-economic cluster had accessibility levels significantly different from the other clusters. The non-parametric Mann–Whitney U test was used to analyze accessibility levels between pairs of socio-economic clusters for the cases where differences at P-level 0.05 were obtained for the Kruskal–Wallis test.

Finally, the multimodal accessibility results for each socio-economic cluster were combined by using a multimodal accessibility benchmarking cube (Silva, 2013), which provides a specific map of multimodal accessibility for each socio-economic population cluster (Fig. 3). A total of eight multimodal accessibility categories were established in the benchmarking cube,

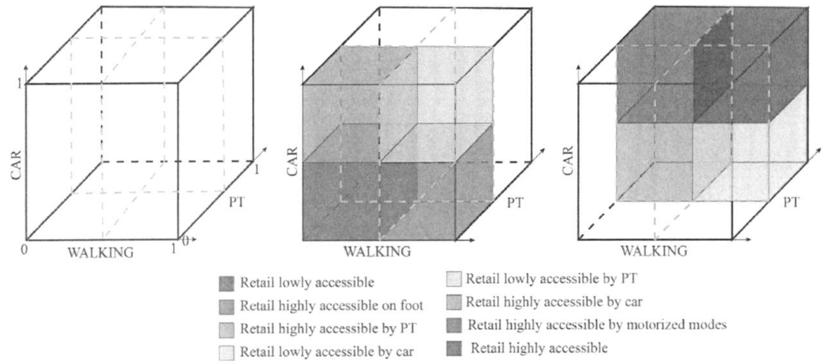

Fig. 3 Benchmarking accessibility cube. Inspired by Silva (2013).

ranging from "low retail accessibility" by any transport mode to "high retail accessibility" by all three transport modes included in the research (car, public transport, and walking).

5. Results

5.1 Sample characteristics

Men and women answers were equally divided, and the mean age of individuals was 50.44 years old. The educational level was distributed in four categories: no studies (14.4%), basic (25.8%), medium (31.9%), and high (27.8%). Regarding the employment status, a total of 35.1% of participants were unemployed or retired, while 64% were employed. However, the household incomes in El Maestrazgo can be considered as low or very low. The most common household incomes were under €1000 (44.3% of participants) and between €1000 and €2000 (46.4%). Only the 9.3% from the sample had a household income over €0.2000. Finally, it highlights that most of people had both driving license (83.5%) and household car availability (84.5%).

5.2 Clustering and distance-decay functions

Based on the questionnaire responses, a total of three socio-economic clusters were identified in the case study (Fig. 4).

- *Cluster #1*, called *the young*, are individuals between 18 and 39 years old, with a job, car availability, and with monthly household incomes between €1000 and €2000.

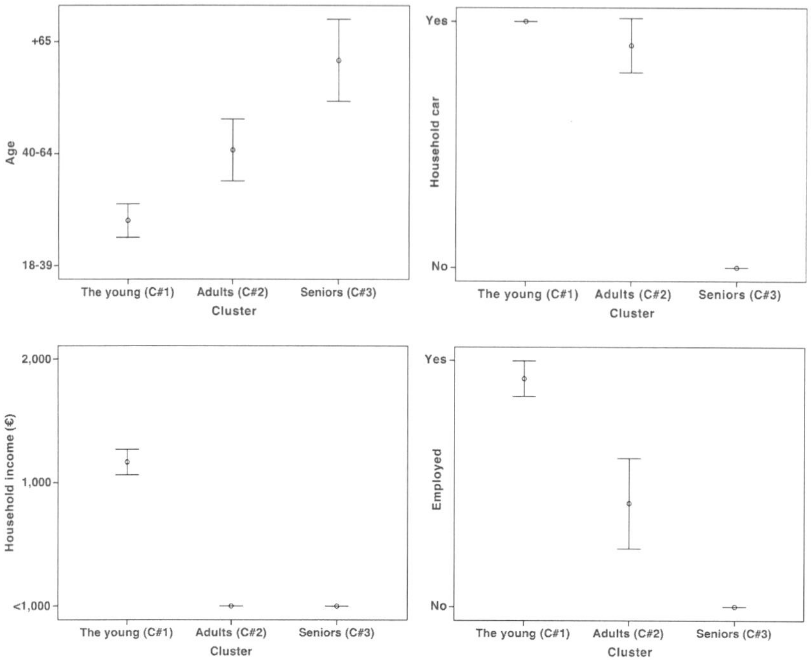

Fig. 4 Error bars (95% IC) to characterize clusters.

- *Cluster #2*, called *adults*, are individuals between 40 and 64 years old, with car availability, monthly household incomes under €1000.
- *Cluster #3*, called *seniors*, are individuals older than 65 years, retired, without access to a car, and with monthly household incomes under €1000.

For each cluster, a set of six distance-decay functions were obtained according to the two types of retail (daily and non-daily) and the three transport modes (car, public transport, walking), providing the basis for the accessibility calculation.

5.3 Mapping relative accessibility

For each socio-economic cluster, accessibility levels for car, public transport, and walking to daily and non-daily retail were finally obtained (Fig. 5). The gravity-based model detailed in Section 3 was used for this purpose.

Car accessibility to daily retail showed the highest values for the target groups the young and adults (Fig. 6), with respective median values of 0.176 and 0.166. The municipalities of Cantavieja, Castellote, and La Iglesuela del Cid had the highest values for car accessibility, since the host

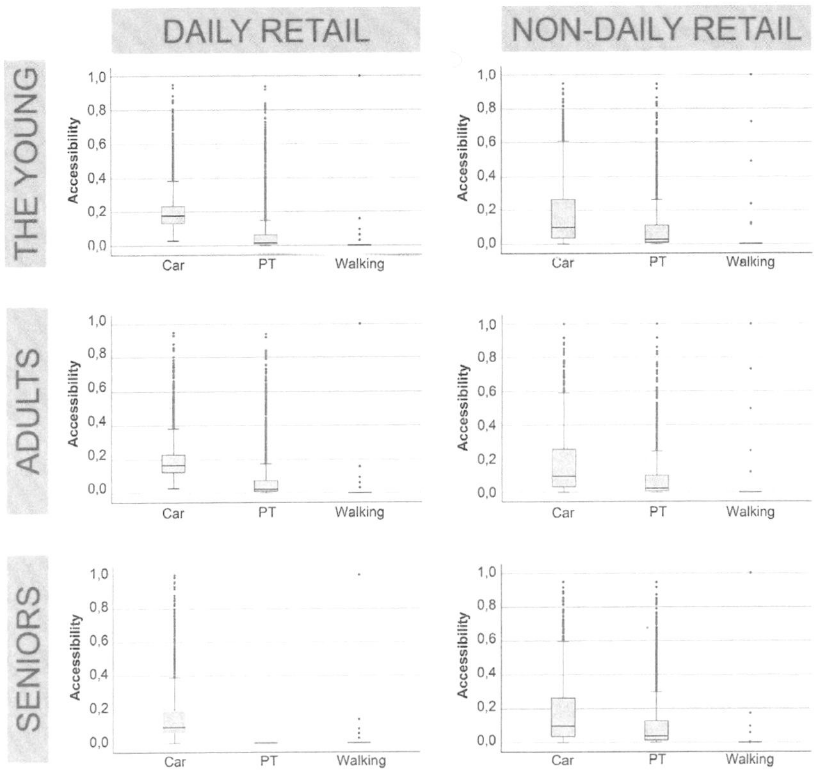

Fig. 5 Accessibility values in the case study (Legend: Points are outliers (>percentile 90th); Upper-part of box plot is 75th percentile; Lower-part of box plot is 25th percentile; line within the box is the median).

most retail opportunities in the region. The rest of the region had medium and low levels of car accessibility, which indicates that an important part of its population travel to other municipalities to reach retail. Unlike these two groups, car accessibility to daily retail for seniors had the lowest values across the Maestrazgo Region, with a median value of 0.095. In this case, the highest values were mainly located in the municipality of Cantavieja, while the others had medium and low car accessibility values. The accessibility variations between socio-economic groups are mainly due to willingness to reach daily retail by car. The young and adults unanimously declared during the fieldwork that they patronize local daily groceries (e.g., bakeries, butchers, greengrocers), but usually travel to shop every fortnight or once a month to Cantavieja and Castellote. Furthermore, they also travel to other towns beyond the region (e.g., Alcañiz, Teruel, Castellón) to shop in big

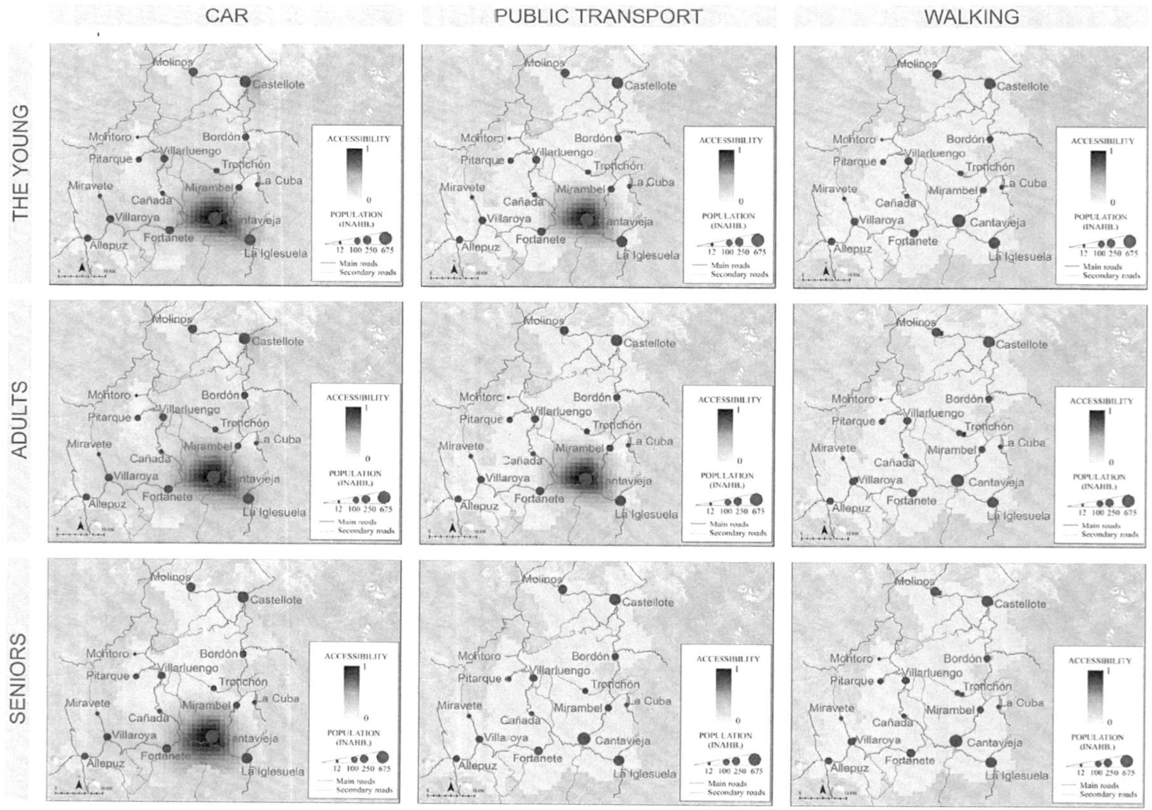

Fig. 6 Relative accessibility to daily retail.

supermarkets and shopping centres in other towns out of the region for big purchases. As a result, both the young and adults asserted that "their daily life was car dependent to access to most of basic needs, such as retail, health care services, and other administrative facilities."

In contrast, seniors buy most often in the stores located in their own municipality, which are complemented with traveling markets once a week for groceries and clothes. Some reasons for this habit are related to not having a drivers' license, insufficient income to fund car ownership, and health barriers to driving. Nevertheless, some seniors declared that they usually take the opportunity to order some products with their relatives who travel to other municipalities beyond the region. In summary, the seniors cohort is drastically disadvantaged compared to the other socio-economic groups, due to being limited to obtain products from daily retail that can be only reached on foot in their own towns or by public transport, which is highly limited in the Maestrazgo. In this respect, the constant decrease of retail locations in smaller towns is increasing the risk of social exclusion of seniors.

Car accessibility to non-daily retail had similar values for all three target groups (Fig. 7), with similar medial values for the young, adults, and seniors of 0.0987, 0.0967, and 0.0977, respectively. While the municipalities of Cantavieja, Castellote, and La Iglesuela del Cid had the highest values, the west of the case study had the lowest values of accessibility due to the non-existence of non-daily retail in those places. The minor accessibility variations between socio-economic groups are mainly due to the low number of non-daily retail opportunities in the region and the poor public transport services, which forces most of the population to use cars to reach non-daily retail. Furthermore, all socio-economic groups declared that "they usually travel to other towns beyond the region to buy non-daily goods, since the supply is clearly higher, and for us it is a way to break with our everyday."

Public transport accessibility to daily retail had the highest values for the target groups of the young and adults (Fig. 6). However, seniors had zero accessibility as they were not willing to reach daily retail locations by public transport, according to the questionnaire responses. The medians for the three target groups were significantly low, 0.014 for the young, 0.022 for adults, and 0 for seniors. In this case, Cantavieja had the highest accessibility values, while the rest of the region had zero accessibility by public transport. This is due to the poor public transport services. The zero accessibility for seniors, who are completely dependent of local daily retail, must be highlighted.

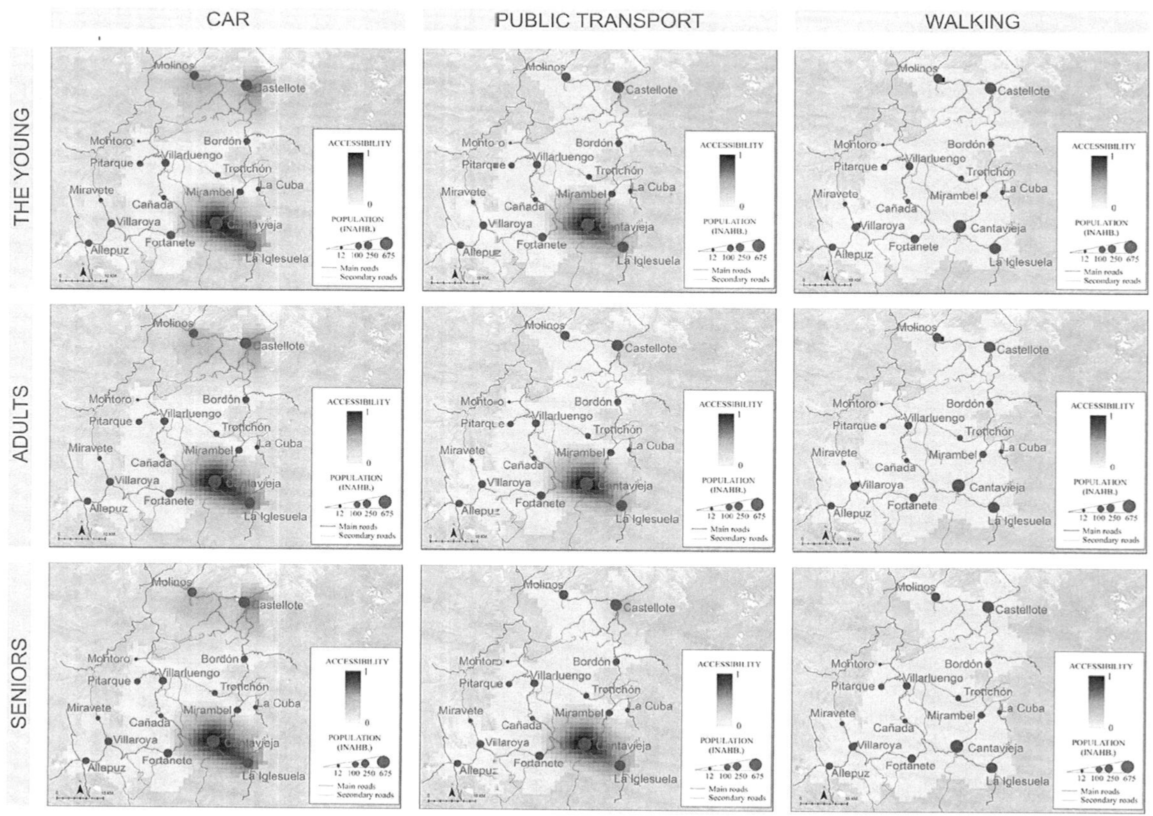

Fig. 7 Relative accessibility to non-daily retail.

The public transport accessibility to non-daily retail showed similar spatial patterns for the three target groups with similar median values (Fig. 7), 0.026 for the young, 0.024 for adults, and 0.037 for seniors. Again, Cantavieja, Castellote, and La Iglesuela del Cid were the municipalities with the highest values. The young and adults declared that "we rarely take the bus to reach non-daily retail activity, since it almost doubles travel time." Although seniors had the highest median, which means the highest willingness to reach non-daily retail by public transport, they used public transport only occasionally, especially for reaching health services located beyond the region (e.g., in the municipalities of Teruel and Alcañiz). The respondents unanimously recognized that "the region has a very poor supply of public transport, and the transport schedules are not appropriate for the ageing population."

In the case of walking accessibility to daily retail (Fig. 6), only cells within municipalities have values over 0. Cantavieja, Castellote, and La Iglesuela del Cid were the municipalities with the highest values for all three socioeconomic groups, while adults and seniors had both the highest and similar values for the rest of municipalities (e.g., Molinos, Bordón, Villarroya de los Pinares). The low walking accessibility values in the smaller municipalities are driven by two main factors. On the one hand, there is a lack of daily retail activity in those places. Some municipalities had only one convenience store with both a limited supply and limited open hours. Even in the smallest municipalities, the only bar corresponds to the convenience store. On the other hand, prices are higher than in retail stores located in the more populated towns. Among other reasons, this is due to the isolated geographical location of the region and the poor road conditions, which increase the cost of freight service. Adding up all these factors, populations from the smallest municipalities preferred to reach retail by car in the biggest municipalities of the region, which offer both higher supply and lower prices. During the fieldwork, the young and adults declared to "only buy daily goods in my municipality if I forgot to buy something in the supermarket." Accordingly, the seniors cohort is again the most disadvantaged, due to having the lowest household incomes and largest car use limitations.

In the case of walking accessibility to non-daily retail (Fig. 7), the situation is even more worrying. Only Cantavieja, Castellote, and La Iglesuela del Cid had a "real" offer of non-daily retail. Other municipalities, such as Molinos, also had a high value of accessibility, but due to the availability of two hairdressers. However, it can be said that the non-daily retail supply did not really exist in the mentioned municipality.

Table 1 Kruskal–Wallis test for accessibility to daily and non-daily retail by multiples transport modes.

	Car	Public transport	Walking
Accessibility to daily retail (*P* value 0.05)	0.000[a]	0.000[a]	1.000
Accessibility to non-daily retail (*P* value 0.05)	0.913	0.000[a]	1.000

[a]Significant values at $P < 0.05$ level.

This finding was supported by the Kruskal–Wallis test, which showed significant differences at *P*-level 0.05 between the three socio-economic clusters for car and public transport accessibility to daily retail (Table 1). This means that at least one socio-economic cluster had significantly different values for car and public transport accessibility to daily retail.

Both the size of the towns and the location of retail activity in the Maestrazgo can help to better understand the obtained results for the Kruskal–Wallis test. On the one hand, the small size of the towns makes it possible for all socio-economic groups to easily reach the existing daily retail locations in their towns on foot, reducing the options to obtain significant walking accessibility differences between them. On the other hand, the low number of non-daily retail opportunities in the region (mostly located in the municipalities of Cantavieja and Castellote), combined with the poor public transport services, forces most residents to use a car to reach non-daily retail, reducing the likelihood to find significant differences for accessibility by car. However, in the case of accessibility to non-daily retail, statistical differences at *P*-level 0.05 between the three socio-economic clusters were only found for public transport accessibility.

Table 2 shows the results for the non-parametric Mann–Whitney *U* test, used to find significant differences between pairs of socio-economic clusters for those accessibility values previously identified as statistically different by the Kruskal–Wallis test. The statistical differences for car accessibility to daily retail and public transport accessibility to daily and non-daily retail show that motorized accessibility for seniors is significantly different from the other groups.

In the last part of the analysis, modal accessibility values for each socio-economic cluster were combined by using the accessibility benchmarking cube (Fig. 8). Although a total of eight multimodal accessibility categories were established in the benchmarking cube (see Section 3 and Fig. 3), only some of them were finally identified in the case study.

Table 2 Mann–Whitney *U* test for car and public transport accessibility to retail.

Car accessibility

	Daily retail		
	C1	C2	C3
C1	–	0.012[a]	0.000[a]
C2		–	0.000[a]

Public transport accessibility

	Daily retail			Non-daily retail		
	C1	C2	C3	C1	C2	C3
C1	–	0.000[a]	0.000[a]	–	0.306	0.000[a]
C2		–	0.000[a]		–	0.000[a]

[a]Significant values at $P < 0.05$ level.

On the one hand, the typologies of multimodal accessibility to daily retail were very similar for the three target groups (Fig. 9). Almost the entire study area had "low retail accessibility", while the municipality of Cantavieja also had "high retail accessibility by motorised transport modes." The most remarkable difference was found for seniors, who had higher values for cells with "high retail accessibly by car."

On the other hand, the typologies of multimodal accessibility to non-daily retail were very similar for all population groups (Fig. 9). In Cantavieja municipality, both "high retail accessibly by car" and "high retail accessibly by motorised modes" were found for all three socio-economic groups. In the case of La Iglesuela del Cid, only "high retail accessibly by car" was found. Finally, in the area that corresponds to Castellote municipality, "high retail accessibly by car" and "low retail accessibility by public transport" were found for all three population groups.

6. Implications for policymaking

How can accessibility levels beyond cities be improved? This is one of the main questions in transport policy and planning in the coming decades (Bruun and Givoni, 2015). In this context, accessibility to basic needs beyond urban areas is crucial for regional development. The exodus of people from the countryside to cities is accelerating urbanization, triggering a

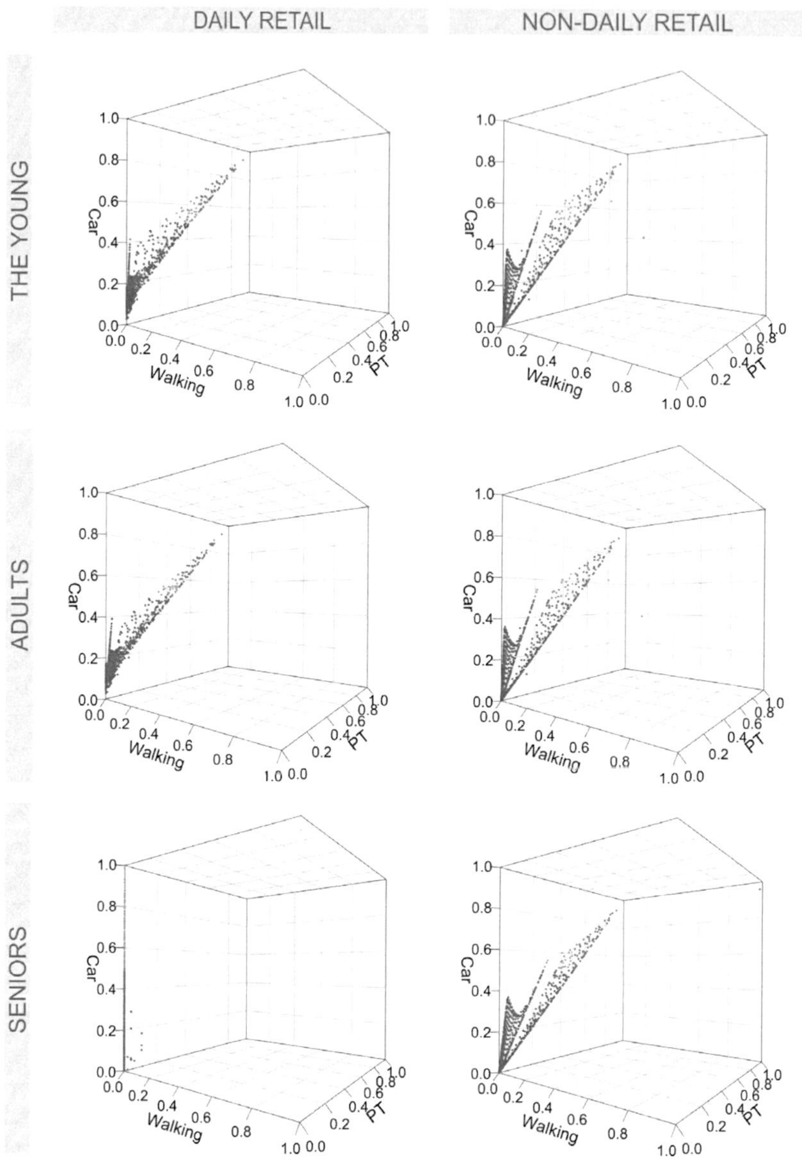

Fig. 8 Multimodal accessibility cube.

rapid growth of megacities, which are plagued by social inequalities and low sustainability standards. Furthermore, depopulation processes can also intensify climate change consequences. For instance, depopulated areas tend to suffer from increased fire risk, reduced river flows, and increased soil erosion

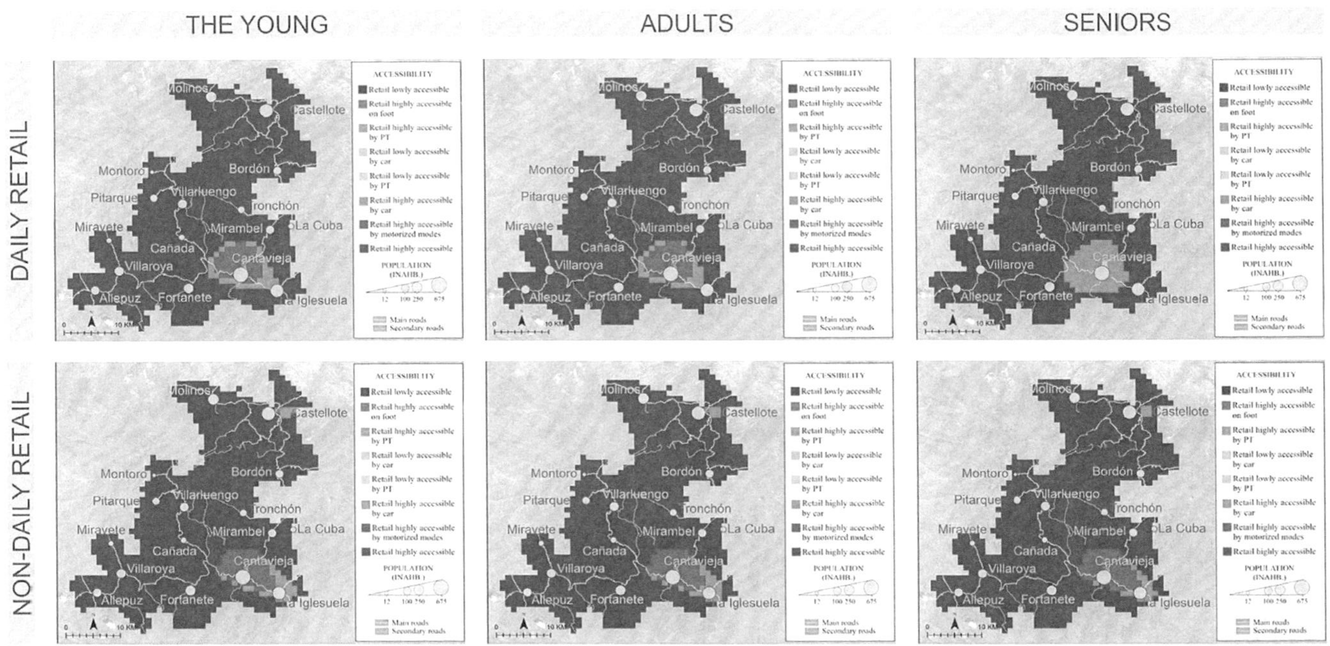

Fig. 9 Multimodal accessibility maps.

(Lasanta et al., 2015). Accordingly, researchers need to generate solutions to improve connections—local, regional, and between cities and their hinterlands—and studies need to be more regionally equitable.

Building on the research findings, this part of the chapter will focus on implications for the process of policy formulation. In particular, three potential ways to increase the accessibility to retail will be discussed in-depth: (i) the role of ICTs; (ii) on-demand transport services; and (iii) planning the city and its hinterland as a whole.

- *The role of ICTs*. ICTs have increasingly become a daily staple of our society in multiple ways. For instance, many people can e-work and e-shop, or can further their education online. The problem is that ICTs are largely ignored in accessibility planning, and academic studies that examine the capacity of ICTs as a transformative instrument in depopulated areas are still limited (Carrasco et al., 2008; Páez and Scott, 2007; van Wee, 2016). Three main problems are related to the use of ICTs to improve accessibility to retail in the context of the case study. First, the internet facilities in the Maestrazgo are quite weak, even despite the repeated promises by the Spanish government to improve those facilities in rural and depopulated areas in the country. For instance, optical fiber and 4G connection are hard to find in the region. Investments in internet facilities do not seem the most expensive part of potential solutions, neither a technical issue, but needed to be solved. Second, a large part of the population is made up of seniors, most of whom have never been connected to the internet or used a smart phone, and this is the group that faces the most severe accessibility limitations due to difficulties to access and use cars. Therefore, one important part of the solution should be focused on reducing the digital divide for this part of the population. Third, a retail scheme based on e-shopping necessitates resolving key logistics' issues. In the context of the Maestrazgo, this is a crucial challenge due to the mountainous topography and the poor transport infrastructures. Investment in infrastructures would be the standard approach, but also the promotion of logistics hubs in the region as well as the development of pilot projects with innovative system (e.g., drone deliveries) should be explored.
- *On-demand transportation services*. The lack of effective public transport is a very important limitation for the Maestrazgo. In particular, seniors (a population that is very willing to take public transport) are adversely affected by the low number of services and itineraries. In the context of low demand for public transport services, the implementation of

on-demand transport solutions can be particularly effective. Potential solutions include designing shared public transport itineraries, where children can travel to schools and residents can travel to retail; ad hoc, door-to-door transport services, under the framework of mobility-as-a-service; car sharing solutions to cover routine travels to retail locations, health services, and other basic needs. Certainly, part of the movements from *seniors* and *adults* is currently running in that way in the case study, but generating ad hoc travels that rely on relatives and friends. However, policy incentives for on-demand transport solutions could generate entrepreneurial business models among young people, which would need to be fostered by public institutions and orientated toward reducing the risk of social exclusion of specific population groups. Such solutions should include door-to-door deliveries in the region and other mobility services.

- *Planning the city and its hinterland as a whole.* Part of the accessibility based problem in depopulated areas is related to the inherent vision of those places as self-sufficient, i.e., the expectations that each region must have the widest range of retail opportunities, all types of health care services, etc. However, a part of these needs can be covered by the nearby main urban areas. Planning the city and its hinterland as a whole could foster accessibility solutions based on proximity when necessary (i.e., for daily retail) and on good connections between the depopulated areas and urban places when convenient (i.e., occasional retail). The main barriers in the Spanish context for implementing a planning process that integrates the city and its hinterland are found in the governance system, which is too rigid between municipalities, regions, etc. Another important problem is the current urban planning system, in which it is difficult to introduce planning instruments that simultaneously combine urban and regional areas.

7. Conclusions

This chapter is aimed at providing additional insights for the debate on accessibility to basic needs in depopulated areas. In particular, it focused on studying how multimodal accessibility to retail varies according to socio-economic groups. Three population groups were studied in this chapter: the young, adults, and seniors. Multimodal accessibility for seniors is remarkably different from the other groups: they are very car dependent for non-daily retail and limited to walking accessibility for daily retail.

The young and adults showed higher accessibility levels due to higher car availability and higher willingness to travel to other municipalities for daily and non-daily retail, even traveling beyond the region.

At the spatial level, the region has two main municipalities, in which the highest values of multimodal accessibility are concentrated: Cantavieja (highest) and Castellote. Both municipalities have the lowest depopulation rates in the region, and public transport services focus on these municipalities as the main destinations. The chapter closed with a few reflections on implication for policymaking, detailing three strategies how to improve accessibility to retail: (i) the role of ICTs; (ii) on-demand transportation services; and (iii) planning the city and its hinterland as a whole. Although, these potential solutions are presented for the specific context of the Maestrazgo, all of them are scalable to other contexts and countries. The need for pilot projects to test potential solutions is crucial in Spain, and stronger efforts from public institutions are expected in this respect. One important element in the design of potential solutions should be the consideration of how socio-economic variations of the population could drastically affect to the effectiveness of the selected policy actions, since one of the main contribution of the present book chapter is the evidence of how accessibility levels are strongly relative and dependent on cultural norms and habits in the context of depopulated areas. In the Maestrazgo case, policy-makers and the regional government should assume future scenarios where population rate will decrease and the elderly population will be higher, being key the design policy packages in the short-, mid-, and long-term. The described problematic is similar to low density areas in other Spanish region, however, the origin of the problematic is quite different and the temporal dynamic of population tends to make the problem stronger. That should be an aspect to take into consideration during the formulation of policy actions.

Finally, the next steps in the research on accessibility to retail in depopulated areas could be based on comparing the obtained results with other depopulated areas in different geographical context (e.g., depopulated places closer to big urban areas). This would facilitate a more-in-depth understanding on how the geographies of location affect accessibility levels and the potential solutions to accessibility challenges. Other research lines can be based on exploring the potentialities of ICTs to access to retail, comparing municipalities with better locations and remote places.

Acknowledgments

This paper has been elaborated under the framework of the following projects: (i) TRANS-URBAN: Simulación de escenarios colaborativos para integrar políticas de transporte urbano sostenible y usos del suelo, funded by the Spanish Government under National R&D Plan (2018 2020). Grant agreement no. CSO2017-86914-C2-2-P; (ii) future studies, transport, and urban planning, funded by the Plan Propio de Investigación de la Universidad Politécnica de Madrid. Grant agreement no. VJIDOCUPM18JASL.

References

Abdullah, J.M., Ahmad, M.M., Saqib, S.E., 2018. Understanding accessibility to healthcare for elderly people in Bangladesh. Dev. Pract. 28 (4), 552–561. https://doi.org/10.1080/09614524.2018.1450845.

Arcury, T.A., et al., 2005. The effects of geography and spatial behavior on health care utilization among the residents of a rual region. Health Serv. Res. 40 (1), 135–155. https://doi.org/10.1111/j.1475-6773.2005.00346.x.

Arranz-López, A., et al., 2018. Measuring relative non-motorized accessibility to retail activities. Int. J. Sustain. Trans. 1–13. https://doi.org/10.1080/15568318.2018.1498563Taylor & Francis, 0(0), in press.

Bertolini, L., 2017. In: Rydin, Y., Thornley, A. (Eds.), Planning the Mobile Metropolis. Transport for People, Places and the Planet. Palgrave.

Bocarejo, S.J.P., Oviedo, H.D.R., 2012. Transport accessibility and social inequities: a tool for identification of mobility needs and evaluation of transport investments. J. Transp. Geogr. 24, 142–154. https://doi.org/10.1016/j.jtrangeo.2011.12.004. Elsevier Ltd.

Boissonnat, J.-D., Cazals, F., 2002. Smooth surface reconstruction via natural neighbour interpolation of distance functions. Comput. Geom. 22 (1–3), 185–203. https://doi.org/10.1016/S0925-7721(01)00048-7.

Bruun, E., Givoni, M., 2015. Sustainable mobility: six research routes to steer transport policy. Nature 523 (7558), 29–31. https://doi.org/10.1038/523029a.

Carrasco, J.A., Miller, E.J., Wellman, B., 2008. How far and with whom do people socialize? Empirical evidence about distance between social network members. Trans. Res. Rec. J. Trans. Res. Board 2076 (1), 114–122. https://doi.org/10.3141/2076-13.

Chaturvedi, A., Green, P.E., Caroll, J.D., 2001. K-modes clustering. J. Classif. 18 (1), 35–55. https://doi.org/10.1007/s00357-001-0004-3.

Escalona-Orcao, A.I., Díez-Cornago, C., 2007. Accessibility to basic services in one to the most sparsely populated areas in Europe: the province of Teruel (Spain). Area 39 (3), 295–309.

Gray, D., Shaw, J., Farrington, J., 2006. Community transport, social capital and social exclusion in rural areas. Area 38 (1), 89–98. https://doi.org/10.1111/j.1475-4762.2006.00662.x.

Handy, S.L.L., Niemeier, D.A.A., 1997. Measuring accessibility: an exploration of issues and alternatives. Environ. Plan. A Commun. 29 (7), 1175–1194. and Regional Planning Program, School of Architecture, University of Texas at Austin, Austin, TX 78712–1160, United States. Available at:https://www.scopus.com/inward/record.uri?eid=2-s2.0-0031441298&partnerID=40&md5=4c971c0e691d04a8c4b31cb3197629c7.

Iacono, M., Krizek, K.J., El-Geneidy, A., 2010. Measuring non-motorized accessibility: issues, alternatives, and execution. J. Transp. Geogr. 18 (1), 133–140. https://doi.org/10.1016/j.jtrangeo.2009.02.002. Elsevier Ltd.

IAEST, 2017. Estadística Local. Trabajo, Salarios y Relaciones Laborales. Afiliaciones en alta a la Seguridad Social. http://www.aragon.es/DepartamentosOrganismosPublicos/Institutos/InstitutoAragonesEstadistica/AreasGenericas/ci.EstadisticaLocal.detalleDepartamento.

INE, 2018a. Encuesta de población activa, Trimestre 1-2018. Resultados Nacionales. Distribución porcentual de los ocupados por sector económico y sexo. https://www.ine.es/dyngs/INEbase/es/operacion.htm?c=Estadistica_C&cid=1254736176918&menu=resultados&idp=1254735976595.

INE, 2018b. Cifras oficiales de población de los municipios españoles: Revisión del Padrón Municipal. https://www.ine.es/dyngs/INEbase/es/operacion.htm?c=Estadistica_C&cid=1254736177011&menu=resultados&idp=1254734710990.

Jordan, H., et al., 2004. Distance, rurality and the need for care: access to health services in South West England. Int. J. Health Geogr. 3 (21), 1–9. https://doi.org/10.1186/1476-072X-3-21.

Lasanta, T., Nadal-Romero, E., Arnáez, J., 2015. Managing abandoned farmland to control the impact of re-vegetation on the environment. The state of the art in Europe. Environ. Sci. Policy 52, 99–109. https://doi.org/10.1016/j.envsci.2015.05.012.

Marquet, O., Miralles-Guasch, C., 2014. Walking short distances. The socioeconomic drivers for the use of proximity in everyday mobility in Barcelona. Transp. Res. A Policy Pract. 70, 210–222. https://doi.org/10.1016/j.tra.2014.10.007. Elsevier Ltd.

McGrail, M.R., Humphreys, J.S., 2009. Measuring spatial accessibility to primary care in rural areas: improving the effectiveness of the two-step floating catchment area method. Appl. Geogr. 29 (4), 533–541. https://doi.org/10.1016/j.apgeog.2008.12.003. Elsevier Ltd.

Morency, C., et al., 2011. Distance traveled in three Canadian cities: spatial analysis from the perspective of vulnerable population segments. J. Transp. Geogr. 19 (1), 39–50. https://doi.org/10.1016/j.jtrangeo.2009.09.013. Elsevier Ltd.

Nemet, G.F., Bailey, A.J., 2000. Distance and health care utilization among the rural elderly. Soc. Sci. Med. 50 (9), 1197–1208. https://doi.org/10.1016/S0277-9536(99)00365-2.

Páez, A., Scott, D.M., 2007. Social influence on travel behavior: a simulation example of the decision to telecommute. Environ. Plan. A 39 (3), 647–665. https://doi.org/10.1068/a37424.

Páez, A., et al., 2010. Relative accessibility deprivation indicators for urban settings: definitions and application to food deserts in Montreal. Urban Stud. 47 (7), 1415–1438. https://doi.org/10.1177/0042098009353626.

Páez, A., Nurul, K.M., Morency, C., 2013. Mode use and trip length of seniors in Montreal. J. Transp. Geogr. 30, 89–99. https://doi.org/10.1016/j.jtrangeo.2013.03.007. Elsevier Ltd.

Shah, T.I., Milosavljevic, S., Bath, B., 2017. Measuring geographical accessibility to rural and remote health care services: challenges and considerations. Spat. Spatiotemporal Epidemiol. 21, 87–96. https://doi.org/10.1016/j.sste.2017.04.002. Elsevier Ltd.

Shergold, I., Parkhurst, G., Musselwhite, C., 2014. Rural car dependence: an emerging barrier to community activity for older people. Transp. Plan. Technol. 35 (1), 69–85. https://doi.org/10.1080/03081060.2012.635417.

Silva, C., 2013. Structural accessibility for mobility management. Prog. Plan. 81 (1), 1–49. https://doi.org/10.1016/j.progress.2012.07.001.

van Leeuwen, E.S., Rietveld, P., 2011. Spatial consumer behaviour in small and medium-sized towns. Reg. Stud. https://doi.org/10.1080/00343401003713407.

van Wee, B., 2016. Accessible accessibility research challenges. J. Transp. Geogr. 51, 9–16. https://doi.org/10.1016/j.jtrangeo.2015.10.018. Elsevier B.V.

Vega, A., 2012. Using place rank to measure sustainable accessibility. J. Transp. Geogr. 24, 411–418. https://doi.org/10.1016/j.jtrangeo.2012.04.008. Elsevier Ltd.

Yeager, C.D., Gatrell, J.D., 2014. Rural food accessibility: an analysis of travel impedance and the risk of potential grocery closures. Appl. Geogr. 53, 1–10. https://doi.org/10.1016/j.apgeog.2014.05.018. Elsevier Ltd.

CHAPTER FIVE

Older drivers in rural areas: Implications for health, social inclusion and caregiving

K. Bruce Newbold*, Anastassios Dardas, Allison Williams
School of Geography & Earth Sciences, McMaster University, Hamilton, ON, Canada
*Corresponding author: e-mail address: newbold@mcmaster.ca

Contents

Abstract

In many developed nations, rural population is both declining and aging rapidly. For the older population that remains in rural areas and small towns where transportation alternatives are more limited and the reliance on the personal automobile is greater, personal transportation is increasingly challenged with age and as health declines. Driving cessation, often due to poor or declining health or eyesight, is particularly troublesome, potentially leading to social isolation. The purpose of this chapter is twofold. First, it will explore changing rural population characteristics in the developed world and the implications for transportation, social inclusion and health. Second, using examples drawn from Canada, the chapter will explore the transportation behaviors and choices of Canada's aging population living in small towns and rural areas, and how their transportation behavior changes according to their specific needs as they age through retirement and approach and complete driving cessation, along with the impacts of driving on their social isolation and opportunities to participate in the community.

Keywords: Rural areas, Canada, Transportation, Driving

Advances in Transport Policy and Planning, Volume 2
ISSN 2543-0009
https://doi.org/10.1016/bs.atpp.2018.09.003

1. Introduction

Within the developed world, driving is the most common and preferred mode of transportation among adults. For the old, the personal automobile is the preferred travel mode choice (Kim and Ulfarsson, 2004; Páez et al., 2007). Indeed, the ability to drive has been linked to independence, greater social participation, community engagement, and better health (Turcotte, 2012), as well as the ability to meet every day needs such as shopping or banking. The fact that the automobile is the preferred travel mode choice is not surprising: today's older adults and aging baby boomers were raised in an automobile culture (Dahan-Oliel et al., 2010; van den Berg et al., 2011).

However, aging populations challenge individual transportation behaviors and the provision of transportation, with the potential need to increase connectivity and mobility opportunities for older adults. As of 2017, 9% of the world's population was aged 65 and over, with the proportion exceeding 18% in the more developed countries (Population Reference Bureau, 2017). Regionally, 20% of Western Europe's population is over 65, and 15% of North America is over 65. While 28% of Japan's population is over 65 (making it the oldest country in the world), population aging is also occurring in other parts of Asia (particularly China given its one-child policy).

Population aging is arguable felt most acutely in rural areas and small towns, where population change is noticeable and has immediate and direct implications on service provision and access to services. However, there are different variations of population change in rural and small towns. For instance, population aging may be associated with the out-migration of younger, labor force aged individuals as they search for education and employment opportunities elsewhere. Consequently, the smaller, dispersed, and older population that remains becomes more difficult to connect through transportation alternatives given the small market opportunities and the high costs of providing transportation services. Alternatively, aging could be due to the in-migration of older adults to a particular area and typically associated with retirement or amenity opportunities (Newbold and Meredith, 2012).

Regardless of how aging occurs, aging populations bring with them their own transportation challenges and differential travel behavior and demands for mobility. Research has demonstrated, for example, that as the populations of the United States, Australia, and some European nations have aged, dependency on the automobile has increased, while demand for public transit has changed little (Collia et al., 2003; Hjorthol et al., 2010; Newbold et al., 2005; Rosenbloom, 2001; Turcotte, 2012). But, aging is also associated with the potential for more limited driving or driving cessation due to poor health, mobility difficulties, or other reasons, raising issues associated with social inclusion, personal health, and caregiving. Given that most older adults want to grow old in their own homes ("aging in place") and actively participate in society, options for mobility beyond the personal automobile, such as public transit or having a friend drive are needed (Schwanen and Paez, 2010).

For the older population resident in rural areas and small towns where transportation alternatives are more limited, reliance on the personal automobile is greater given distances and the more dispersed settlement pattern. Consequently, personal transportation (and driving specifically), is increasingly challenged with age and declining health. Driving cessation, often due to poor or declining health or eyesight, is particularly troublesome, potentially leading to social isolation and further declines in health. As societies continue to age, an increasing proportion will cease to drive due to health concerns (Kim, 2011; Waldorf, 2001). Consequently, the rural old will likely face greater transport challenges due to much more limited services and mobility options, meaning that they are typically more reliant on the personal automobile for travel than their urban counterparts. Evidence from the United States and elsewhere, for example, suggests that older rural women tend to travel less than their urban counterparts (Fortuijn, 1999; Hildebrand et al., 2004; Hough et al., 2008).

Given the challenges rural older adults face in terms of transportation, the purpose of this chapter is twofold. First, it will discuss the transportation behaviors of aging populations and the social and health implications of limited transportation options among the old, contrasting residents in rural and urban locations. Second, using data drawn from Statistics Canada's 2009 Canadian Community Health Survey (CCHS) Annual Component subsample, the chapter will explore the transportation behaviors and choices of Canada's aging population and how their transportation behaviors changes with age and location. The conclusion offers insights into caregiving and health issues in these situations.

2. Background: Setting the context

While the majority (78%) of the old in the developed world live in urban areas, the rural population is not inconsequential. Moreover, a growing proportion of old means that an increasing number of older adults will reside in small urban and rural areas as they age in place, with this increasing number also including those with more limited transportation options. Public transit services are typically minimal to non-existent in rural areas given low population density, large distances and geographies and the correspondingly small ridership, resulting in a high cost to provide transportation options. In places where public transit options do exist, trip frequency and timing are often limited, and older adults are typically less likely to use public transit services as compared to younger cohorts (Newbold and Scott, 2018). Likewise, other forms of transportation, including active transportation, are of limited use given distances and poor infrastructure typically found in small urban or rural areas, while weather related issues such as winter further discourage both active and public transportation opportunities. Consequently, individuals residing in rural areas and small towns are more likely to rely on the personal automobile for transportation to social activities, health care, work, and shopping given longer trip distances and more dispersed residences and activity sites in rural areas (Pucher and Renee, 2005).

Aging in place implies the importance of transportation options, including having access to a personal automobile as an important aspect of quality of life. Indeed, the car remains the preferred travel mode for older adults, with much lower rates of public transit use and active transportation relative to younger generations (Newbold and Scott, 2017; Schwanen et al., 2004; Turcotte, 2012). But, for residents in rural environments, more limited transportation options further challenges the mobility and accessibility of the old, along with their inclusion within the broader society. In addition, the use of a personal automobile may be limited in some instances, including cases where individuals self-regulate their driving behaviors, choosing to not drive in, for example, poor weather conditions, at night, or on busier routes and limited access highways. These capability (or personal choice) constraints among the old, including physical and psychological constraints, will alter driving choices (Marottoli et al., 2000; Turcotte, 2012; Waldorf, 2001). Consequently, aging in place becomes difficult for individuals who are no longer able to drive if a car is their only available means of transportation, limiting their social interaction. In particular, older females are often faced with fewer transportation options (relative to males) since they are historically less likely to have a driver's license (Fuels Institute, 2014), they are more likely to live alone, more likely to live longer, and are less affluent (Kim, 2011).

Irrespective of location, the ability to travel across these long distances in a rural setting is vital, with transportation providing the link to health services and socialization opportunities. Indeed, there is an extensive literature that explores the transportation barriers for individuals seeking health care in a rural setting (i.e., Arcury et al., 2006; Heckman et al., 1998; Mattson, 2011). Arcury et al. (2006), for example, noted that individuals with a driver's license who resided in rural areas were more likely to access health care than those who did not. Similarly, access to a private automobile and a driver's license is associated with higher rates of social participation and community engagement, particularly among older adults (Turcotte, 2012). Conversely, social exclusion, which could occur due to lack of transportation, is associated with poorer health outcomes (Sacker et al., 2017).

However, increasing age is associated with greater health and functional limitations that may limit the ability to drive. While individuals may lose their license because of health issues, the loss of a driver's license is often associated with multiple negative outcomes, including poorer health status (Edwards et al., 2009), reduced participation in out-of-home activities (Marottoli et al., 2000), and greater rates of depression (Fonda et al., 2001). Moreover, older adults without a license and living in rural areas or small towns may be more likely to experience these adverse outcomes given the lack of alternative transportation options (Miller, 2017). The inability to drive also impacts the ability to care for oneself and the need for caregiving. In particular, the lack of a valid driver's license may lead to their potential isolation and complete dependency on caregivers. For those rural individuals without a license, it is more likely that they are less able to care for their social and health needs themselves, given that they have limited mobility when compared to their urban counterparts who have access to various forms of public transportation. This problem is accentuated by the limited access to health and social services in these often medically underserved rural geographies (Schuurman et al., 2010). As a consequence, health and pharmaceutical needs may not be addressed in a timely manner, and social isolation may engender possible mental health concerns. The comparatively poorer health status of rural populations when compared to urban populations corroborates this (Williams and Kulig, 2012).

3. Data and methods: The canadian context

Like many other countries, Canada's population is also aging rapidly. Currently representing approximately 17% of Canada's population (as of the

2016 census), the old (aged 65+) are expected to grow to over 25% of the nation's total population by 2036. At the same time, the vast majority (83%) of Canadians live in urban places, with Canada's rural population largely located in the peripheral areas around urban areas. Despite the large proportion of Canada's population that lives in urban areas, nearly 17% live in rural and small town Canada (Statistics Canada, 2016) where transportation options are more limited given no or limited public transit opportunities. In fact, Canada's rural population is older than the urban population and is aging faster than their urban counterparts (Dandy and Bollman, 2008).

At the same time, the preference for aging in place will mean that the number of older Canadians that will face transportation challenges due to living in rural areas will increase. Canada's aging population means that the travel behaviors and demands for mobility among older adults will continue to evolve. Indeed, individuals aged 65 and older represent the fastest growing segment of Canada's driving population; a trend that raises significant personal and public health issues given that older drivers (and particularly those aged 70 and over) are more likely to be involved in multi-vehicle collisions (Burkhardt et al., 1998; Dobbs, 2008). Further, an increasing number and proportion of older Canadians will be less likely to drive or will cease driving completely due to health or other concerns (Kim, 2011; Waldorf, 2001).

The balance of the chapter explores the transportation behaviors and choices of the old in the Canadian context, with a particular focus on the urban/rural divide. Data are drawn from Statistics Canada's 2009 Canadian Community Health Survey (CCHS) Annual Component sub-sample. The CCHS gathered information regarding health status, healthcare utilization, health determinants, and transportation-related data for Canadians. The dataset has an unweighted sample size of 30,865, which when weighted represents >13 million Canadians aged 45 and over, with the current analysis focusing on individuals aged 65 and over. The survey excludes persons living on Native reserves, the institutionalized, and members of the Canadian Armed Forces. Access to the data was obtained through Canada's Research Data Center (RDC) protocols,[1] and all results are weighted according to Statistics Canada guidelines.[2]

[1] RDCs enable researchers to access survey microdata in a secure university setting. Researchers must receive approval for research projects and abide by confidentiality rules.

[2] See: http://www23.statcan.gc.ca/imdb/p2SV.pl?Function=getSurvey&SDDS=3226 (Accessed 15 August 2018).

Given the likelihood that residents of urban and rural areas will face different transportation challenges and therefore have different driving behaviors, we focus on urban-rural differences. Descriptive statistics are used to explore the presence of a valid driver's license (yes/no) and frequency of driving in the past 12 months by age cohort, and gender, and location (urban vs. rural).[3] In addition, the frequency of driving and the prevalence of specific chronic conditions by age cohort, gender, and geographic setting were evaluated. Age cohorts are defined by 5 year age groups, ranging from age 65–69 to 85–89, with an open-ended 90+ age cohort. We used individual self-reports of having a "valid driver's license" to measure driving cessation, although this may capture both individuals who have had to give up their license (i.e., due to health) or have never held a driver's license. Unfortunately, the CCHS did not ask if the person had ever had a valid driver's license, meaning we cannot distinguish those who have never driven from those that may have more recently given up their license due to health or other reasons. Finally, logistic regression was used to identify the correlates of holding a valid driver's license (yes/no) among the old, with correlates including sociodemographic (age, gender, marital status), socioeconomic (income, education), and health effects, including vision status, self-assessed health, and the presence of specific health outcomes including high blood pressure, back pain, osteoporosis, and diabetes.

4. Results

Table 1 records the presence of a valid driver's license by age cohort. Across age groups, the majority of participants report having a valid driver's license. As expected, the proportion of older adults holding a valid driver's license decreases with increasing age, dropping from 87% among 65–69 year olds to just 25.4% in the oldest cohort (90+). Males are typically more likely to hold a valid driver's license as compared to females, likely reflecting historically lower levels of licensure among women in older

[3] Statistics Canada defines an urban area ("population centre") as having a population of at least 1000 and a density of 400 or more people per square kilometer. All areas outside an urban area are defined as rural. Clearly, the definition of rural used in this chapter is limited and portrays a homogenous version of rurality while failing to distinguish concepts such as remote rural from rural areas that are peripheral to urban areas or differences in their demographic composition, including whether they were growing due to in-migration of older adults or out-migration of younger adults. In particular, out-migration continues from remote rural locations dependent on resource extraction. In contrast, rural areas near cities have experienced population growth due to in-migration as urban areas have decentralized (Bryant and Joseph, 2001).

Table 1 Presence of a valid driver's license by cohort, gender and location (%).

	Age					
	65–69	70–74	75–79	80–84	85–89	90+
Valid Driver's License (All)	87.0	81.6	76.3	61.7	45.8	25.4
Males	95.1	92.4	90.0	82.4	73.1	46.1
Females	80.3	72.5	65.5	46.7	30.6	16.1
Urban resident	85.1	79.6	75.4	58.2	41.8	23.9
Rural resident	92.6	88.0	77.9	72.4	57.1	30.7

Table 2 Main form of transportation (%) by age, sex, and geographic setting.

			Driving	Passenger	Public transit	Other
Male	Urban	65–74	77.5	11.0	5.8	5.7
		75–84	70.4	13.3	9.7	6.6
		85+	50.8	31.9	9.1	8.2
Male	Rural	65–74	85.7	11.4	—	2.3
		75–84	85.9	13.8	—	—
		85+	69.7	24.3	—	5.6
Female	Urban	65–74	52.8	30.1	9.9	7.3
		75–84	40.3	35.6	12.3	11.9
		85+	21.1	43.3	14.7	20.9
Female	Rural	65–74	57.0	40.8	—	1.9
		75–84	57.5	37.6	—	4.3
		85+	55.1	36.6	—	6.9

Note: — indicates cell frequency too small for release.

cohorts (Fuels Institute, 2014), with the gap between males and females growing as age increases. Rural residents were also more likely to hold a valid driver's license as compared to urban residents, regardless of age group, potentially reflecting their greater reliance on the personal automobile for transportation.

Table 2 reports the main form of transportation by age, gender and urban/rural setting. In this case, age cohort was aggregated to 10 year age cohorts, (65–74, 75–84, and an open-ended 85+ cohort) to avoid small sample numbers and disclosure issues. In addition, public transit, active transit and other transit were aggregated into one category for rural residents. Three broad observations can be drawn from the table. First, driving represented the majority of out-of-home trips across all age groups and locations. However, increasing age is associated with a declining proportion of both males and females that drive, while the proportion participating in trips as a passenger increases. For instance, 85.7% of males aged 65–74 and living in a rural area drove, while approximately 70% of those aged 85 and over drove. Concurrently, those participating in trips as passengers grew from 11.4% to 24.3%. Second, females living in urban areas were somewhat more likely to report using public transit as compared to their male urban counterparts. While the proportion of trips by public transit increased with increasing age, public transit trips still represented a comparatively small proportion of all trips made by the old. Third, given that public transit was not an option for residents in rural areas, the proportion of trips where the individual reported driving was higher for residents of rural areas. For example, 69.7% of males aged 85+ in rural areas reported driving compared to 50.8% of urban males. Likewise, just 21.1% of females lagged 85+ and living in urban areas reported driving, while 55.1% of females aged 85+ living in rural areas did so. In addition, older rural adults (especially those aged 85+) were also more likely to report being a passenger relative to residents of urban areas, with results pointing to the reliance on the personal automobile for residents in rural areas. Unfortunately, the data do not provide insight into whether switching to other modes of transportation, and particularly car as passenger, provided a sufficient substitute for driving. However, it is reasonable to assume that trip needs are not met among those without a driver's license given their reliance on other drivers and limited alternatives.

Table 3 reports the frequency of driving (car as driver) for those with a valid driver's license, with the table again distinguishing between urban and rural residents and by broad age cohort. Among individuals who reported having a license, most used their vehicle 6–7 times per week, although women reported a lower frequency of driving than men. Echoing results from Table 2, males were broadly more likely to drive than their female counterparts, with the frequency of trips tending to decline with increasing age and observed in almost all instances. For example, males were likely to drive on a daily (6–7 days per week) basis as compared to females, although females were somewhat more likely than males to drive less frequently. Increasing age was also associated with fewer trips per week. Indeed, while near daily trips (6–7 trips per week) tended to decline with increasing age,

Table 3 Frequency (%) of driving in the past 12 months by age, gender, and geographic setting.

			6–7 days/ week	4–5 days/ week	1–3 days/ week	1–3 days/ month	Not in the past month
Male	Urban	65–74	74.5	11.8	9.3	2.4	1.9
		75–84	63.8	15.6	15.8	2.0	2.7
		85+	46.7	14.1	30.0	2.6	6.7
Male	Rural	65–74	71.1	14.3	12.3	1.6	0.7
		75–84	67.9	19.3	9.4	3.4	—
		85+	45.7	29.5	15.1	9.7	—
Female	Urban	65–74	49.5	18.7	17.8	5.9	8.0
		75–84	34.4	23.0	26.0	7.0	9.7
		85+	27.3	23.0	31.3	6.3	12.1
Female	Rural	65–74	34.8	22.2	30.6	11.0	1.5
		75–84	34.2	20.9	36.3	6.9	1.7
		85+	13.6	11.4	62.0	10.3	2.6

Note: — indicates cell frequency too small for release.

less frequent trips per week (i.e., 4–5 trips per week, 1–3 trips per week) tended to increase with age. Among those with a valid license, there was a small percentage of individuals who indicated not driving at all in the month preceding the interview, with the proportion increasing with age.

Table 4 reports the prevalence of specific health conditions across cohorts with and without a valid driver's license. Not surprisingly, arthritis, heart disease, high blood pressure (HBP), and the use of high blood pressure medication increases with age. On average, however, the proportion of respondents reporting the presence of a chronic condition was nearly identical for those with and without a valid driver's license. However, turning to self-rated health, individuals with a valid license tended to be somewhat more likely to report excellent, very good or good general health as compared to those without a valid license, with the exception of those in the oldest age groups. In other words, people who report better health are more likely to have their driver's license. While non-driver's tended to be somewhat more likely to report specific conditions such as diabetes, heart disease, and high blood pressure that could reduce their ability to drive relative to those with a valid driver's license, differences were not large, echoing results by Siren et al. (2004).

Table 4 Health outcomes (%) by age cohort with a valid driver's license.

	Age					
	65–69	**70–74**	**75–79**	**80–84**	**85–89**	**90+**
With valid driver's license						
Chronic condition	86.3	90.7	90.5	90.3	91.8	91.3
Excellent/Very good/good health	84.5	80.3	78.9	76.7	76.2	69.0
Asthma	7.5	6.7	6.9	10.8	6.9	3.4
Arthritis	35.6	42.1	44.8	48.3	47.9	50.1
Back problems	26.3	29.6	28.2	26.4	31.2	26.7
Diabetes	15.0	17.9	17.8	15.0	10.4	12.2
Heart disease	15.2	20.3	24.3	31.2	31.2	40.0
High blood pressure	43.4	47.5	54.5	52.0	50.1	49.7
HBP medication	43.3	48.2	56.0	55.9	54.8	51.9
Without valid driver's license						
Chronic condition	88.4	90.2	95.3	91.5	91.7	91.3
Excellent/Very good/good health	71.7	64.7	64.2	61.2	59.9	68.9
Asthma	13.2	11.0	9.5	10.1	8.1	6.6
Arthritis	41.8	46.8	48.5	51.9	53.1	50.6
Back problems	26.7	33.2	31.3	31.3	27.2	32.4
Diabetes	24.3	26.5	22.0	18.7	17.1	11.0
Heart disease	13.0	22.0	26.1	31.9	32.9	32.7
High blood pressure	55.6	52.8	61.3	56.5	57.1	48.9
HBP medication	54.7	54.2	63.1	59.3	57.8	50.7

Finally, we turn to logistic analysis of the factors associated with having a valid driver's license (Table 5). Two models are presented, with the first model incorporating sociodemographic and socioeconomic effects, and the second model introducing a set of specific health measures including whether or not the respondent reported diabetes, osteoporosis, high blood pressure, or heart disease. Overall, results are comparable between both models. Of particular interest is where individuals reside, with the results indicating that residents of urban areas were less likely to have a valid driver's license as compared to their rural counterparts, reinforcing earlier descriptive results and likely reflecting alternate transportation choices beyond their personal automobile.

Table 5 Logistic analysis of the factors associated with having a valid driver's license.

	Model 1		Model 2	
Variable	**Estimate**	**Pr (>|t)**	**Estimate**	**Pr (>|t)**
Intercept	1.629[a]	0.000	1.705[a]	0.000
Age (*Ref*=65–69)				
70–74	−0.231	0.082	−0.233	0.079
75–79	−0.489[a]	0.000	−0.490[a]	0.000
80–84	−1.404[a]	0.000	−1.393[a]	0.000
85–89	−2.087[a]	0.000	−2.091[a]	0.000
90+	−2.771[a]	0.000	−2.774[a]	0.000
Gender (*Ref*=female)				
Male	1.509[a]	0.000	1.515[a]	0.000
Marital status (*Ref*=not married)				
Married	0.240[b]	0.014	0.243[b]	0.013
Geography (*Ref*=rural)				
Urban	−0.814[a]	0.000	−0.804[a]	0.000
Income (*Ref*=<$50k)				
>$50K	0.736[a]	0.000	0.720[a]	0.000
Education (*Ref*=trades certificate or less)				
College and University	0.277[c]	0.009	0.284[c]	0.007
Bachelor's or higher	0.131	0.278	0.117	0.331
Self-perceived health (*Ref*= fair or less)				
Excellent/very good/good	0.574[a]	0.000	0.535[a]	0.000
Vision (*Ref*= unable to see without glasses/contacts)				
Can see with glasses/contacts	0.253[b]	0.019	0.265[b]	0.014
Health issues (*Ref*= does not report)				
Osteoporosis			−0.139	0.209
Back problems			0.180	0.087
High blood pressure			0.006	0.948

Table 5 Logistic analysis of the factors associated with having a valid driver's license.—cont'd

	Model 1		Model 2	
Variable	**Estimate**	**Pr (>|t)**	**Estimate**	**Pr (>|t)**
Diabetes			-0.318^{b}	0.012
Heart disease			−0.123	0.266
Pseudo R-squared	0.421		0.424	
Likelihood ratio	10.9		11.4	

[a] $P < 0.1\%$.
[b] $P < 5\%$.
[c] $P < 1\%$.

Turning to other sociodemographic and socioeconomic effects, increasing age is not surprisingly associated with a greater likelihood of not having a driver's license. Furthermore, the likelihood of not having a license increased at an increasing rate with age. Individuals with incomes greater than $50,000 and those who are married (or common-law) were more likely to report having a valid driver's license. Educational level was not statistically significant, although individuals who reported better self-assessed health (excellent, very good or good) and better vision (i.e., able to see with glasses or contacts) were more likely to have a valid driver's license.

With respect to specific measures of health (Model 2), only individuals reporting osteoporosis were less likely to hold a valid driver's license (at $P < 0.1\%$). Other specific indicators, including back problems, high blood pressure, diabetes and heart disease did not have a significant impact at the $P < 5\%$ level.

5. Conclusion and implications

It is vitally important to recognize that older rural residents are frequently disadvantaged in terms of access to transportation and transportation alternatives beyond the personal automobile. Even in societies such as Canada that are highly urbanized, demographic change—driven by aging populations—means that the number of old living in rural areas will increase, with individuals aged 65 and older the fastest growing segment of Canada's driving population.

In looking at older rural driver's, this chapter has reviewed the transportation behaviors and choices of aging populations and the social and health implications of limited transportation options among the old. In addition, it has explored the case of Canada's older rural drivers relative to their location. In the Canadian context, results reveal that a large proportion of older adults report having a valid driver's license, with males more likely to report having a valid driver's license as compared to women. However, increasing age is associated with a declining proportion of licensed drivers and a widening gap between males and females. While the gap between men and women likely reflects historical differences between men and women in obtaining a license, women with a license also reported driving less frequently than men, which likely reflects situations where the husband drives more if they are married. However, given differences in longevity between women and men, the lack of a valid license among women, along with declining health and mobility with age, is worrisome. Given the reliance on driving a vehicle as the primary mode of transportation, public transit continues to be used by only a small proportion of older Canadians. Not surprisingly, public transit was used more by residents of urban areas as compared to rural areas. Instead, participating in car trips as a passenger was the second most common mode of transportation, while active transportation represented only a small share of total trips among older adults.

For those living in rural areas, the reliance on the personal automobile is illustrated with higher licensure rates among rural residents (including females) and a greater proportion reporting car as the primary means of transportation. Such results are hardly surprising, given that public transportation options are less common in rural areas, placing greater reliance on the personal car. Further, the results suggest that rural drivers without a license make fewer trips than their urban counterparts. The greater reliance on the personal automobile among females and rural residents is problematic, suggesting a heavy reliance on caregivers for meeting transportation needs.

For those living in rural areas without a driver's license, the risk of social isolation and dependency on other drivers is elevated as compared to their urban counterparts who likely have a greater variety of transportation options, including public transit and ride sharing services, but also easier access to health and social services. Furthermore, rural non-drivers may be less able to care for their social and health needs themselves, a problem that is accentuated in underserved rural geographies, further threatening their physical and mental health. Consequently, access to transportation options is critical to ensure personal health and well-being and ongoing and meaningful participation in one's community.

Given the limited locus of control that these rural drivers without a license have—specific to their mobility, they are more reliant, and often fully dependent, on informal caregivers—whether a family member, friend, or neighbor. This has the potential to be problematic given that these caregivers can often live far distances and have to make long drives to care; this prohibits timely access when emergencies strike. Further, with the majority of caregivers being female and thereby more likely to not drive, they may have to depend on others for transportation needs. In addition, the growing uncertainty of climate and weather conditions, particularly in winter months, adds an additional layer of concern for safety regarding rural driving. Future research directions therefore include intervention research which examines the feasibility of: offering innovative community ride share/ car-pooling services; in-home social and health services/support; innovative living arrangements for older rural adults (such as cohousing) and; rural caregiver supports.

Finally, limitations of this chapter should be noted. First, the distinction between urban and rural used in this chapter is relatively crude and fails to distinguish between individuals who are in remote rural areas vs. those that are (for example) in rural areas that are relatively close to urban opportunities. Second, the work is cross-sectional, meaning that we cannot determine the factors that resulted in the lack of a valid license (or whether the individual ever had a valid license at any point in their life), along with the relationship between changing health and driving behaviors. Consequently, longitudinal data are required to tease out such relationships. Third, culture has not been accounted for; this is significant given that indigenous peoples are the fastest growing segment in Canadian society and largely represented in rural geographies.

Acknowledgment

This research was supported by a grant from the Social Sciences and Humanities Research Council of Canada (SSHRC, Grant # 435-2017-1141).

References

Arcury, T.A., Preisser, J.S., Gesler, W.M., Powers, J.M., 2006. Access to transportation and health care utilization in a rural region. J. Rural Health 21 (1), 31–38.

Bryant, C., Joseph, A.E., 2001. Canada's rural population: trends in space and implications in place. Can. Geogr. 45 (1), 132–137.

Burkhardt, J.E., Berger, A.M., Creedon, M., McGavock, A.T., 1998. Mobility and Independence: Changes and Challenges for Older Drivers. Ecosometrics, Bethesda, MD.

Collia, D.V., Sharp, J., Giesbrecht, L., 2003. The 2001 national household travel survey: a look into the travel patterns of older Americans. J. Safety Res. 34, 461–470.

Dahan-Oliel, N., Mazer, B., Gélinas, I., Dobbs, B., Lefebvre, H., 2010. Transportation use in community-dwelling older adults: association with participation and leisure activities. Can. J. Aging 29 (4), 491–502.

Dandy, K., Bollman, R.D., 2008. Seniors in Rural Canada. Rural and Small Town Canada Analysis Bulletin, vol. 7. Statistics Canada, Ottawa. No. 8. Catalogue no. 21–006-X.

Dobbs, B.M., 2008. Aging baby boomers—a blessing or challenge for driver licensing authorities. Traffic Inj. Prev. 9 (4), 379–386.

Edwards, J.D., Lunsman, M., Perkins, M., Rebok, G.W., Roth, D.L., 2009. Driving cessation and health trajectories in older adults. J. Gerontol. Med. Sci. 64, M1290–M1295.

Fonda, S.J., Wallace, R.B., Herzog, A.R., 2001. Changes in driving patterns and worsening depressive symptoms among older adults. J. Gerontol. Soc. Sci. 56, S343–S351.

Fortuijn, J.D., 1999. Daily life of elderly women in a rural area in the Netherlands. GeoJournal 48, 187–193.

Fuels Institute, 2014. Driver Demographics: The American Population's Effect on Vehicle Travel and Fuel Demand. fuelsinstitute.org/ResearchArticles/DriverDemographics.pdf.

Heckman, T.G., Somlai, A.M., Peters, J., Walker, J., Otto-Salaj, L., Galdabini, C.A., Kelly, J.A., 1998. Barriers to care among persons living with HIV/AIDS in urban and rural areas. AIDS Care 10 (3), 365–375.

Hildebrand, E.D., Gordon, M.J., Hanson, T., 2004. In: Understanding the Travel Behavior of the Rural Elderly. Proceedings of the 39th Annual Conference of the Canadian Transportation Research Forum. Revolutions in Transportation, Calgary, Alberta, Canada, pp. 236–252.

Hjorthol, R.J., Levin, L., Sirén, A., 2010. Mobility in different generations of older persons. The development of daily travel in different cohorts in Denmark, Norway and Sweden. J. Transp. Geogr. 18, 624–633.

Hough, J.A., Cao, X., Handy, S.L., 2008. Exploring travel behavior of elderly women in rural and small urban North Dakota: an ecological modeling approach. Transp. Res. Rec. 2082, 125–131. https://doi.org/10.3141/2082-15.

Kim, S., 2011. Transportation alternatives of the elderly after driving cessation. Transp. Res. Rec. 2265, 170–176. https://doi.org/10.3141/2265-19.

Kim, S., Ulfarsson, G.F., 2004. Travel mode choice of the elderly: effects of personal, household, neighborhood, and trip characteristics. Transp. Res. Rec. 1894, 117–126.

Marottoli, R.A., de Leon, C.F., Glass, T.A., Williams, C.S., Cooney, L.M., Berkman, L.F., 2000. Consequences of driving cessation decreased out-of-home activity levels. J. Gerontol. B Psychol. Sci. Soc. Sci. 55 (6), S334–S340.

Mattson, J., 2011. Transportation, distance, and health care utilization for older adults in rural and small urban areas. Transp. Res. Rec. 2265, 192–199.

Miller, B., 2017. No Place to Grow Old: How Canadian Suburbs Can Become Age Friendly. Report published by the Institute for Research and Public Policy. http://on-irpp.org/2A3ngIs.

Newbold, K.B., Meredith, T., 2012. Where Will you Retire? Seniors' Migration within Canada and Implications for Policy. IRPP Study 36. Institute for Research on Public Policy, Montreal.

Newbold, K.B., Scott, D.M., 2017. Driving over the life course: the automobility of Canada's millennial, generation X, baby boomer and greatest generation. Travel Behav. Soc. 6, 57–63.

Newbold, K.B., Scott, D.M., 2018. Insights into public transit use by millennials: the Canadian experience. Travel Behav. Soc. 11, 62–68.

Newbold, K.B., Scott, D.M., Spinney, J.E.L., Kanaroglou, P., Páez, A., 2005. Travel behavior within Canada's older population: a cohort analysis. J. Transp. Geogr. 13, 340–351.

Páez, A., Scott, D., Potoglou, D., Kanaroglou, P., Newbold, K.B., 2007. Elderly mobility: demographic and spatial analysis of trip making in the Hamilton CMA, Canada. Urban Stud. 4, 123–146.
Population Reference Bureau, 2017. World Population Data Sheet. Available at: https://www.prb.org/wp-content/uploads/2017/08/2017_World_Population.pdf. Accessed 27 March 2018.
Pucher, J., Renee, J.L., 2005. Rural mobility and mode choice: evidence from the 2001 National Household Travel Survey. Transportation 32, 165–186.
Rosenbloom, S., 2001. Sustainability and automobility among the elderly: an international assessment. Transportation 28, 375–408.
Sacker, A., Ross, A., MacLeod, C.A., Netuveli, G., Windle, G., 2017. Health and social exclusion in older age: evidence from understanding society, the UK household longitudinal study. J. Epidemiol. Community Health 71, 681–690.
Schuurman, N., Berube, M., Crooks, V.A., 2010. Measuring potential spatial access to primary health care physicians using a modified gravity model. Can. Geogr. 54, 29–45.
Schwanen, T., Paez, A., 2010. The mobility of older people—an introduction. J. Transp. Geogr. 18, 591–595.
Schwanen, T., Dieleman, F.M., Dijst, M., 2004. The impact of metropolitan structure on commute behavior in the Netherlands: a multilevel approach. Growth Change 35 (3), 304–333.
Siren, A., Hakamies-Blomqvist, L., Lindeman, M., 2004. Driving cessation and health in older women. J. Appl. Gerontol. 23 (1), 58–69.
Statistics Canada, 2016. Focus on Geography Series, 2016 Census. https://www12.statcan.gc.ca/census-recensement/2016/as-sa/fogs-spg/Facts-can-eng.cfm?Lang=Eng&GK=CAN&GC=01&TOPIC=1.
Turcotte, M., 2012. Profile of Seniors' Transportation Habits. Canadian Social Trends, Statistics Canada. Catalogue no. 11-008.
van den Berg, P., Arentze, T., Timmermans, H., 2011. Estimating social travel demand of senior citizens in the Netherlands. J. Transp. Geogr. 19, 323–331.
Waldorf, B., 2001. Anticipated mode choice following driving cessation. Eur. Res. Reg. Sci. 11, 22–40.
Williams, A.M., Kulig, J.C., 2012. Health and place in rural canada. In: Kulig, J.S., Williams, A.M. (Eds.), Health in Rural Canada. UBC Press, Vancouver, BC, pp. 2–19.

Further reading

Mercado, R., Paez, A., Newbold, K.B., 2010. Transport policy and the provision of mobility options in an aging society: a case study of Ontario, Canada. J. Transp. Geogr. 18 (5), 649–661.
Okola, A., 2003. Departure time choice for recreational activities by elderly nonworkers. Transp. Res. Rec. J. Transp. 1848, 86–93. Paper No. 03-3870.
Scott, D.M., Newbold, K.B., Spinney, J.E.L., Mercado, R.G., Páez, A., Kanaroglou, P.S., 2009. New insights into senior travel behavior: the Canadian experience. Growth Change 40, 140–168.

CHAPTER SIX

Adapting transport related innovations to rural needs: Smart Mobility and the example of the Heinsberg region, Germany

Sophia Gross-Fengels, Martina Fromhold-Eisebith*
Chair of Economic Geography, Department of Geography, RWTH Aachen University, Aachen, Germany
*Corresponding author: e-mail address: martina.fromhold-eisebith@geo.rwth-aachen.de

Contents

Abstract

Mobility and transportation innovation in recent years make more intensive use of modern information and communication technologies (ICT). The term Smart Mobility has come to signify the use of ICT for organizing shared personal transportation tailored to individual needs. Smart Mobility has so far mostly been adopted in urban areas. However, rural areas can also potentially reap benefits from adopting Smart Mobility. When applied in, and adapted to rural regions, Smart Mobility elements offer to reduce several typical disadvantages of rural living and working conditions, such as deficient public transport supplies and older people's restricted access to various amenities. This chapter explores how Smart Mobility can help to align improved job and service accessibility conditions, as well as entrepreneurial initiatives, with environmental, economic, and societal sustainability goals. The chapter first outlines some conceptual considerations that highlight (1) typical rural transport demands, (2) rural context conditions that shape the implementation of digitally enhanced sustainability innovations, and (3) conceptual elements required to study the rural adoption of Smart Mobility

Advances in Transport Policy and Planning, Volume 2
ISSN 2543-0009
https://doi.org/10.1016/bs.atpp.2018.09.007

solutions. The innovation-decision-model of Rogers (2003) and the macro-, meso-, micro-level approach of Esser (1999) serve as cornerstones for conceptualization and research methodology. Then empirical results of an ongoing case study are presented. The case study consists of Smart Mobility-related developments in Heinsberg County, Germany, a rural region in the west of the country. A mixed methods approach combines qualitative and quantitative means of data acquisition and analysis. The findings reveal some interesting clues toward the adaptation and adoption of Smart Mobility in rural areas. Major promoting factors, but also impediments are identified, relating to interdependent macro-, meso- and micro-level characteristics. Finally, some policy conclusions are drawn.

Keywords: Smart Mobility, Rural development, Rural context, Adoption of innovation, Adaptation, Promoting factors, Impediments, Germany

1. Introduction

Transportation and mobility are among the key challenges that need to be tackled in order to sustain attractive living and working conditions in rural areas, and to prevent further population losses (Chambers, 2013; Hoggart et al., 2014; Küpper, 2017). For the geographically dispersed population of rural regions it is not only important to have access to basic amenities and infrastructure within their region of residence, but also to be connected to adjacent agglomerations that offer a broader range of workplaces, as well as higher level consumption and service opportunities (Ward and Brown, 2009; Woods, 2005). Mobility per se rarely poses a major problem to people living in rural areas in affluent European economies due to mass motorized individual transport. More recently, however, there are also calls for mobility alternatives that can lead to more efficient and sustainable rural development (Bryden et al., 2011). The task of transforming travel behavior in these regions is particularly pressing, given the long commuting distances of rural residents and the scarcity in these regions of public mass transport (Herget, 2016; Osti, 2010). The rapidly ageing population further motivates to extend rural transportation opportunities (Ahern and Hine, 2012). Furthermore, mobility systems should be advanced in ways that generally support residential qualities of rural areas, rather than encouraging peoples' movement out of them (Milbourne and Kitchen, 2014). Accordingly, the mobility options for people in rural areas should be developed in ways that support environmental, economic, and social sustainability. Therefore, it is important to not only implement novel mobility solutions that use less fossil fuel, but that also contribute to economic revitalization and social coherence in rural areas.

Modern digital technologies, particularly ICT, now offer interesting possibilities toward more sustainable mobility systems for rural areas, but yet they have only recently started to gain scholarly attention (e.g., Cohen-Blankshtain and Rotem-Mindali, 2016; Fournier et al., 2018). This is in contrast to the more extensive literature on Smart Mobility devoted to the notorious personal mobility and traffic congestion problems of urban areas (e.g., Jeekel, 2018; Papa and Lauwers, 2015; Wolter, 2012). Often embedded within broader "Smart City" strategies, the digitally enhanced coordination and systemic bundling of "cleaner" transport processes relating to goods and people are seen as integral part of the ideal type sustainable city of the future (Ahvenniemi et al., 2017). But why should this trend only be viable for urban settings? Could it not, suitably adapted, be viable too for rural areas?

Smart Mobility can in general be defined as a category of novel means of personal transport that use ICT applications to provide low-emission, secure, comfortable, and cost-effective mobility optimized to people's needs (Wolter, 2012), The thesis of this chapter is that Smart Mobility solutions, increasingly implemented in urban agglomerations, offer options to also make rural regions more sustainable and, hence, attractive settlement places—turning them into "Smart Rural Areas" (Trapp and Swarat, 2015). At the same time, however, we advocate that the Smart Mobility notion requires adaptations and interpretations in order to be applicable to a broader range of rural areas. This is due to the specific mobility demand patterns in these regions (Herget, 2016; Osti, 2010) as well as the idiosyncrasies of rural context for sustainability-related innovation (Fromhold-Eisebith and Dewald, 2018). This chapter elaborates on these propositions by first rolling out some conceptual considerations and then presenting empirical insights based on a case study. Section 2 introduces the conceptual framework for the research. Then the case of Heinsberg, a rural region in the west of Germany, is used to show in more detail which Smart Mobility elements can support sustainable rural development and which factors specifically foster or restrict innovation diffusion (Section 3). We conclude with some policy recommendations (Section 4).

2. Conceptually framing studies on rural conditions for Smart Mobility solutions

To provide a solid conceptual base for the case study we first need to offer a definition for "rural areas" and how their specific mobility needs can be characterized according to the literature, mainly referring to the situation in Germany (Section 2.1). Second, the contextual qualities of rural areas for implementing sustainability innovations are explored (Section 2.2).

Finally, several theoretical threads are pulled together to form a conceptual framework that integrates major aspects to be included in studies on the adaptation, adoption, and diffusion of Smart Mobility innovations in rural areas (Section 2.3).

2.1 Rural transport demands

Scientific debates in Germany have still not arrived at a conclusion on how to uniquely define and classify "rural areas" (Grabski-Kieron, 2007; Küpper, 2017; Woods, 2005). Definitions can either be structural or functional in nature. Functionally, rural areas "are significantly characterized by agriculture and forestry-based industries, disperse settlement structures, primary small- to medium-sized, non-central towns, indicating—depending on the location within the development axis—differences in development dynamics and a mostly peripheral location in distance to greater agglomeration areas" (Grabski-Kieron, 2007: 602ff, translated). Public German institutions and ministries, in turn, usually employ a definition of rural regions that concentrated on settlement structure, setting the criterion of a population density below 150 inhabitants per km^2. Accordingly, nearly 60% of Germany's space is rural and 26.6% of Germans live in rural areas (BMVI and Infas, 2018: 39ff).

Rural areas are characterized by transport demands that differ significantly from those of urban areas. Low population densities and disperse settlement structures are associated with lower accessibility (Farber and Páez, 2011; Pucher and Renne, 2005; Ward and Brown, 2009). At the same time, rural areas are often characterized by significant outmigration and demographic change, resulting in both lower demand and availability of public transportation (Gather et al., 2008). Due to the distances to be covered and low densities, rural transportation networks are marked by low demand and high operating expenses. Further, the centralization of service facilities and closure of local supply outposts additionally challenge actors in rural regions. For these reasons, rural areas are particularly dependent on sufficient supplies of public transport to maintain accessibility, as politically required according to the principle of equal living conditions (Küpper, 2017; Segert, 2009). Derived from the German basic principles of the welfare state, "equal living conditions" refers to "a supply of sufficient infrastructure in relation to a fixed reference (i.e., per habitant)" (Flex and Lamker, 2012: 76; translated).

Rural populations, often marked by low birth rates and high shares of elderly people, also suffer from the outmigration of young, highly qualified people to urban areas, which further propels rural population decrease

(Ahern and Hine, 2012; Segert, 2009). Consequently, numbers and shares of pupils decline as well, yet actually still stand for up to 90% of rural transportation demand and widely keep public bus services alive (Gather et al., 2008). Public transport thus faces simultaneously significant cuts in public subsidies and challenges to maintain service qualities, as service must be provided even to remote, peripheral locations with declining demand. Still, decreasing public transport demand combined with tight municipal funding cause retrenchments of inefficient lines and services, which further reduce the attractiveness of public transport. Deficient infrastructure supplies, both physical and digital, aggravate inadequate transport conditions and inhibit the expansion of digital services in the countryside.

Furthermore, in rural areas the lack of job opportunities and low presence of industry, in line with the increasing flexibility of work environments, nurture high commuter rates to surrounding cities (Chambers, 2013). Globalization trends and the dissolving Fordist economy lead to dispersed "industrial sprawl" and increased rural traffic. Although rural dwellers generally commute less frequently than urban citizens, they do so for longer distances (Osti, 2010). These arguments further support the importance of mobility opportunities and supplies that represent crucial factors of industrial location and, more broadly, of quality of life (Goldman and Gorham, 2006; Segert, 2009).

Insufficient provision of public transportation increases the attractiveness of individual car traffic opposed to public services, which in turn promotes a shift toward private transport modes. It is no wonder that private car usage shares are particularly high in rural areas, as inhabitants considerably rely on this mode to maintain mobility and to "escape isolation" (Osti, 2010: 301; see also Milbourne and Kitchen, 2014). Rural people are accustomed to using their own car, while showing to be relative insensitive to the fuel costs accompanying car ownership (Dargay, 2002; Segert, 2009). In Germany's countryside, more than 60% of all routes are travelled by car (compared to 40% in cities), which significantly contributes to carbon emissions (infas and DLR, 2010: 43ff).

Non-automotive user groups are particularly disadvantaged in rural areas, especially elderly people, disabled, children and the mobility impaired. Alternative transport modes for rural areas must not only meet people's everyday mobility demands but should also be accompanied by monetary restraints to individual motorized traffic (Kenyon et al., 2002). The spatially dispersed patterns typical of rural areas, however, hamper the pooling of public transport supplies and hinder the emergence and diffusion of new transport related business models (Ward and Brown, 2009). Overall, rural transport systems may not be under as much pressure to act as urban ones (Pangbourne et al., 2018; Spickermann et al., 2014). But against the backdrop of ecological and other sustainability challenges, a transition of the rural transport system away from motorized individual traffic is still sorely needed.

Public transport in the German countryside currently consists mainly of bus services, sometimes supplemented by "collected taxi services," as well as some train connections from a few country towns to larger urban areas. But rural areas still mostly lack shared mobility services, intermodal transport, and on-demand services (Jeekel, 2018). Nevertheless, Lenz and Fraedrich (2015: 176) observe a "behavioral change" in society, as people become increasingly flexible in their choice of transportation modes and tend toward multimodal travel, switching between different means of transport. Consequently, in line with proliferating digitalization and ICT use, opportunities for implementing alternative, digitally-enhanced transportation services open up various promising opportunities for introducing Smart Mobility elements to the countryside (Dorner and Berger, 2017). Technology progress allows electric (e-)cars and e-bikes to cover longer distances, and rural regions, other than cities, are much better endowed for providing the necessary infrastructure, as e-vehicles can easily be charged on private premises. Collaborative mobility and shared transport concepts, such as car-sharing, offer various options in line with the changing user behavior in rural areas, particularly for community-based services (Pucher and Renne, 2005).

2.2 Rural contexts for digital sustainability innovations

The conditions that affect transport needs and trends in rural areas also create the context for the implementation of ICT based sustainability innovations. The importance of context factors is emphasized in sustainability transitions research (Dewald and Fromhold-Eisebith, 2015; Truffer and Coenen, 2012), which suggests that the operation of actors is shaped by context in a multi-level setting. This setting is thought to be composed of a dominating "regime" of established routines, an overarching "landscape" of broader regulation and orientation marks, and "niches" that provide options for developing and testing novel solutions (MLP approach; Geels and Schot, 2007; Van Bree et al., 2010). The particular challenges, opportunities, and support requirements of rural areas with respect to sustainability innovations, however, have rarely been identified (Fromhold-Eisebith and Dewald, 2018; Hoggart et al., 2014; Stephens et al., 2013). Due to their distinctive natural, societal, and economic qualities, rural spaces can be assumed to significantly deviate from urban ones in terms of adopting and disseminating new technologies. Although it is important to acknowledge differences between rural regions (e.g., Terluin, 2003), these are not further explored here. While this may seem too broad, considering the dangers of stereotypes that could potentially overlook important heterogeneities, here we concentrate on common factors supported by scholarly research (Hoggart et al., 2014; Woods, 2005). We argue that the context characteristics of rural areas should be considered when assessing how modern ICT-based, sustainability oriented personal transport concepts could be applied.

In general, the digital turn offers ample opportunities for improving living and working conditions also in the (German) countryside (Stiftung, 2017). Options for digital enhancement and upgrading relate to many functions and challenges typical for rural areas (Grabski-Kieron, 2007; Küpper, 2017). Most notably, agriculture has profited from ICT innovations for quite some time, allowing, for instance, to instantly monitor weather and market price developments, raise productivity through precision farming, or manage the farms' bureaucracies (Bramley, 2009; Walter et al., 2017). Now digitalization promises to support sustainability transformation in rural areas in more systemic ways, including a broader range of activities. One is the increasing engagement of rural spaces in regenerative energy production, feeding into the smart grids of ICT-coordinated energy supplies for larger, functionally complementary areas (Boehner et al., 2016; Fromhold-Eisebith and Dewald, 2018). Other ICT-driven improvements relate to the provision of services such as distance learning, online shopping and e-health (Stiftung, 2017; Trapp and Swarat, 2015). Last but not least, Smart Mobility approaches can be promoted too, as elaborated below.

The particular qualities and prerequisites of rural areas for implementing digital sustainability innovations refer to the five major dimensions of topography and settlement patterns, economic structure, innovation system qualities, socio-economic entrepreneurship, and community and environmental ethics (see Table 1). The second column of Table 1 is the general characteristics of rural contexts that matter for the issue at stake, whereas the third indicates in which respects the introduction of ICT-enhanced services can potentially support sustainable development of rural areas. The table partly draws on a review of the literature of sustainable solar energy innovations in rural and urban contexts (Fromhold-Eisebith and Dewald, 2018), but extends conceptual assumptions toward broader issues of disseminating ICT-based sustainability innovations to rural areas.

Table 1 Rural context qualities and digital sustainability innovations.

Dimension	Rural context qualities	Digitalization and sustainability implications
Topography and settlement patterns	Sparsely populated with small population numbers; abundance of free, extensively used space; sparse infrastructure endowment	Digital services diminish disadvantages of distance and remoteness, improve intra-/inter-regional communication; but relatively high cost of building up digital infrastructure for all
Economic structure	Focus on agriculture and raw materials production, small supply of personal services; functional dependency on surrounding cities; long commuting distances to jobs	Better access to qualification and jobs, broadening sectoral opportunities and especially service provision; impulses for new entrepreneurship in the region; reduction of commuting needs and related environmental, social detriments
Innovation system qualities	No regional innovation system; difficult access to top class knowledge and human capital; scarce endowment with higher level qualification institutes	Dependency on externally developed technologies and related services; but impulses to locally adapt, further develop solutions; better access to higher level qualification options
Socio-economic entrepreneurship	Alternative, social economies based on community entrepreneurship, rural ethics, milieus and hybrid institutions	Activation of social innovations that enable people to jointly profit from new digital services; impulses to develop rural specific user platforms
Community and environmental ethics	Solidarity, tradition and social cohesion mark the way of life; closeness to nature; interest in preserving the environment	Reputation and self-esteem of rural people is raised; digital services allow to creatively combine rural and modern lifestyles, help realize environmental protection goals; but also resistance to drastic changes can be expected

Source: Compilation by the authors, partly drawing on Fromhold-Eisebith and Dewald (2018), as well as Stiftung (2017), Bryden et al. (2011), Chambers (2013), Gibson-Graham and Roelvink (2009), Hoggart et al. (2014), Stephens et al. (2013), Terluin (2003), and Woods (2005).

As detailed in the table, rural areas offer various advantages for adopting and applying novel digital technologies and services, respectively. In principle, the implementation of innovative ICT-based services can help to diminish some of the major disadvantages still associated with living and working in rural areas, and can also support environmental, economic and societal sustainability goals. Therefore, it seems possible, on the one hand, to combine improved access to education, jobs, and other important amenities, with an impulse toward endogenous economic revitalization and the activation of local innovation dynamics. On the other hand, the cost of bringing new digital services to the countryside also tends to be higher. And the specific societal settings of the rural context need to be considered. This is important because said settings in some respects favor, yet in others also obstruct the adoption and wide use of digital innovations.

2.3 Conceptualizing the adaptation of Smart Mobility to rural needs

After discussing broader conceptual issues in the preceding section, we now turn to synthesizing various aspects that interdependently help assess the adoption and adaptation of Smart Mobility approaches in rural areas. Conceptual tasks are, first, to acknowledge rural sustainability needs as they relate to transport and mobility innovations; second, to provide a refined definition of Smart Mobility; third, to frame a study on the adoption and diffusion of mobility innovations in rural areas; and fourth, to propose how the factors that shape the implementation of Smart Mobility in rural areas could be categorized for assessment.

The transportation sector in Germany causes over 18% of all greenhouse gas emissions (UBA, 2018), which calls for improvements perhaps assisted by technology. The transportation situation in urban agglomerations tends to receive more attention and greater pressure to action due to traffic congestion, air pollution and other detrimental effects (Jeekel, 2018). This often translates into greater public financial support compared to rural areas (i.e., EU-funded research under the Horizon 2020 scheme). The trend toward the Smart City approach to sustainable urban development has especially propelled this funding bias (Ahvenniemi et al., 2017; Vanolo, 2013). Within the broad literature field of rural transportation demands (e.g., Herget, 2016; Woods, 2005), the issue of rural mobility innovations has only been treated marginally so far (Bochner et al., 2016; Fournier et al., 2018; OECD, 2006). Recently, however, conceptual ideas like "Smart Countryside" or "Smart Rural Areas" (Fraunhofer IESE, 2017; Trapp and Swarat, 2015) have contributed to shedding more light on this sustainability issue.

Addressing socio-economic sustainability objectives, the public supply of transportation infrastructure forms part of fulfilling people's elementary requirements, yet poses distinctive challenges for rural areas, as explained above (Section 2.1). Concerning problems of outmigration (Kholodilin, 2017), rural areas can become more attractive locations by investing in mobility options that are responsive to specific rural demands. As transport development generally influences regional economic performance, rural regions can gain broader benefits from improving accessibility by means of transportation and mobility infrastructure, which in turn could enhance endogenous regional progress (Olsson, 2009). Overall, mobility is a key factor for the living quality and attractiveness of an area (Goldman and Gorham, 2006; Jeekel, 2018). And it also allows for economic opportunities, such as offering test sites to mobility providers that want to test new products or services while taking advantage of small rural traffic volumes and extensive land availability (for examples, see Wittlich shuttle, https://ioki.com/wittlich/; Odenwald Mobil, https://www.odenwaldmobil.de/).

To define the concept of Smart Mobility, we must refer to literatures on mobility innovations in urban contexts (Jeekel, 2018). Drawing on the standards set by the Oslo Manual (OECD, 2005), mobility innovations can generally be conceived as marketable services or processes that are—at least relatively—new to firms and consumers. The conceptualization of Smart Mobility (Flügge, 2016; Papa and Lauwers, 2015) is closely related to terms like "alternative mobility" (Manders et al., 2018), "intelligent mobility" (Beckmann and Klein-Hitpaß, 2013), or "sustainable mobility" (Banister, 2008; Cohen-Blankshtain and Rotem-Mindali, 2016; Nykvist and Whitmarsh, 2008). Surprisingly, the Smart Mobility term itself still lacks a consistent definition (Flügge, 2016; Noy and Givoni, 2018; Vanolo, 2013). While "sustainable mobility" signifies the "ultimate goal of mobility, which is accessibility [...], by improving access while simultaneously reducing environmental and social impacts by managing traffic congestion, [...] encouraging modal shift [...] to achieve greater efficiency in the transport system" (Papa and Lauwers, 2015: 543), Smart Mobility is simply regarded as means to digitally improve existing transportation services. Following Wolter (2012), this chapter conceives Smart Mobility as low-emission, secure, comfortable, and cost-effective mobility that optimizes existing services through the application of ICT. Computer-based services are used to augment existing systems, thus allowing more effective usage of public as well as private transportation (i.e., shared and pooled services). In detail,

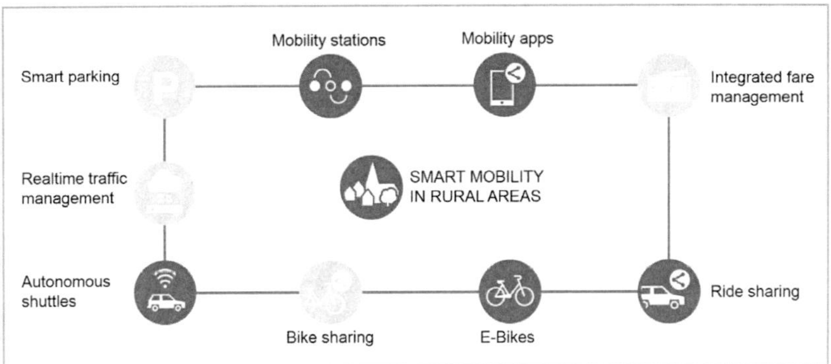

Fig. 1 Features of Smart Mobility. *Source: Depiction by the authors. Dark icons: Smart Mobility solutions that particularly apply to rural areas.*

Smart Mobility comprises various elements and technology combinations, creating opportunities not only for urban, but also rural areas (Fig. 1).

The Smart Mobility approach implies both a "techno-centric" and a "consumer-centric" perspective (Papa and Lauwers, 2015: 543; see also Noy and Givoni, 2018). This understanding once again underscores that the typical socio-economic context of rural spaces must explicitly be considered when transferring novel mobility solutions from urban to rural areas (Section 2.2). A user-focused approach seems appropriate to analyze the transfer and diffusion of mobility innovations, under the understanding that innovation is an "idea, practice, or object that is perceived as new by an individual, group or organisation" (Rogers, 2003: 12). Accordingly, the novelty of a product or process not only relates to its objective characteristics, but also the subjective perception of its attributes and components by the users, influenced by personal and context variables (Langert, 2008). This chapter therefore refers to Rogers' (2003) innovation-decision-model. This model consists of five stages, each representing a set of adopters' decisions and actions: from the first awareness of the innovation in the knowledge stage (1) over the persuasion stage (2), the decision stage (3) whether to adopt the innovation or not, and the implementation stage (4), finally to the confirmation stage (5). As the study presented below aims at analyzing factors that determine the adoption of mobility innovations, research concentrates only on the stages 3 (decision) to 5 (confirmation) of Rogers' model, in which consumers decide whether to adopt or reject an innovation.

Other studies indicate that the process of innovation diffusion is influenced not only by the users but also by several other factors and innovation qualities, although the user's decision to accept an innovation strongly determines successful adoption (Franke et al., 2006; Rogers, 2003). Further, region specific capacities to effectively implement and diffuse an innovation are crucial. This article therefore takes up the idea of "absorptive capacities" (Zahra and George, 2002) applied to the regional level (e.g., Cooke and Morgan, 1998; Grabher and Stark, 1997). "Even given common access to technology, regional differences in labour market and industrial organisation, institutional structures, regulatory frameworks and social conventions may lead to very different outcomes" (Roper and Love, 2006: 438). This statement supports our proposition that rural regions are, compared to urban ones, marked by specific factors impeding or promoting innovation implementation and diffusion.

To better understand and categorize the factors that influence innovation adoption regionally, this conceptual framework presumes a level-based approach, sorting impeding and promoting factors according to vertical macro-meso-micro logics (Esser, 1999). The macro-level (1) comprises the supreme factors associated with environment and society, the intermediate meso-level (2) lies between the overarching macro conditions and individual agency, covers regional institutions and organizations, and the micro-level (3), or actor level, includes the actions and interactions of users as consumers as well as adopted products or services. This approach is distantly related, yet logically not identical to the MLP concept depicted above (Section 2.2), also widely applied in literatures on sustainability transitions and innovation diffusion (Dewald and Fromhold-Eisebith, 2015; Geels and Schot, 2007). Below we name several factors that influence the adoption of (mobility) innovations, which can be shaped by macro-spatial conditions, such as historical and political backgrounds, meso-regional economic and cultural settings and institutional frameworks, as well as micro-individual values and standards (drawing on Manthey-Kloppenburg, 2018).

Policies and regulations, which operate at the macro-level, are manifested in political enactments, legislation, and regulatory agencies or accreditations standards, and can positively influence innovation diffusion (Wisdom et al., 2014). Referring to the "new rural governance" concept (Drabenstott et al., 2004; Little, 2001; OECD, 2006), policy mechanisms that aim at fostering partnerships, community participation, and local cooperation become increasingly popular instruments for regional development support. These mechanisms establish important links to meso-level agency. The "new rural governance" concept grants a central role to governments for managing the transition toward Smart Mobility, and the ability to actively shape its spatial impacts and strengthen associated governance capacities. Institutional settings generally play a crucial role when implementing innovations regionally (Docherty, 2018; Wisdom et al., 2014), shaped by organizational characteristics such as size, knowledge, skills, expertise, values and leadership (i.e., championing adoption) of institutions that support innovation dissemination on the meso-level. Successful integration of new mobility services into existing infrastructure components as well as fare and ticketing systems are essential for fostering user acceptance and the adoption of mobility innovations, too (Goldman and Gorham, 2006). As public budgets for investments in transportation infrastructure are scarce, the regional funding capacities for investing in new technologies are critical. Other factors relating to the meso-level, for instance, looking at regional innovation system qualities, are mentioned in Table 1 (Section 2.2).

On the micro-level, the characteristics of individuals, as well as their values and attitudes toward innovation, are important for implementing mobility innovations (Aarons et al., 2011). Further, societal factors, such as a social system's norms, structures and opinion leaders (key actors), are major drivers of diffusion processes, in addition to the innovativeness of the system members themselves (Rogers, 2003). Especially communication between members of a social system, besides other factors (time, relative advantage, compatibility, complexity, testability and observability), is a decisive driver of innovation diffusion (Hägerstrand, 1967; Rogers, 2003). Communication, either face-to-face or via social networks and mass media, improves also the observability of a new technology and may encourage other consumers to use the innovation. Finally, studies underscore the importance of opportunities for users to test and experiment with a technology in the decision phase of the innovation-decision-process, which increase the probability of users adopting the innovation—with the consequent acceleration of the diffusion processes (Arts et al., 2011; Rogers, 2003).

3. Case study: Smart Mobility in the region of Heinsberg, Germany

A case study serves to illustrate the conceptual framework developed in the preceding sections. This shows how rural transportation demand and conditions for digital sustainability innovation mark the implementation and diffusion of selected Smart Mobility solutions. The Heinsberg region, situated in the Western corner of the state of North Rhine Westphalia (Fig. 2), displays many of the typical rural settings and conditions outlined

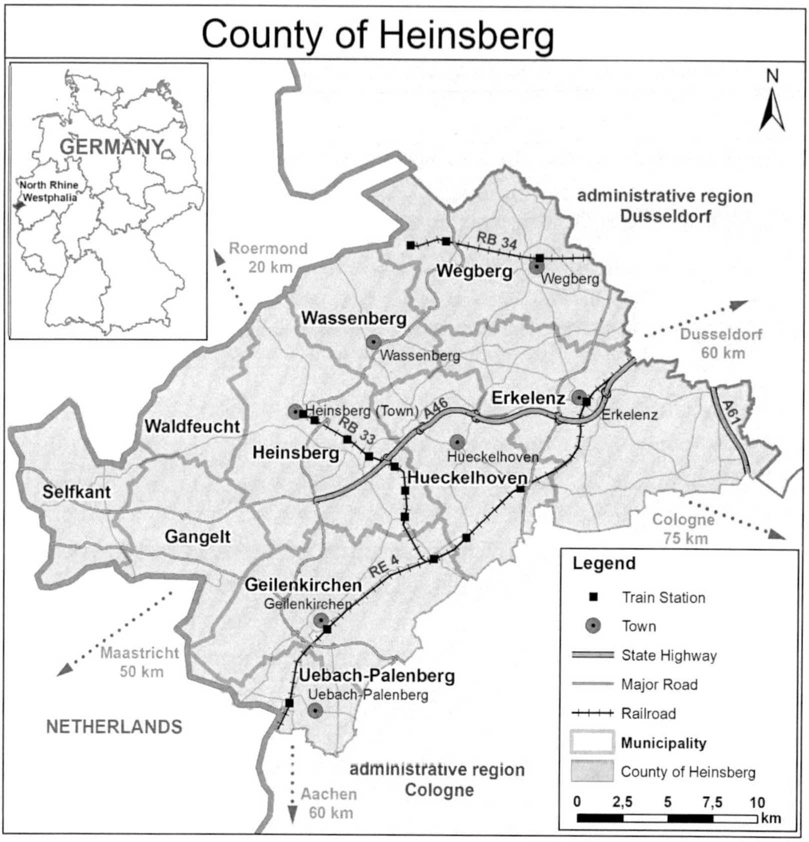

Fig. 2 The County of Heinsberg, Germany. *Source: Depiction by the authors; cartography: P. Büldt.*

in previous sections. The region has been studied using a mixed-methods approach (Section 3.1). After characterizing the setting and mobility situation of the study area (Section 3.2), empirical results are presented that provide insights into which factors support or impede the adoption and implementation of Smart Mobility innovations (Section 3.3).

3.1 Methodology

The case study adopts Creswell's (2003) mixed methods approach and adapts it to the requirements of this particular project. The combined strength of qualitative and quantitative methods allows for better exploring the research problem. To add scientific value, the rigorous use of qualitative and quantitative methods is combined with integrating and combining different kinds of information (Flick, 2009). This research design offers various advantages, as it not only solidifies the results through mixing methods, but also neutralizes each other's deficiencies (Tashakkori and Teddlie, 2003). Typical advantages of qualitative methods, such as revealing subjective personal knowledge, experiences and views, can be complemented by quantitative, potentially more objective data referring to reliably captured standardized response categories (Gläser and Laudel, 2010). As qualitative statements can be validated by quantitative data, more comprehensive, generalizable conclusions on complex social science issues can be derived.

The data used for this study stem from three different empirical approaches:

(1) Qualitative semi-structured expert interviews ($n = 28$; September 2017 to June 2018).

(2) Standardized survey among users and non-users of the on-demand service "Multibus" in the Heinsberg area ($n = 196$; Gäbel, 2018).

(3) Several standardized surveys embedded in a university project course that analyzes various mobility issues in the Heinsberg region (June–July 2018).[a]

Consequently, the research design combines experts' opinions and assessments with data collected on users of transportation, eventually leading to conclusions that are relevant for policies. In the following, the data collection methods are described in more detail.

The 28 qualitative interviews (dataset 1), which provide the core information for this article, included 34 experts (sometimes more than one expert participated in a conversation). Participants were selected according to their "privileged access to information" (Bogner et al., 2009: 72) as well as their position, specific knowledge and expertise in the field of study. Respondents could provide their specialists' interpretations, views, and attitudes. Among the interviewed experts, a majority are representatives of transport companies (26.5%, $n = 9$) and consultancies and federations (26.5%, $n = 9$), followed by public administration (23.5%, $n = 8$), and start-ups and service providers (23.5%, $n = 8$).[b] The classification of these four actor groups also forms the basis for the subsequent empirical analysis.

Especially start-ups, that seem to particularly matter for new mobility concepts and often drive social innovations (Butzin et al., 2013), deserve more attention in this field of research. To place the issue of innovation adoption in rural areas into a broader picture, a few of the interviewed

[a] The surveys were conducted by university students participating in the project course "Mobility in Rural Areas" (summer term 2018), B.Sc. Applied Geography, RWTH Aachen University.

[b] This group includes all companies that provide mobility services in an early state of business development and are not tied to a traditional transportation company.

experts are from outside the Heinsberg region. The semi-structured interview questionnaire covered four main content categories that reflect major aspects of the innovation adoption and diffusion process.

Based on the interview transcripts, data were analyzed by using MaxQDA, performing qualitative content analysis and combining qualitative and quantitative operations according to Mayring (2015) (a saturated system of categories (coding scheme) was set up). Based on the semi-structured layout of the questionnaires (similar questions were asked in each interview), quantitative statements about the frequency of responses mentioned by each actor group were acquired employing MaxQDA's group comparison tool. The cross tabulations indicate the bivariate distributions of factor frequencies mentioned by each actor group, here referring to the overall share of this specific variable (factor) among all variables mentioned by the specific actor group. Variables (codes) were only counted once per interview for achieving accurate statements. In order to circumvent typical caveats of quantifying qualitative contents (such as overlooking the ambiguity of terms in different contexts, content references of terms, problems with substitutive words and dialectical meanings; see Mayring, 2015), a random review of text samples in their specific context as well as a triangulation of differing expert statements were conducted beforehand.

The logical classification of factors of Smart Mobility adoption (Section 3.3) draws on the multi-level approach by Esser (1999), which originates from systems theory, but is widely applied in the social and political sciences (e.g., Dederichs and Florian, 2013). The approach assumes three levels (macro-meso-micro) that follow a vertical logic (Esser, 1999), as previously discussed. As multi-level logics were already purposefully employed in other mobility studies (Nykvist and Whitmarsh, 2008; Van Bree et al., 2010), they also seem adequate for the case of Heinsberg.

Other quantitative data (dataset 2) were retrieved from a standardized oral survey in the study region collected for a Master thesis on a local on-demand service called "Multibus" (Gäbel, 2018). These data capture socio-demographic variables of respondents, actual use of the service and requested improvements, mode choice restrictions, and attitudes toward alternative mobility services. The dataset (covering 109 users and 87 non-users; $n_{\text{total}} = 196$) was analyzed with SPSS. According to the age distribution of the sample, a majority of younger users were included (32% are 18–30 years old), while older age groups (51–65 years and older) are less represented. As only very few results of dataset 3 (student project course) are used for this study, the varied collection methods and sample structures are not described here.

3.2 Regional setting and mobility situation

The County of Heinsberg ("Kreis Heinsberg," hereafter simply "region") is a fairly peripheral district located some distance away from major economic and cultural centers (Fig. 2). Although surrounded by several large and mid-sized cities (Cologne and Dusseldorf, Monchengladbach and Aachen), the region itself bears rural qualities. Despite directly bordering to the Netherlands, the region does not offer good transport connections to the nearest larger Dutch cities (Roermond, Maastricht). More broadly, the region barely touches the major European development axis spreading between Cologne, Maastricht and Liége, and forms a transit area also on the regional axis between Monchengladbach and Aachen. The region is characterized by a polycentric, heterogeneous settlement structure composed of some more densely populated mid-sized country towns (Erkelenz, City of Heinsberg, Hückelhoven) and veritably rural communities (Selfkant, Gangelt, Waldfeucht). Especially in those parts of the region typical rural features dominate (outlined in Section 2.1), such as peripheral village settlements, single-family housing, low job densities, and major shares of employment in agriculture. The region's heterogeneous settlement structure, which lacks a clear rural-suburban distinction, is also reflected in regional statistics: the entire county has 252,000 inhabitants (data for 2016), hence a population density of about 400 inhabitants/km^2 (IT.NRW, 2017), alluding to a partially suburban rather than solely rural character. The German Federal Institute for Building, Urban Affairs and Spatial Development BBSR typifies Heinsberg as a county with urban influences and partly rural settlement structures (https://www.bbsr.bund.de/BBSR/DE/Home/bbsr_node.html).

In contrast to many other European rural areas, Heinsberg's population is not declining, but instead has shown a small increase since 2012 due to positive net migration (IT.NRW, 2017). Forecasts, however, expect a population decline of approximately 3% until 2030, in line with steady demographic change due to ageing dynamics that exceed German average (Stiftung, 2018). Heinsberg shows further typical rural characteristics, such as high commuter rates, deficient broadband internet connection, skills shortage, lack of medical specialists, and a scarce endowment with schools (BMEL, 2016). Wide parts of the county (64.5%) are extensively used for mixed farming (NABU, 2016). All these features underscore that the region faces some distinctive rural transportation challenges and demands, making it an appealing case study area for the future of rural mobility.

Given the region's dispersed settlement structure and insufficient coverage by public transport services, high car availability and dependency can be expected. As a regional mobility survey revealed (Kreis Heinsberg, 2012), 92% of all households have at least one car available, and 57% of inhabitants never use public transport at all. Modal split data show a car usage rate of nearly 70%, whereas 13% of the distances travelled in the region are covered by foot, 10% by bike, and only 9% by public transport. Evidence for high car dependency in the region can also be found with respect to the choice of transportation mode: 69% of respondents use the car on a daily or weekly basis, but only 14% use public transportation (all data taken from Kreis Heinsberg, 2012). Heinsberg's dominating focus on using cars becomes particularly obvious when comparing it to the all-German average car use rate of only 43% (BMVI and Infas, 2018). Although settlements and the infrastructure for supplying goods and services are geographically dispersed in the region, Heinsberg's relatively flat landscape offers good context conditions for alternative means of personal transport (i.e., electric bikes).

Nevertheless, the region can be considered to be fairly well connected by public transportation services. Four regional hubs, which again offer local bus lines for more fine-grained linkages, connect the county's medium-sized centers via train and bus services with the bigger cities around. This includes, among other lines, a revitalized train route (RB33) to Aachen especially serving commuters and students. Future plans for 2020 intend to launch an additional service of the Rhein-Ruhr-Express (RRX1), offering more frequent connections from the city of Heinsberg to Aachen and Monchengladbach (https://www.rrx.de/konzept/betrieb/#&gid=1&pid=1). Yet, the heterogeneous settlement pattern of the Heinsberg region implies a remarkably unequal accessibility of its different parts: small towns along the Monchengladbach-Aachen axis are significantly better connected than the places close to the western international border, where public transport supplies are poor. Schoolchildren and students, respectively, are the main user groups of regional public transport (the age group 6–18 uses public transport for nearly 30% of all their trips, whereas 25–45 years old people only for 4%; Kreis Heinsberg, 2012). The connection times and timetables of the county's major transport hubs are not coordinated with regional lines, which causes long transfer waiting times especially outside major operating hours. Although Heinsberg is part of the greater ticket zone of the Aachen Transport Federation (AVV), the attractiveness of regional public transport remains low, and incentives to shift from private cars to public transport are missing. Moreover, alternative mobility options for non-automotive user groups (youths, families, and elder people) are hardly provided; an exception is the recently introduced "Senior Ticket" for people aged 63 and above (AVV, 2018).

The region's economic situation has been shaped by substantial industrial restructuring for the past three decades, as coal mines had to close and textile companies shifted activities to locations abroad. Recently, however, large corporate investments, often involving high labor demand, have instigated promising trends reflected in a decreasing unemployment rate (now around 7%; Agentur für Arbeit, 2018). Structural deficiencies of the regional labor market prevail, though, as the region's high commuter rate indicates: 43% of inhabitants commute daily in order to work outside the region (IT.NRW, 2017), mainly travelling to Monchengladbach, Aachen and Dusseldorf thanks to Heinsberg's good highway connections. Further, the tourism sector is growing slowly, especially short bike trips, pushed by a recent marketing campaign and new mobility offers, such as e-bike rentals (https://heinsberger-land.de).

Spatial mobility patterns in the Heinsberg region are also strongly influenced by the polycentric settlement structure, which causes imbalanced and spatially dispersed transport demands. Various demographic challenges, such as the expected decline of population and workforce in line with an ageing population, which raise the need for health and care services as well as more flexible work environments, and decreasing numbers of schoolchildren that require transportation significantly add to the mounting tasks for local governments and transportation companies. As typical in this situation (Gather et al., 2008), shrinking public transport demand inevitably entails rising communal subsidies, or transportation services in the Heinsberg region must be further reduced and continue losing attractiveness for users.

These challenges call for thoroughly rethinking of public transportation services along with the simultaneous adoption and expansion of novel mobility solutions. As the following list shows, Heinsberg already offers some alternative mobility schemes, which enrich the region's mobility system. But only very few alternative solutions independent from private cars were regionally introduced so far. All of them are small-scale, lack digital support, and are at best only vaguely integrated in existing transportation networks:

- *The "Multibus":* this on-demand public transportation service provided by a local company operates several mini busses. On weekends, additional bike transport (Fahrradbus) is available. Aligned with existing transport lines, the busses call at regular bus stops, and the fare is included in the AVV's overall ticketing system. As booking works via telephone only (online booking is planned to be launched soon), time flexibility is limited (orders must be placed at least 60 min in advance), and there is no service outside major operating hours.

- *Carsharing*: this service provided by a local car dealer requires online-booking only, as well as pre-registration. There is no integration in regional transportation networks or ticketing systems. Only three rental stations are offered (Heinsberg Königs, Heinsberg town hall, Geilenkirchen station), equipped with just three cars (compact and mid-size cars) for the entire region.
- *Ridesharing*: the County of Heinsberg is registered in two nationwide online ridesharing platforms. But links to the platform are only provided via the county government's homepage, and the service is not integrated into the regional transport federation's mobility platform, which limits its visibility to potential users.
- *E-Mobility:* Electric charging services are provided by a private energy supplier, offering 10 charging points within the region, mostly concentrated in the city of Heinsberg. These installations are neither integrated in existing loading networks nor do they provide technical interfaces with other common charging systems.

Plans exist to further support alternative, more sustainable regional mobility approaches in the near future, including the installation of three "mobility stations" at the most frequented train stations (city of Heinsberg, Geilenkirchen, Erkelenz). These mobility stations are multimodal connection points that both pool public transportation services and offer mode-switching opportunities using shared bikes and cars. For that purpose, bike- and car-sharing stations will be implemented that have not been provided in the region so far. In terms of a simple mobility solution, some rural communities also plan to introduce a "Mitfahrbank": a public bench, equipped with a stop sign which can be used by potential co-riding passengers to indicate their intended travel direction, until a passing car offers them a free lift.

The fact that these novel mobility services are not integrated in a common booking platform, and the lack of their adequate marketing and promotion are surprising: the regional transport federation company AVV has recently implemented an app-based mobility platform (AVV connect) that provides a basis not only for giving access to full transport information and booking services, but also offers best options for customer-oriented marketing and communication activities (AVV, 2018). Another booking platform with e-mobility focus was proposed by some stakeholders residing in the most rural parts of the region (Westzipfel region, 2015), but has not been introduced so far.

As the recent developments show, the regional and local public transportation companies represent the main actors of advanced mobility and transport provision in the Heinsberg region, in line with very few private companies. The latter, though, do not boast extensive experience in the field. To date no young entrepreneurs or start-ups have entered the mobility market in Heinsberg yet. The regional expansion of mobility services has been supported by some public support programs in the past: the introduction of the "Multibus," for instance, was funded by a national program launched by the central Ministry of Education and Research BMBF in 2001–2003. Currently VITAL.NRW promotes local initiatives in Heinsberg's rural parts, including mobility issues among others (Westzipfel region, 2015). Besides the industrial promotion services provided by the regional development agency (Wirtschaftsförderung Heinsberg), centers for knowledge and innovation transfer are missing in Heinsberg. These deficiencies are key, since the promotion of mobility innovations and the support for implementing and adapting new products and services are highly dependent on local cooperation and institutional initiatives (Rogers, 2003; Wisdom et al., 2014). An open question is to which extent copying mobility innovations originating from urban agglomerations is unequivocally desirable for rural areas like Heinsberg, given the significant differences between rural and urban context conditions and transport demands.

3.3 Drivers and impediments for implementing Smart Mobility

This section describes the empirical findings that help develop strategies for successfully implementing Smart Mobility solutions in the rural context of the Heinsberg region. It reveals major promoting and impeding factors. These factors are differentiated with respect to perceptions by the four main actor groups included in the study (Figs. 3 and 4), combining insights gained through the 28 conducted expert interviews (dataset 1, coded as I1–I28) with user related results (datasets 2 and 3, as outlined in Section 3.1). According to the multi-level logics introduced above (Section 2.3) and applied for data classification (Section 3.1), Table 2 provides an overview of identified impeding and promoting factors, which are further explained in the following.

3.3.1 The macro-level (environment, society)

The factors that characterize conditions at the macro-level relate to, and depend on, political enactments, legislation and regulatory agencies. They can only be changed by means of strong political intervention, for instance, on the meso-level. Insufficient infrastructure, both physical (i.e., conditions and capacity of train or bus stations and service lines) and digital

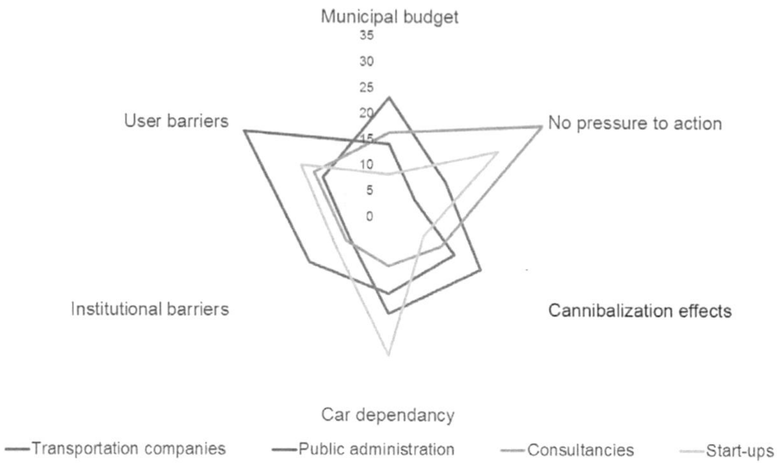

Fig. 3 Adopting Smart Mobility innovations in the rural Heinsberg region: impeding factors (% of respondents). *Source: Depiction by the author, based on analyzed expert interview data 2017–2018.*

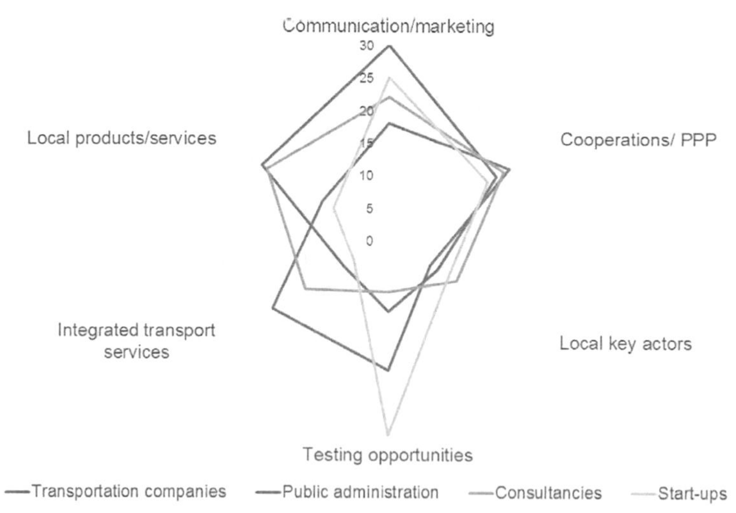

Fig. 4 Adopting Smart Mobility innovations in the rural Heinsberg region: promoting factors (% of respondents). *Source: Depiction by the author, based on analyzed expert interview data 2017–2018.*

Table 2 Implementation of Smart Mobility in the Heinsberg region: impeding and promoting factors.

	Impeding factors	Promoting factors
MACRO Environment, society	• Legislation • Infrastructure • Disperse settlement structures	• Physical, topographical qualities • Digitization
MESO Regional institutions, policies	• Institutional barriers • Regional funding • Cannibalization effects • Lack of pressure to action	• Policy measures • Local cooperation and partnerships • System integration
MICRO Actor, product	• Car dependency • Usability barriers/comfort • Limited openness for innovations • Last mile coverage	• Communication, marketing • Testing opportunities • Local services • Local key actors • Civil participation

Source: Depiction by the author based on expert interviews 2017–2018. Only factors with a minimum count of $n = 7$ are listed.

(i.e., broadband connections, WLAN hotspots), is a crucial impeding factor that can hamper implementing (digital) mobility services. And covering the so-called last mile (connection from a hub to the final destination) counts as a major challenge for installing Smart Mobility solutions in rural Heinsberg. This factor is particularly significant for introducing on-demand or ride sharing services in the region's dispersed settlement context (factor mentioned in 8 out of 28 interviews):

> *The commuting peaks and the imbalanced pupil traffic make the introduction of a smart on-demand system unrealistic by now. We still need to find the perfect match between sufficient supplies for the people that live geographically disperse and profitability for transportation providers at the same time (interview I6, translated).*

Conversely, the physical, i.e., topographical qualities of the region with its extensive land availability and low traffic volumes are also conducive to expediently implementing mobility innovations. Endowed with ample space, this rural region offers better opportunities for installing mobility and car-sharing stations or setting up e-charging infrastructure than urban agglomerations. Yet, these procedures require intricate negotiation processes between land owners and public authorities (as expressed by I3).

Several experts (in 9 out of 28 interviews) confirm that legal restrictions obstruct the diffusion of innovations (Aarons et al., 2011; Wisdom et al., 2014). In Germany, the ongoing debate about the law on passenger transport (PBfG) reveals how powerfully this regulation has prevented the diffusion of alternative pooling-on-demand services so far.

> *Germany is a highly regulated country. If policies are not defining a clear framework to let new technologies freely develop and innovations diffuse, whilst adapting the regulations of the PBfG, Smart Mobility will not work (I3, translated).*
> *The amendment of the PBfG will cause a massive innovation boost (I14, translated).*

Currently, tests of new on-demand or pooling services are only permitted within the frame of a special legal clause ("experimental clause; VDV, 2015), which allows practical trials of new transportation services only for a duration of up to 4 years and as long as public interests are not violated.

The digitization of products and services forms the basis for various technical improvements, and clearly counts as a main driver of innovation diffusion (confirmed in 10 interviews); it is *"enabling the change"* (I14, translated). As the experts advocate in the interviews, public authorities and institutions are requested to invest heavily in digital infrastructure and broadband expansion in the countryside to provide a solid base for future developments (I2, I18, I22, I28). Especially in the field of mobility, well equipped digital amenities are key to enabling customers to use online services (BMEL, 2016; Flügge, 2016). The importance of this factor for motivating users to adopt mobility innovations was confirmed by Gäbel (2018), showing that the expansion of related digital services can strongly promote the use of Smart Mobility solutions: passengers explicitly demand reliable booking options via smartphone app or instant messaging, as well as booking and information services offered via a common platform based on registered personal user accounts. The platform infrastructure could be used beyond mobility services, for example, providing information about natural hazards and epidemic diseases (I8). Findings of dataset 3 confirm this requirement, exposing that all age groups consider the equipment of planned mobility stations in the Heinsberg region (Section 3.2) with WLAN hotspots and digital sharing services as highly relevant.

3.3.2 The meso-level (regional institutions, policies)

According to the applied multi-level logics, regional institutions are important agents at the meso-level, including interactions with the superior macro-level (environment, society) as well as the actor-oriented micro-level. At large, crucial interdependencies between developments at the different levels can be detected, which at times render clear distinctions difficult.

In the Heinsberg case, communal budgets are constricted, and infrastructure investments are in general particularly costly. Hence, regional funding is the chief impeding factor when it comes to implementing mobility innovations, as stated in over half of the interviews (19). Further, public transport services in this rural area are financially highly deficient (I1, I2, I8). Therefore, budgets for introducing alternative mobility concepts that add to existing services require extra support by federal funds (I5), for instance, when installing the particularly expensive autonomous driving systems (I17).

Institutional barriers and weak local governance can also be important hindrances to the implementation and diffusion of Smart Mobility innovations. Many interviewees (13) assert that in the case of Heinsberg, insufficient knowledge and expertise, blockading initiatives (for example, by parties in chambers or parliaments) or harmful subsidies obstruct innovation diffusion (confirming Docherty, 2018; Wisdom et al., 2014). On the contrary, policy measures can in other guises also promote the adoption of alternative mobility services, such as the reservation of parking lots for e-cars only, traffic priority for car pools (HOV lanes), or sharing models that combine both communal and private car users (I3, I10).

Fig. 3 illustrates interesting, albeit unsurprising differences between actor groups with respect to assessing impeding factors for Smart Mobility adoption: representatives of public administration regard meso-level institutional barriers much less as an impediment to introducing mobility innovations in the Heinsberg region, in contrast to actors from consultancy and start-up companies.

Looking at major factors that are assumed to support the regional implementation of Smart Mobility, the local cooperation of public administration, transportation and taxi companies, other regional firms, associations, and citizens stand out (18 interviews). Communal governments feature as important managers for sustainability developments, fostering local collaboration and partnerships among actors of different levels (i.e., cargo-bikes by local retailers for neighborhoods), in line with the "New Rural Governance" approach (Drabenstott et al., 2004; Little, 2001; OECD, 2006). In the countryside, productive governance networks can easier and faster be established than in cities, due to typical rural socio-cultural features (as conceptualized in Section 2.2), based on the region's smaller population size and fewer actors involved:

> *Actors in rural areas are much clearer about what they need for their community, however, that does not make things simple, as economic power and sufficient funding are often missing (I11, translated).*

The successful adaptation of mobility services to rural demands often implies rescaling them (due to dispersed transport demand, wide operating areas; Section 2.1), thus *"actors need to unite, join forces and combine efforts in order to be able to generate economies of scale"* (I7, translated). Requisites to further improve cooperation among different actors in Heinsberg seem favorable, as all actors agreed on the importance of that factor (see Fig. 4). Furthermore, new services must be integrated into, and adjusted to the existing transportation network in order to avoid isolated solutions (9 interviews), to provide secured connecting services and to coordinate transfer times and time tables in the region or even beyond (7 interviews).

Further support for innovation adoption can emerge from open attitudes of regional actors toward external market entrants, such as private mobility companies. Private firms can relieve tight public budgets by offering additional transportation services and improving regional accessibility. *"In cities, market demands are fully covered, but in the countryside, the situation is different"* (I18, translated). An expanded range of service supplies and mobility options can instigate a behavioral change of citizens toward easier adopting mobility innovations, as long as new offers meet the users' demands well (Lenz and Fraedrich, 2015). Private companies, though, mainly focus on country towns so far, as transport demand and volumes are higher here than in more peripheral parts of the rural region:

> *When a private company or a start-up comes up to a municipality and offers the implementation of new mobility services in cooperation with the local transportation providers, it is a win-win-situation for both (I18, translated).*

A growing number of competitors can also improve the general quality of mobility services offered, in terms of competitive pressure (I13). Start-ups are not obliged to comply with the principles of the welfare state, which is why some experts see chances that these firms *"revolutionize the mobility market"* (I14, translated) much more than public transportation companies.

> *They [start-ups] are neither engaged in servicing all parts of the region due to their private commission, nor must they cover deficit routes; thus their role in the transformation of the mobility sector in the countryside is not negligible (I14, translated).*

Experts therefore see opportunities in fostering the *"innovation atmosphere whilst using the various advantages (i.e., low rents, special properties for co-working) of the countryside"* (I24a, translated; the project "CoWork land" gives an example, https://www.region-digital.de/coworkland/das-projekt/). The planned establishing of innovation and knowledge-transfer centers in the Heinsberg region (Section 3.2) holds promises to raise the development of the entire region by *"boosting the regional entrepreneurship movement"* (I24, translated).

Other experts, in turn, doubt that these prospects exist, as *"success is more than just launching an app for the countryside, while being originally located in urban environments"* (I19, translated). This statement also supports the importance of adapting mobility innovations before implementing them in rural contexts. As Fig. 3 shows, open attitudes toward new market entrants are not shared by all actor groups alike. Transportation companies fear cannibalization effects (losses of their own market share to new market entrants; factor named in 15 interviews). Start-up firms, in contrast, do not perceive the risk of cannibalization effects as a factor that hampers the introduction of new mobility services, but rather detect business development opportunities for themselves (see Fig. 3). Looking at sustainability goals, the risk of inducing rather than reducing traffic and emissions prevails, as digital services can increase the appeal of shared cars, for instance, which spurs the demand for individual mobility (I12). The introduction of new services should not only be left to private companies, though. Market share losses of public transportation not only lead to higher ticket prices, but also threaten to neglect basic principles of the welfare state.

> *It is the task of the public transport authority to support the successful implementation of innovations; in the optimal case, they even become the main drivers of this development (I4, translated).*
> *Transportation companies have to go where their rival is about to take over and, by using their local knowledge advantage, offer the service themselves (I8, translated).*

Resonating the rural transport challenges described above (Section 2.1), over half of the experts (in 17 out of 28 interviews) state that lack of pressure toward a smart, sustainable transformation of rural mobility is currently the biggest impeding factor that hinders mobility innovations to be implemented and adopted in the Heinsberg region (generally confirming Pangbourne et al., 2018; Spickermann et al., 2014; Wittowsky and Hoenninger, 2018). However, there are remarkable discrepancies in the opinions of the actors groups (see Fig. 3). The perceived reasons for the limited pressure to action in the rural transportation sector are diverse: Due to the relatively small traffic volumes, people's environmental motives to use alternative mobility solutions are virtually absent. And the rural region does not directly suffer from, for instance, particulate matter pollution, driving bans, or mobility restrictions through the introduction of environmental zones (I7, I5).

> *Even if electronic busses were never implemented in rural areas, this would be fine, as investments in technological developments are disproportionate to the missing emission-related challenges (I8, translated).*

People are not as aware of sustainability issues as in cities, either (I1, I9, I26). Due to the broad availability of cars, accessibility is, because covered by private transport, *"not a pain"* (I6, translated) for rural inhabitants. *"The car still works perfectly in the countryside"* (I5, translated), "*they (rural users) do not have the pressure to accept innovations*" (I12, translated). When going by car in rural areas, typical collateral costs incurring from traffic jams, finding a parking lot or high parking fees do not apply either (I23, I7). These arguments render debatable to what extent the introduction of Smart Mobility services to rural areas like Heinsberg is desirable: *"Up to now I am not convinced that we need smartification in the countryside"* (I6, translated). It remains unclear *"how this pressure to action should be triggered and who should do this"* (I14, translated).

Mobility service users, in contrast, perceive the need for action and a transition of the mobility situation in Heinsberg differently (Gäbel, 2018). And the students' surveys (dataset 3) also detected problems like a missing accessibility to train stations for handicapped passengers as well as lacking intermodal mobility options and incentives for increased (e)-bike use (i.e., secure public bicycle stands). To transform the modal split in the region in favor of environmental concerns, connecting times, service frequencies and travel times with public transport need to be improved: *"uncoordinated timetables of busses and trains"* was the chief critical factor mentioned by 35% of interviewed users (students' survey; $n = 162$). Especially the rural Western parts of the Heinsberg region suffer from poor connections and limited accessibility (I9, I22, I23). According to the representative mobility survey of the county government, the services of public transportation earned an overall grade of only 3.7, i.e., "not satisfying" (Kreis Heinsberg, 2012).

3.3.3 The micro-level (actor, product)

Finally, factors at the micro-level are outlined, which influence the adapted implementation of mobility innovations in the rural area of Heinsberg. Referring to Rogers' (2003) innovation-decision-model, the micro-level factors are divided into product and adopter (consumer) specific categories.

Again we must point out that the dominance of private cars in rural mobility represents one of the most crucial hindering factors for implementing mobility innovations in the countryside (as mentioned in 14 out of 28 expert interviews). Especially start-up firms and transportation companies as mobility service providers emphasize this disadvantage (see Fig. 3). The high dependency of people on private cars not only is aligned with a low frequency of public transportation services in general, but also lowers the demand for alternative mobility options. In Heinsberg, 92% of all inhabitants own a car (Kreis Heinsberg, 2012). This distinctly rural situation is both reflected in Heinsberg's modal split rates (as shown in Section 3.2) and can be found in other datasets used for this study. Gäbel (2018), for instance, reveals particularly low rates of using alternative modes of transport (the 'Multibus') compared to private cars.

For the entire process of Smart Mobility implementation in rural context, communication and marketing measures are assessed as the most important promoting factor (stated by 20 experts), in line with Rogers' (2003: 18) statement: "Communication is the quintessence of the diffusion process, where individuals inform each other about the innovation". Communication and marketing campaigns are decisive means not only to inform potential consumers about new products or services, but also to enhance their acceptance; also testing opportunities can contribute to strengthening the consumers' compliance. Although actors on the meso-level initiate and supervise such campaigns, the consumers on the micro-level are the target groups of these activities, as outlined in the following paragraphs.

Fig. 4 underscores the importance of the communication and marketing factor for the Heinsberg case, as all actor groups agreed on its significance within the innovation adoption process.

> *Governments and transportation associations have to invest not only into infrastructure, but also in minds, hearts and attitudes (I1, translated).*
> *Saving on the marketing budget is one of the biggest drawbacks of public transportation companies (I10, translated).*
> *People have to believe and understand that the innovation offers them relative advantages to their prior mobility choices, therefore investments in marketing campaigns are not optional (I11, translated).*

In addition to digital forms of marketing (i.e., social media, videos) other tailor-made measures could also address the specific needs of rural areas, such as advertisements of services on weekly markets, in elderly homes or with personal ambassadors from door to door (I25). Eventually, the importance of communication for raising user rates and the utilization of mobility services are confirmed by our students' surveys, too, which tell that alternative mobility services already existing in the Heinsberg region (i.e., the bike Multibus) are only sparsely used so far because they remain widely unknown. Likewise, the students found out that people are not well informed about the mobility stations soon to be installed. There is only some marginal interest of Heinsberg's inhabitants in alternative modes of transport (Gäbel, 2018). All these deficiencies could probably be improved by tailor-made marketing campaigns.

Many experts confirm (12 interviews) that the personal issues of customer comfort, skeptical attitudes and traditions of usage are important actor-based factors that impede the rural adoption of mobility innovations. In contrast to urban travelers, rural people often display skepticism toward alternative and shared mobility services.

> *People in the countryside have a very distant attitude towards sharing. 'My home is my castle', they hold their own house, their own car, they don't want to share this with others (I3, translated).*

Thus *"citizens must be sensitized for new forms of mobility, [...] new generations grow up, and their view of ownership is generally different"* (I11, translated). Especially when using an innovation (i.e., pooling-on-demand service) for the first time, various barriers apply, often relating to a lack of accompanying digital support. As shown for Heinsberg (Gäbel, 2018), usage of the on-demand minibus "Multibus" could potentially be improved by complementing telephone-based booking services with online booking options. The thesis also suggests that better coordination and alignment between alternative mobility providers and public transportation players could reduce barriers to use.

Since rural users may not be as familiar with innovative, digital transportation services as urban consumers, the offer to test novel mobility options, to try new products and services is regarded as a main promoting factor for implementing Smart Mobility in the countryside (stated in 9 interviews, confirming Arts et al., 2011; Rogers, 2003). Especially start-ups, which display a particularly strong customer-service orientation, advocate this factor (see Fig. 4). Based on the fairly strong social cohesion and bonding to traditions in rural areas (Section 2.2), mobility services that are marked by a local connection—be it to a neighborhood, community or person—have a higher probability of being successfully implemented (as mentioned in 8 interviews). Locally based services that are offered by well-known actors or institutions will not only meet the need for the passengers' security but can also better promote the users' identification with this innovation (I4, I9, I13, I28).

> *Concepts that are closely related to citizens' needs and rooted in well-known settings are much more likely to be adopted than concepts originating from outside the region. [However] integration of the concept into the regional network needs to be ensured, too (I9, translated).*

Besides customer acquisition, the testing of Smart Mobility solutions also provides bright opportunities for rural areas to more broadly function as testing arenas in the future, opening up chances to support overall regional economic development.

> *The motivation to install testing opportunities and pilots in rural areas is that scaling here is extremely easy, because the utilization potential is particularly great. I think it is far easier to introduce a pilot in a rural area than in a city (I11, translated).*

Some other rural regions have already made use of their structural advantages of land availability, low traffic volumes, and high scaling potential for functioning as test fields (i.e., "test field e-mobility south west," cluster intelligent move Baden-Wurttemberg, established 2015). Yet, no coherent (nationwide) political requirements for the installation of "test fields or arenas" have been elaborated by the German government so far. If incentives were provided, rural regions could profit not only from state funding but also from arranging agreements with private mobility providers about the subsequent use of tested and proven concepts, potentially leaving loss-making service operations to the private provider (I7). Testing opportunities and pilot projects can also multiply user rates and employ "customers win customers" campaigns (I1; in line with Arts et al., 2011; Rogers, 2003). Start-ups particularly see opportunities here (Fig. 4). They may accelerate the adoption process, too, as the visibility and observability of novel mobility initiatives further influence the innovation decision of users (according to Rogers, 2003): *"Those [testing opportunities] must be designed so eye-catching and obvious that the user must actively resist against using them"* (I1).

When implementing Smart Mobility, the (mobility) behavior of local key actors probably fosters the broader adoption of new products and services (stated in 13 interviews). Outstanding personalities like mayors, councilors, or directors of prominent companies can promote the use of innovations by serving as role models and by publicly supporting new mobility ideas in local parliaments and within other decision-making processes.

> *If people [users] know someone within their community who also uses alternative modes of transport, chances for adoption are much higher (I18, translated).*
> *At the same time the courage [of actors] in the countryside to implement new, innovative services that people are not familiar with and that might be loss-making is much lower than in cities (I10, translated).*

How the extent and point of time of civil participation and enactment influence innovation implementation remains unclear, though, as engaging the general public bears both chances (*"activating the knowledge of the local crowd*", I24) and risks ("*participation of the general public does not occupy pooling vehicles*", I7). Still, many experts (7 interviews) consider civil participation as a promoting factor for adopting mobility innovations. Surprisingly, social innovations associated with novel mobility solutions remain undeveloped in Heinsberg, yet bear particular chances to encourage people to jointly profit from new digital services, drawing on the typically strong social cohesion in rural areas (I7, 28, I19; see also Butzin et al., 2013).

4. Conclusions

The main thesis of this chapter is that rural areas could reap substantial benefits from adopting and adapting digitally supported services, tools and platforms, in fact offer widely unexplored territory for ICT-based initiatives. One promising issue is innovative Smart Mobility solutions which—mostly used in urban agglomerations hitherto—use digital means for organizing shared transportation adapted to individual needs (Papa and Lauwers, 2015). When applied in the countryside, Smart Mobility could help to reduce several disadvantages of living and working conditions in rural areas, allowing for a combination of improved job and service accessibility for the rural population and entrepreneurial stimuli. At the same time, they could advance environmental, economic, and social sustainability goals, just as modern governance concepts require (Docherty, 2018). Conceptual considerations and empirical findings based on mixed methods show for the case of Heinsberg in Germany that there are in fact some interesting starting points for improving shared and bundled people's transportation means in rural areas. In some respects, these regions offer topographical, settlement and societal conditions that are particularly conducive to testing and adopting novel ICT coordinated mobility systems. Favorable factors relate to the overarching macro-, regional meso- and individual micro-levels of socio-political dynamics (Esser, 1999). This approach, used as a heuristic framework for data analysis in this study, reveals that intricate interdependencies between these levels make clear distinctions difficult, yet methodologically still viable. We must concede, though, that the rural implementation of Smart Mobility solutions is also hampered by various obstacles on these levels, both in general and specific terms.

These insights pose significant challenges for deriving promising Smart Mobility policy recommendations, which could form part of broader "Smart Countryside" or "Smart Rural Area" development strategies (as called for by Fraunhofer IESE, 2017). Most notably, it will be difficult to convince wider parts of the rural population that "smartified" means of public mass transport should be preferred to the use of private cars for individual trips because of broader welfare and sustainability values attached to the former compared to the latter. Alas, this paper once again confirms car-centric modal split patterns typical for rural contexts (Farber and Páez, 2011; Pucher and Renne, 2005). But maybe it requires really smart approaches to finally move out of the trap?

Above all, our findings indicate that related developmental and policy tasks must refer to more than just a suggestion to further increase public as well as private corporate engagement and financial investments in setting up state-of-the-art ICT infrastructure for mobility innovations in rural areas like Heinsberg. Still, macro-level legislative settings as well as meso-level institutional and policy initiatives in the region are crucial, as they need to create supportive framework constellations and incentives for promoting the rural adoption, adaptation and proliferation of suitable Smart Mobility approaches, also integrating them into the overall system of intra- and inter-regional personal transportation. On the macro- and meso-levels, also new business partners must be attracted or endogenously generated in order to revitalize and diversify rural mobility.

The most difficult challenges, however, loom at the micro-level of individual user decisions (in line with the diffusion model by Rogers (2003)). Only when a growing wave of Smart Mobility participation by rural residents can be set into motion, new transportation offers can feasibly be established and effective rural development impulses launched. Personal digital devices and apps in principle are well suited for instigating this wave toward broader uses of shared mobility options, potentially creating contagious Smart Mobility user cultures locally. Yet, appealing and functional tools that initiate such a trend still remain to be developed and implemented in the rural Heinsberg region and beyond. Besides offering comprehensive information and complete transport booking options, tailor-made Internet platforms could, for instance, include attractive award and incentive elements for Smart Mobility users, combine route planning with other rural sharing and consumption needs, or even take in entertaining game components that draw on rural favorites. In any case, it is again the agency at the macro- and meso-levels which must pave the way for change, enabling and inspiring new actor collectives to develop truly smart trajectories toward Smart Mobility for an attractive, livable countryside.

Acknowledgements

The authors gratefully acknowledge financial support by the State of North Rhine Westphalia for the ongoing research project, as the first author is member of the publicly funded PhD Graduate School (Forschungskolleg) "ACCESS!."

References

Aarons, G.A., Hurlburt, M., Horwitz, S.M., 2011. Advancing a conceptual model of evidence-based practice implementation in public service sectors. Adm. Policy Ment. Health Ment. Health Serv. Res. 38, 4–23.

Agentur für Arbeit, 2018. Statistik Regionen. Kreis Heinsberg. https://statistik.arbeitsagentur.de/Navigation/Statistik/Statistik-nach-Regionen/Politische-Gebietsstruktur/Nordrhein-Westfalen/Heinsberg-Nav.html (last accessed: 01.08.2018).

Ahern, A., Hine, J., 2012. Rural transport—valuing the mobility of older people. Res. Transp. Econ. 34, 27–34.

Ahvenniemi, H., Huovila, A., Pinto-Seppä, I., Airaksinen, M., 2017. What are the differences between sustainable and smart cities? Cities 60, 234–245.

Arts, J.W., Frambach, R.T., Bijmolt, T.H., 2011. Generalizations on consumer innovation adoption: a meta-analysis on drivers of intention and behavior. Int. J. Res. Mark. 28, 134–144.

AVV (Aachener Verkehrsverbund), 2018. AVV Connect. https://avv.de/de/fahrplaene/app-avvconnect (last accessed 12.10.2017).

Banister, D., 2008. The sustainable mobility paradigm. Transp. Policy 15, 73–80.

Beckmann, K.J., Klein-Hitpaß, A. (Eds.), 2013. Nicht Weniger Unterwegs, sondern Intelligenter? Neue Mobilitätskonzepte. Difu, Berlin.

BMEL (Bundesministerium für Ernährung und Landwirtschaft), 2016. Ländliche Regionen verstehen. Fakten und Hintergründe zum Leben und Arbeiten in ländlichen Regionen. Berlin.

BMVI (Bundesministerium für Verkehr und digitale Infrastruktur), Infas, 2018. Mobilität in Deutschland. Kurzreport. Verkehrsaufkommen—Struktur—Trends. Bonn and Berlin.

Boehner, V., Franz, P., Hanson, J., Gallart, R., Martínez, S., Sumper, A., Girbau-Llistuella, F., 2016. Smart Grids for Rural Conditions and E-Mobility-Applying Power Routers, Batteries and Virtual Power Plants. Actas CIGRE, pp. 1–9. 2016.

Bogner, A., Littig, B., Menz, W. (Eds.), 2009. Das Experteninterview. Theorie, Methode, Anwendungsfelder. VS Verlag, Wiesbaden.

Bramley, R., 2009. Lessons from nearly 20 years of precision agriculture research, development, and adoption as a guide to its appropriate application. Crop Pasture Sci. 60, 197–217.

Bryden, J.M., Efstratoglou, S., Ferenczi, T. et al., (Eds.), 2011. Towards Sustainable Rural Regions in Europe. Exploring Inter-Relationships Between Rural Policies, Farming, Environment, Demographics, Regional Economies and Quality of Life Using System Dynamics. Routledge, Abingdon.

Butzin, A., Terstriep, J., Welschhoff, J., 2013. Nachhaltige Mobilität durch soziale Innovationen!? Verkehrsprobleme und alternative Ansätze zu ihrer Lösung. Forschung Aktuell 02/2013, Institut Arbeit und Technik, Gelsenkirchen.

Chambers, R., 2013. Rural Development: Putting the Last First. Routledge, London.

Cohen-Blankshtain, G., Rotem-Mindali, O., 2016. Key research themes on ICT and sustainable urban mobility. Int. J. Sustain. Transp. 10, 9–17.

Cooke, P., Morgan, K., 1998. The Associational Economy: Firms, Regions, and Innovation. Oxford University Press, Oxford.

Creswell, J., 2003. Research Design: Qualitative, Quantitative, and Mixed Methods Approaches. Sage, Thousand Oaks.

Dargay, J.M., 2002. Determinants of car ownership in rural and urban areas: a pseudo-panel analysis. Transport Res E-Log 38, 351–366.

Dederichs, A.M., Florian, M., 2013. Felder, Organisationen und Akteure—eine organisationssoziologische Skizze. In: Ebrecht, J., Hillebrandt, F. (Eds.), Bourdieus Theorie der Praxis: Erklärungskraft·Anwendung Perspektiven. Springer, Berlin, pp. 69–96.

Dewald, U., Fromhold-Eisebith, M., 2015. Trajectories of sustainability transitions in scale-transcending innovation systems: the case of photovoltaics. Environ. Innov. Soc. Trans. 17, 110–125 (Dec.).

Docherty, I., 2018. New governance challenges in the era of 'smart' mobility. In: Marsden, G., Reardon, L. (Eds.), Governance of the Smart Mobility Transition. Emerald Publishers, London, pp. 19–32.

Dorner, F., Berger, M., 2017. Kombiniertes Carsharing und Ridesharing: eine gemeinschaftsbasierte Mobilitätslösung für den ländlichen Raum? In: REAL CORP 2017–A World in Constant Motion. Proceedings of 22nd International Conference on Urban Planning. Regional Development and Information Society, Vienna, pp. 319–328.

Drabenstott, M., Novack, N., Weiler, S., 2004. New Governance for a New Rural Economy: Reinventing Public and Private Institutions—A Conference Summary. Federal Reserve Bank of Kansas City Economic Review 4th Quarter, pp. 55–70.

Esser, H., 1999. Soziologie. Allgemeine Grundlagen, third ed. Campus Verlag, Frankfurt.

Farber, S., Páez, A., 2011. Running to stay in place: the time-use implications of automobile oriented land-use and travel. J. Transp. Geogr. 19 (4), 782–793.

Flex, F., Lamker, C., 2012. Verantwortung, Versorgung, Entwicklung—Daseinsvorsorge zwischen Kooperation und Wettbewerb. In: Growe, A., Heider, K., Lamker, C., Paßlick, S. (Eds.), Polyzentrale Stadtregionen: Die Region als planerischer Handlungsraum. ARL Verlag, Hannover, pp. 75–85.

Flick, U., 2009. Sozialforschung. Methoden und Anwendungen. Rowohlt Taschenbuch Verlag, Reinbek.

Flügge, B. (Ed.), 2016. Smart Mobility. Trends, Konzepte, Best Practices für die Intelligente Mobilität. Springer Vieweg, Wiesbaden.

Fournier, G., Baumann, M., Gasde, J., Kilian-Yasin, K., 2018. Innovative mobility in rural areas—the case of the black forest. Int. J. Automot. Technol. Manag. 18, 247–269.

Franke, N., Von Hippel, E., Schreier, M., 2006. Finding commercially attractive user innovations: a test of lead-user theory. J. Prod. Innov. Manag. 23, 301–315.

Fraunhofer IESE (Institut für Experimentelles Software Engineering), 2017. Smart Rural Areas. https://www.iese.fraunhofer.de/de/innovation_trends/sra.html. (last accessed 21.07.2017).

Fromhold-Eisebith, M., Dewald, U., 2018. Urban innovation or rural dedication? Contrasts in socio-technical niche development and the case of photovoltaics in Germany. In: Van Geenhuizen, M., Holbrook, J.A., Taheri, M. (Eds.), Cities and Sustainable Technology Transitions. Leadership, Innovation and Adoption. E. Elgar, Cheltenham, pp. 109–133.

Gäbel, L., 2018. Integrierte Verkehrskonzepte für ländliche Regionen: Der Multibus als Lösung für bedarfsorientierte Verkehre im ländlichen Raum? In: Untersuchung am Beispiel des Kreises Heinsberg. RWTH Aachen University, Aachen. Unpublished Master thesis, Dept. of Geography.
Gather, M., Kagermeier, A., Lanzendorf, M., 2008. Geographische Mobilitäts- und Verkehrsforschung. Borntraeger, Berlin and Stuttgart.
Geels, F.W., Schot, J.W., 2007. Typology of sociotechnical transition pathways. Res. Policy 36 (3), 399–417.
Gibson-Graham, J.K., Roelvink, G., 2009. Social innovation for community economies. In: Mac-Callum, D., Moulaert, F., Hillier, J., Haddock, S.V. (Eds.), Social Innovation and Territorial Development. Ashgate, Farnham, pp. 25–37.
Gläser, J., Laudel, G., 2010. Experteninterviews und Qualitative Inhaltsanalyse. Springer-Verlag, Berlin.
Goldman, T., Gorham, R., 2006. Sustainable urban transport: four innovative directions. Technol. Soc. 28, 261–273.
Grabher, G., Stark, D., 1997. Organizing diversity: evolutionary theory, network analysis and postsocialism. Reg. Stud. 31, 533–544.
Grabski-Kieron, U., 2007. Geographie und Planung ländlicher Räume in Mitteleuropa. In: Gebhardt, H., Glaser, R., Radtke, U., Reuber, P. (Eds.), Geographie. Springer-Spectrum, Heidelberg, pp. 602–615.
Hägerstrand, T., 1967. Innovation Diffusion as a Spatial Process. The University of Chicago Press, Chicago.
Herget, M., 2016. Mobilität von Familien im ländlichen Raum. Springer VS, Wiesbaden.
Hoggart, K., Black, R., Buller, H., 2014. Rural Europe. Identity and Change. Routledge, London.
infas, DLR, 2010. Mobilität in Deutschland 2008. Ergebnisbericht. Struktur—Aufkommen—Emissionen—Trends. Institut für angewandte Sozialwissenschaft, Deutsches Zentrum für Luft- und Raumfahrt, Bonn and Berlin.
IT.NRW, 2017. Kommunalprofil Heinsberg. Landesdatenbank NRW, Düsseldorf.
Jeekel, H., 2018. Cities and adoption of innovation in passenger mobility. In: van Geenhuizen, M., Holbrook, J.A., Taheri, M. (Eds.), Cities and Sustainable Technology Transitions. Leadership, Innovation and Adoption. E. Elgar, Cheltenham, pp. 167–188.
Kenyon, S., Lyons, G., Rafferty, J., 2002. Transport and social exclusion: investigating the possibility of promoting inclusion through virtual mobility. J. Transp. Geogr. 10, 207–219.
Kholodilin, K.A., 2017. Wanderungen in die Metropolen Deutschlands. Der Landkreis 87, 44–47.
Kreis Heinsberg, 2012. Mobilitätsuntersuchung 2012. Planersocietät, Dortmund.
Küpper, P., 2017. Herausforderungen bei der Entwicklung ländlicher Räume—eine Bestandsaufnahme. Der Landkreis 87, 252–260.
Langert, M., 2008. Der Anbau nachwachsender Rohstoffe in der Landwirtschaft Sachsen-Anhalts und Thüringens: eine innovations-und diffusionstheoretische Untersuchung. VDM-Verlag, Saarbrücken.
Lenz, B., Fraedrich, E., 2015. Neue Mobilitätskonzepte und autonomes Fahren: Potenziale der Veränderung. In: Maurer, M., Gerdes, J.C., Lenz, B., Winner, H. (Eds.), Autonomes Fahren. Technische, rechtliche und gesellschaftliche Aspekte. Springer, Berlin, pp. 175–195.
Little, J., 2001. New rural governance? Prog. Hum. Geogr. 25, 97–102.
Manders, T.N., Wieczorek, A.J., Verbong, G.P.J., 2018. Understanding smart mobility experiments in the Dutch automobility system: who is involved and what do they promise? Futures 96, 90–103.

Manthey-Kloppenburg, C., 2018. Die Diffusion von Eco-Innovationen im Spannungsfeld von Staat und Markt—Das Beispiel des Elektroautos in ausgewählten europäischen Ländern. PhD Dissertation, Department of Geography, RWTH Aachen University, Aachen.

Mayring, P., 2015. Qualitative Inhaltsanalyse. Grundlagen und Techniken, 12th ed. Beltz, Weinheim.

Milbourne, P., Kitchen, L., 2014. Rural mobilities: connecting movement and fixity in rural places. J. Rural. Stud. 34, 326–336.

NABU (Naturschutzbund), 2016. Landwirtschaft im Kreis Heinsberg. https://www.nabu-heinsberg.de/naturblatt-2016/landwirtschaft-im-kreis-heinsberg/ (last accessed: 18.02.2018).

Noy, K., Givoni, M., 2018. Is 'smart mobility' sustainable? Examining the views and beliefs of transport's technological entrepreneurs. Sustainability 10 (2), 422 (no. 10020422).

Nykvist, B., Whitmarsh, L., 2008. A multi-level analysis of sustainable mobility transitions: niche developments in the UK and Sweden. Technol. Forecast. Soc. Chang. 75, 1373–1387.

OECD (Organisation for Economic Co-operation and Development), 2006. The New Rural Paradigm. OECD, Paris.

OECD, 2005. Oslo Manual. Guidelines for collecting and interpreting innovation data. OECD, Paris.

Olsson, J., 2009. Improved road accessibility and indirect development effects: evidence from rural Philippines. J. Transp. Geogr. 17, 476–483.

Osti, G., 2010. Mobility demands and participation in remote rural areas. Sociol. Rural. 50, 296–310.

Pangbourne, K., Stead, D., Mladenović, M., Milakis, D., 2018. The case of mobility as a service: a critical reflection on challenges for urban transport and mobility governance. In: Marsden, G., Reardon, L. (Eds.), Governance of the Smart Mobility Transition. Emerald Publishers, London, pp. 33–48.

Papa, E., Lauwers, D., 2015. Smart mobility: opportunity or threat to innovate places and cities. In: 20th International Conference on Urban Planning and Regional Development in the Information Society. CORP—Competence Center of Urban and Regional Planning, Ghent.

Pucher, J., Renne, J.L., 2005. Rural mobility and mode choice: evidence from the 2001 National Household Travel Survey. Transportation 32, 165–186.

Rogers, E., 2003. Diffusion of Innovations, fifth ed. Free Press, New York.

Roper, S., Love, J.H., 2006. Innovation and regional absorptive capacity: the labour market dimension. Ann. Reg. Sci. 40, 437–447.

Segert, A., 2009. Mobilitätsorientierungen—eigenständiger Faktor für die Entwicklung nachhaltiger Mobilität in ländlichen Räumen. Ländlicher Raum, pp. 1–17. Jg. 2009.

Spickermann, A., Grienitz, V., Heiko, A., 2014. Heading towards a multimodal city of the future?: multi-stakeholder scenarios for urban mobility. Technol. Forecast. Soc. Chang. 89, 201–221.

Stephens, H.M., Partridge, M.D., Faggian, A., 2013. Innovation, entrepreneurship and economic growth in lagging regions. J. Reg. Sci. 53, 778–812.

Stiftung, B., 2017. Digitale Zukunft auf dem Land. Wie ländliche Regionen durch die Digitalisierung profitieren können. Bertelsmann, Gütersloh.

Stiftung, B., 2018. Statistische Daten. Bevölkerungsvorausberechnung—Relative Entwicklung der Altersgruppen. Kommunen im Kreis Heinsberg, Bertelsmann, Gütersloh.

Tashakkori, A., Teddlie, C., 2003. Handbook of Mixed Methods in Social & Behavioral Research. Sage, Thousand Oaks.

Terluin, I.J., 2003. Differences in economic development in rural regions of advanced countries: an overview and critical analysis of theories. J. Rural. Stud. 19, 327–344.
Trapp, M., Swarat, G., 2015. Rural Solutions: Smart Services für ein Land von morgen. IM+io Fachzeitschrift für Innovation, Organisation und Management. Fraunhofer IESE, Kaiserslautern, pp. 33–38. 2/2015.
Truffer, B., Coenen, L., 2012. Environmental innovation and sustainability transitions in regional studies. Reg. Stud. 46, 1–21.
UBA (Umweltbundesamt), 2018. Emissionsquellen. https://www.umweltbundesamt.de/themen/klima-energie/klimaschutz-energiepolitik-in-deutschland/treibhausgas-emissionen/emissionsquellen#textpart-2 (last accessed: 14.01.2018).
Van Bree, B., Verbong, G.P.J., Kramer, G.J., 2010. A multi-level perspective on the introduction of hydrogen and battery-electric vehicles. Technol. Forecast. Soc. Chang. 77, 529–540.
Vanolo, A., 2013. Smartmentality: the smart city as disciplinary strategy. Urban Stud. 51, 883–898.
VDV (Verband Deutscher Verkehrsunternehmen), 2015. Flexible Bedienungsformen. Genehmigung und Rechtsfolgen. Thesenpapier zur Fachtagung am 3. Februar 2015. Berlin.
Walter, A., Finger, R., Huber, R., Buchmann, N., 2017. Opinion: smart farming is key to developing sustainable agriculture. Proc. Natl. Acad. Sci. U.S.A. 114 (24), 6148–6150.
Ward, N., Brown, D., 2009. Placing the rural in regional development. Reg. Stud. 43, 1237–1244.
Westzipfel region, 2015. GIEK—Gebietsbezogenes Integriertes Entwicklungskonzept. Zur Bewerbung als Leader-Region in NRW 2014-2020. Erkelenz.
Wisdom, J.P., Chor, K., Hoagwood, K., Horwitz, S., 2014. Innovation adoption: a review of theories and constructs. Admin. Pol. Ment. Health 41, 480–502.
Wittowsky, D., Hoenninger, P., 2018. Integrierte Mobilitätskonzepte in Räumen schwacher Verkehrsnachfrage. Verkehr Technik 71, 3–8.
Wolter, S., 2012. Smart mobility—intelligente vernetzung der verkehrsangebote in Großstädten. In: Proff, H., Schönharting, J., Schramm, D., Ziegler, J. (Eds.), Zukünftige Entwicklungen in der Mobilität. Springer Gabler, Heidelberg, pp. 527–548.
Woods, M., 2005. Rural Geography. Processes, Responses and Experiences in Rural Restructuring. Sage, London.
Zahra, S.A., George, G., 2002. Absorptive capacity: a review, reconceptualization, and extension. Acad. Manag. Rev. 27, 185–203.

CHAPTER SEVEN

Change versus decline: The suburbanization of jobs in U.S. shrinking cities

Joanna Ganning*
Department of Urban Studies, Levin College of Urban Affairs, Cleveland State University, Cleveland, OH, United States
*Corresponding author: e-mail address: j.ganning@csuohio.edu

Contents

Abstract

Spatial mismatch theory hypothesizes that as jobs suburbanize, minorities and low-income households will disproportionately lose access to economic opportunity. This paper hypothesizes that the context of urban decline also challenges job accessibility. In shrinking cities, growth at the urban fringe not only expands the footprint of the region's urbanized area, but unlike in most strong market settings, it simultaneously hollows out the core, challenging job accessibility for residents. This paper tests this hypothesis by presenting a block-group level model of job accessibility in the Principal Cities of 349 Metropolitan Statistical Areas (MSAs). The model finds that the context of urban decline reduces job accessibility for residents by 6.9%, other things equal. Descriptive statistics are employed to analyze spatial changes in job location over time. The results suggest that as development pushes outward in strong market settings, the core shares in the growth, while in shrinking cities, spatial deconcentration

Advances in Transport Policy and Planning, Volume 2
ISSN 2543-0009
https://doi.org/10.1016/bs.atpp.2018.09.006

disproportionately weakens the core. This process is hypothesized to lead to the decreased job accessibility found in shrinking cities.

Keywords: Deconcentration, Shrinking cities, Job accessibility, Inequality, Spatial mismatch

1. Introduction

The vast literature on spatial mismatch theory hypothesizes that as jobs suburbanize, racial and ethnic minorities will become spatially and economically disconnected from economic opportunity, leading to adverse outcomes in employment status, poverty status, and related socioeconomic status measures (i.e., Gobillon and Selod, 2014; Kain, 1968). Researchers have identified a range of causal mechanisms through which spatial mismatch produces these adverse outcomes, including mechanisms pertaining to job search efficiency and cost, commuting costs, location-based cost disincentives (including housing discrimination), and commuting-based declines in productivity. The latter two of these mechanisms have not, however, been thoroughly studied (see Gobillon and Selod, 2014 for a review). Relating most closely to the causal mechanism on location-based cost disincentives, the spatial mismatch literature also has not considered whether the context of urban decline may exacerbate or add to the inequalities of spatial mismatch.

That spatial mismatch might occur more intensely in the context of urban decline—or "shrinking cities" as they are often called—follows a simple logic. The spatial deconcentration process moves population and jobs away from the core and into suburban, lower-density areas, developing those areas and expanding the footprint of the region. On the whole, the region becomes less dense. In a growing metropolitan region, these newly developed areas might be—at least theoretically—wholly or predominantly accommodating new residents or jobs, rather than simply relocating existing residents from the traditional urban core. However, in a shrinking city, where regional population growth is either slow or negative, relocation of people or jobs to the suburban fringe means a net loss of people and/or jobs from the urban core. For example, from 1970 to 2010, the five-county region that today comprises the Cleveland-Elyria, OH MSA declined in population by approximately 10.5%, but all four of the suburban counties gained population. Those left behind, it logically follows, will face worse job accessibility than would their counterparts in strong market metropolitan regions. Making matters worse, the theory of housing filtering posits that those left behind will have lower incomes than those who left (i.e., Margulis, 1998).

This paper focuses on the city-level implications of the context of urban decline rather than on processes that occur within neighborhoods—which is not to say those processes are inconsequential or unrelated. While the vast majority of spatial mismatch literature finds that it disproportionately impacts low-income and minority neighborhoods, the intersection with urban decline invokes unique features into this process that warrant examination in their own right. As Galster (2012) details in Detroit and Tighe and Ganning (2015) in St. Louis, the process of decline uniquely invokes "policies, prejudices, and plans interacted with broad economic restructuring to devastate poor and minority communities, while leaving White and middle-class communities largely intact" (Tighe and Ganning, 2015, p. 654). Further research is warranted to study the distinct processes and outcomes of job accessibility for low-income and minority neighborhoods within shrinking cities, as distinct from those processes within strong market cities. This paper seeks to facilitate that future research by advancing our understanding of the effects of urban decline on job accessibility in a generalizable sense, from which those more nuanced questions might arise.

Testing the hypothesis that urban decline exacerbates job accessibility through deconcentration bears important implications. First, metropolitan regions situated around shrinking central cities are aware of the threat of deconcentration on regional economic health (Galster, 2012; Northeast Ohio Sustainable Communities Consortium, 2014). Regional planning organizations in such settings may benefit from knowledge that can assist in establishing effective incentives for core-based and node-based urban development. Second, and relatedly, companies considering moving to suburban locations may be influenced by information campaigns regarding the social costs of such decisions. Although economics texts emphasize that information campaigns tend to be less effective than prescriptive or market-based interventions (e.g., Keohane and Olmstead, 2016), Home Rule authority renders information campaigns necessary by removing or weakening other levers of regional control. Third, improved knowledge regarding the effects of deconcentration on job accessibility for shrinking city residents may guide strategic planning efforts around land use, zoning, and transportation, or provide support for transit riders' unions to lobby for additional funding.

Finally, the results of this research will apply to a not insignificant group of cities. Research on what constitutes a shrinking city is nascent, but one recent effort to reach a consensus (Ganning and Tighe, 2018) identifies 80 such cities in the United States alone. Scholars have most frequently studied those located in the United States or Europe (Pallagst, 2009), but such cities exist elsewhere as well (Martinez-Fernandez and Wu, 2009).

This paper employs two research methodologies to analyze the impact of urban decline on job accessibility for central city residents. In the first approach, this paper uses regression to model job accessibility at the Census block group level, using the job accessibility estimates from the Environmental Protection Agency's (EPA) Smart Location Database (SLD) as the dependent variable. The model estimates that the context of urban shrinkage imposes a 6.9% penalty on job accessibility for city residents, other things constant. In the second research methodology, this paper uses Longitudinal Employer-Household Dynamics (LEHD)-Origin-Destination Employment Statistics (LODES) from the U.S. Census Bureau to estimate job accessibility at the central point of Principal Cities for 3 years: 2005, 2010, and 2015. An analysis of changes in total jobs and job accessibility shows that when Non-Shrinking Principal Cities add jobs regionally, the core shares in the benefits of greater job accessibility. However, when Shrinking Principal Cities decline, job accessibility losses are experienced disproportionately in the core.

2. Literature review

2.1 Shrinking cities and equity

The terms "shrinking cities" and "Rust Belt" often appear together, but using these terms interchangeably over-simplifies urban decline. While urban decline is believed to stem most commonly from deindustrialization, it can also be caused by violent conflicts, natural disasters, suburbanization, or economic crisis, all of which affect different segments of the population differently (Rieniets, 2009). While shrinking cities tend to be located in the northeast, tend to have seen their peak decennial Census population in either 1950 or 1960, tend to have manufacturing histories, and tend to have disproportionately African American populations, still much distinguishes each from the next (Mallach, 2014; Rieniets, 2009). In some MSAs, all counties have declined (e.g., Youngstown, OH-PA), while a few, like Philadelphia, are seeing population growth after a long period of decline. Co-mingling "shrinking cities" and "Rust Belt" also over-simplifies the geography of urban decline. In their conceptual piece systematically identifying U.S. shrinking cities, Ganning and Tighe (2018) identify 80 cities from Massachusetts to Texas, with one in California (Inglewood).

Researchers have previously argued that urban decline processes might produce inequitable outcomes for minorities and low-income households. Galster (2012) narrates a process in which metropolitan Detroit has engaged in, effectively, decades-long turf wars, carving out hyper-local identities to bolster self-image. Residential segregation has been maintained through intimidation, steering, and other discriminatory practices. Newer and bigger is perceived to be better, and largely out of fear (of a variety of things, including potential losses in property values), affluent, predominantly white households continually push the urban fringe outward, taking their tax dollars with them.

In regions with very slow growth or even decline, suburban development has effectively meant gutting the central cities—the Cities of Detroit, Cleveland, St. Louis, and their counterparts elsewhere. It has also meant confining a disproportionate number of the region's African Americans to those central cities through red lining, steering, and a range of other discriminatory practices. An analysis of U.S. Census Bureau PL-94 data and the group of U.S. shrinking cities recently identified by Ganning and Tighe (2018) shows that nationally, African Americans account for 17.6% of the Non-Shrinking Principal Cities of MSAs. Yet African Americans account for 41.6% of the populations of the 63 Principal Cities that are also shrinking cities. This discrepancy cannot be explained solely by a difference in demographics in the metropolitan regions of these two groups. The Black or African American alone population comprises 12.7% of the population of MSAs without shrinking cities, and 15.8% of the population of MSAs containing shrinking cities.

The effects of urban decline have equity implications not only for racial minorities, but also for low-income households. As those with more residential mobility options departed, those left behind have endured the declining budgets associated with lost local tax revenue and the reality that shrinking the physical footprint of a city or its infrastructure stock presents enormous challenges. Local budgets were further impacted by the urban austerity regimes launched in earnest in the United States by President Reagan in the 1980s (Goldsmith, 2016). Combined, these cuts have meant fewer and lower quality public services for households, especially affecting lower-income households who are more reliant on public services for mobility, food security, public education, public health services, and other public services (Beauregard, 2013; Thomson, 2012). The resulting decades-long population loss is suggestive of Myrdal's (1957) cumulative causation, by which services decline, taxes must be raised, and more businesses and households relocate. The process of decline itself may, therefore, impact job accessibility for city residents, by pushing jobs away from the core. This paper seeks to analyze that impact, hoping to lay the groundwork for future work that will take a closer focus on the closely-intertwined equity concerns.

2.2 Spatial mismatch

"Spatial mismatch relates the unemployment and poverty of vulnerable population groups to their remoteness from job opportunities" and has a decades-long literature described as "very abundant" (Gobillon and Selod, 2014, pp. 93–94). Several review pieces exist, summarizing the literature in different ways. Notable recent reviews include Geurs and Van Wee (2004), Gobillon and Selod (2014), and Geurs et al. (2015).

Researchers commonly study spatial mismatch through analyses of job accessibility within regions. As Neudorf (2014) explains, job accessibility metrics and models are usually (though not exclusively) broken down into two types: cumulative opportunity models and gravity models. Each method bears its own strengths, shortcomings, and variations in implementation. The many studies employing variations of these two approaches seek to include some combination of four critical factors: (1) "the amount, quality and spatial distribution of opportunities; (2) the transportation component describing the disutility of travel in terms of time, cost and effort; (3) the temporal component reflecting the temporal constraints and variability; and (4) the individual component reflecting the needs and abilities of individuals" (Geurs et al., 2015, p. 82).

The simplicity of that list of factors belies an incredible range of progress along each theme. For an example of the first factor, Halás and Klapka (2015; see also Halás et al., 2014) argue that the distance decay function—meaning the distance before which a job is not considered accessible to a worker—varies with the size of the economy and other localized features. Other literature (e.g., Wang and Chen, 2015) advances the spatial econometric specifications of job accessibility modeling in various capacities. As an example of the second factor (travel time, cost, and effort), consider recent work by Tasic et al. (2017) that challenges multimodal estimates of accessibility, and aptly observes that more accurately calculating such estimates requires enormous quantities of ever-changing data on local transit systems.

Also along this theme, but looking at different research questions, Wiersma et al. (2016) analyze transportation modes according to (among other variables) metropolitan spatial structure, finding that transit improves accessibility the most in polycentric settings. Along the third theme (temporal constraints and variability), studies of "time-of-day variations in road network accessibility" (Geurs et al., 2015, p. 83) have been facilitated by GPS data sources. Finally, along the fourth theme (needs and abilities of individuals), recent research calls out the importance of segmenting analysis to reflect the attributes of jobs and workers to estimate job accessibility more accurately (e.g., Cheng and Bertolini, 2013; Merlin and Hu, 2017).

This brief illustration of the diversity of scholarly work in this literature suggests that tremendously and variously detailed estimates of job accessibility are possible for a variety of analyses—and they are, for case studies. In fact, virtually all papers reviewed herein use case study cities or regions. Simply stated, the data requirements to advance any one of the four themes strongly discourage multi-region analysis. For instance, computing network distance or travel time between points is incredibly computationally demanding for large geographic areas (for example, all tract-tract pairs within a state). Moreover, network distance is necessary but insufficient; estimating travel times along a network is tedious and expensive in the absence of a calibrated regional travel demand model. Thus, producing accessibility metrics for large groups of cities, such as the group of U.S. shrinking cities, often falls short of accomplishing the accuracy or conceptual clarity demonstrated in much of the literature's current work. This is less a criticism of the literature itself as an explanation of an existing technical barrier to implementing the literature's advancements in cross-sectional research.

Illustrating this, two federal agencies in the United States—the Department of Housing and Urban Development (HUD) and the Environmental Protection Agency (EPA) have published job accessibility databases built from gravity models at the block group level. The HUD job accessibility index is part of its Location Affordability Index (LAI) (Department of Housing and Urban Development, n.d.). The HUD index has distinct benefits. First, it is replicable using R and ArcGIS for any year after 2002,[1] and is calculable for multiple Census geography types, such as the block group or Census tract. Second, a researcher could segment the index by worker salary

[1] The LAI uses an input database which most states participate in from 2002 onward. However, a few states joined later, such as Arizona in 2004, and Massachusetts in 2011. Wyoming is missing its 2014 data. For a full accounting of data availability, see https://lehd.ces.census.gov/data/lodes/LODES7/LODESTechDoc7.2.pdf.

(by place of residence or by place of work) or industry. However, it does not take into consideration road or transit networks, and in recalculating it, calculating accessibility of jobs across state lines is especially time-consuming. The EPA index, on the other hand, uses both road and transit networks to calculate accessibility. However, the EPA index is available for only 1 year (most of its inputs reflect 2010), and though it comes with data on worker and job characteristics within each block group, the index itself is not segmented to consider their match. Thus, while the literature on job accessibility and spatial mismatch is technically sophisticated in terms of spatial econometrics, segmentation, and other features, our ability to apply those advances to multi-city studies remains a challenge.

This paper approaches doing just that—producing generalizable estimates of job accessibility across cities by type—by leveraging the EPA database, while acknowledging its shortcomings. Following that estimation, the paper turns toward using block group-level estimates of jobs (provided through Census LODES data) to estimate job accessibility in the urban core for Shrinking and Non-Shrinking Principal Cities, informing on the role of suburbanization in job accessibility.

3. Methods

This paper first uses a quasi-experimental research design to estimate the effects of urban decline on job accessibility in central cities. Then, the paper uses descriptive statistics to examine one hypothesized causal pathway for differential job accessibility between shrinking and non-shrinking cities. In the first analysis, job accessibility is modeled at the block group-level within the Principal Cities of 349 MSAs in the United States, including 63 shrinking cities (the other 17 shrinking cities identified by Ganning and Tighe (2018) are not Principal Cities). As outlined in the literature review, job accessibility is hypothesized to be worse in shrinking cities than non-shrinking cites. The second analysis evaluates the hypothesis that shrinking Principal Cities have lower job accessibility due to the suburbanization of jobs.

3.1 Sample selection

Principal Cities are identified using the July 2015 delineation file provided by the U.S. Census Bureau's Population Division, in collaboration with the Office of Management and Budget. This file includes 686 Principal Cities of MSAs. Using Principal Cities ensures relative comparability between cities;

using Principal Cities prevents comparison of central cities to suburban cities, where job densities (McMillen, 2006), land use, and commuting dynamics vary markedly from those of central cities. The use of Principal Cities also seeks to avoid comparing suburbs to suburbs when the focal point of the paper is on the effects of the spatial deconcentration of jobs away from the core.

Both the regression and the descriptive statistics analyses use block group-level data. For the regression, block groups are selected for inclusion if the block group's geographic centroid falls within the boundary of any Principal City. These block groups are identified using GIS and the TIGER/Line Place shapefiles, available through the U.S. Census Bureau. Using this approach, the regression sample includes 54,639 block groups. From those, 509 block groups are dropped due to incomplete data, leaving 54,130 block groups.

The descriptive statistics analysis takes a markedly different approach to selecting block groups. In this analysis, all block groups in the United States are included unless the Principal City to which one is closest lacks data for any year studied (2005, 2010, or 2015; variables included are presented below). This more inclusive sample includes 182,021 block groups.

The list of shrinking cities is taken from the literature (Ganning and Tighe, 2018). A complete list of these cities is provided in Table A1. In general terms, their method selects Census Designated Places that had at least 50,000 people in 1970 and which experienced a net loss in occupied housing units to 2010, using a fixed 1980 boundary. This approach identifies places which have seen population loss extensive enough to impact local real estate markets. Of the 80 identified Shrinking Cities, 63 are also Principal Cities; the remaining 17 are not included in the analyses that follow (those dropped are identified in Table A1). Notably, the analyses include Macon, GA, although the city consolidated with Bibb County in 2014.

3.2 Employment access measurement and model

This paper seeks first to find generalizable results for groups of cities. To do this, this paper uses the SLD destination accessibility database. The SLD was developed in response to research on the relationships between land use, transportation, and affordability. More specifically, the SLD "is a nationwide geographic data resource for measuring location efficiency" (Environmental Protection Agency, 2018a). Location efficiency refers to the idea that households should consider transportation costs in addition to housing costs when making decisions about the affordability of neighborhoods (Department of Housing and Urban Development, 2018). Where HUD's LAI focuses on promoting location affordability in its own right and stems from the Obama administration's Partnership for Sustainable Communities, the SLD emerges from Smart Growth partnerships and research efforts. The Smart Growth agenda promotes development that invests in existing infrastructure, provides multimodal transportation options, includes a mix of housing types, promotes resident involvement in decision making, and promotes economic competitiveness (Environmental Protection Agency, 2018b). Online, the EPA presents the SLD alongside two related tools: The Access to Jobs and Workers via Transit Tool and the National Walkability Index.

The SLD is leveraged here for its data regarding the number of jobs accessible to workers living within identified block groups. Yet the SLD provides substantially more data than this, including urban design metrics, employment statistics, counts of housing units and households, and other variables. Unlike HUD's LAI, the SLD incorporates road networks into its data, ensuring the reflection of impedance in the calculation of accessibility—a key reason the SLD is used in the analyses presented in this paper. Further, with the LAI, job accessibility calculations would include only those jobs located in the block groups chosen for analysis. By contrast, the SLD's accessibility measures include *all* jobs to which workers living in the selected block groups have access—whether those jobs exist in selected block groups or elsewhere.

For the sample of 54,130 block groups used in the first, regression-based analysis, SLD job accessibility is modeled using variables that cut across virtually all job accessibility sub-literatures (Eq. 1): total MSA employment, the percent non-white alone population, and the share of workers that is low wage. The key independent variable *SC* (a dummy variable denoting a Shrinking City) is added to indicate whether and to what extent, globally, the context of urban decline influences job accessibility. The dependent variable, *D5ar*, is the SLD's code meaning "Jobs within 45 min auto travel time, time-decay (network travel time) weighted." Table 1 follows with descriptive statistics for each variable.

$$D5ar = \partial + \beta_1 MSA\_EMP + \beta_2 NWA + \beta_3 NLOWWG + \beta_4 SC + e \quad (1)$$

where:

D5ar = SLD distance-weighted job accessibility within 45 min by automobile,

Table 1 Descriptive statistics for SLD variables.

	Mean	Standard deviation	Description and source
D5ar	231,780	230,010	Auto-based job accessibility with 45-min, distance decay, using road network. Source: EPA-SLD
MSA_EMP	2,300,903	2,657,439	Total employment in the MSA. Source: EPA-SLD
NWA	0.4444	0.2979	The block group's percent population that is non-white alone, expressed as a decimal. Source: U.S. Census 2010 PL-94
LOWWG	0.2681	0.0687	The percentage (expressed as a decimal) of low wage workers in the block group. Defined as number of workers (by place of residence) earning $1250/month or less. Source: EPA-SLD

MSA_EMP=number of jobs located within the MSA,
SC=dummy variable representing a Shrinking City,
NWA=Non-white alone population share,
LOWWG=Share of workers (by place of residence) earning $1250 per month or less

3.3 Descriptive statistics analysis of job suburbanization

Following the regression-based analysis, this paper tests the hypothesis that job accessibility is lower in Shrinking Principal Cities due to job suburbanization without replacement in the core. This descriptive analysis uses a measure of job accessibility for each Principal City for 2005, 2010, and 2015. The Principal Cities are identified as given above, from the U.S. Bureau of the Census July 2015 definition file. The Principal Cities are, as before, distinguished as Shrinking Cities or Non-Shrinking Cities using the Ganning and Tighe (2018) list of U.S. shrinking cities. Since the SLD is published for only 1 year and thus not usable for a time series analysis, job accessibility is measured using LODES data from 2005, 2010, and 2015.

To calculate each city's accessibility metric, each block group in the United States is associated with its closest Principal City. Then, job accessibility is calculated from the central point of each Principal City (defined by the point shapefile of places available from the Minnesota

Population Center's NHGIS) to the jobs located in the block groups associated with each city. The following steps outline how this is accomplished.

A point shapefile of all Census Designated Places, available from the Minnesota Population Center's National Historical Geographic Information System (NHGIS) database, is first limited to include only Principal Cities, then appended to include the dummy variable indicating whether each Principal City is also a Shrinking City. Second, the Work Area Characteristics LODES files for each state for 2005, 2010, and 2015 were downloaded. The LODES data, downloaded at the block level, were then summarized to produce an estimate of the total number of jobs at the block group level for each year. Third, these estimates were appended to block group shapefiles for each state. Fourth, the block group shapefiles (with employment data attached) were projected to the UTM zone appropriate for each state, to improve the accuracy of distance measurements, which follow. Pennsylvania was divided in half, designating county-by-county as UTM zone 17 N or 18 N. Other states that cross UTM zones were assigned based on the zone in which the majority of the state's land and population reside. Using geographic projection systems suited to each state works to reduce the spatial measurement error in distance measurements.

UTM Zone 10 N is used to illustrate the process from here. Zone 10 N contains two states: Washington and Oregon. First, the point shapefile of Principal Cities is projected to UTM 10 N. Then, *R* identifies the closest Principal City to each Washington and Oregon block group centroid and records the geographic identifier for the closest Principal City. Following, *R* is used to calculate and record the Great Circle distance from each block group centroid to the identified closest Principal City. From here, the shapefiles are dropped, leaving only tabular data inclusive of: block group identifier, geographic identifier of closest Principal City, and distance to closest Principal City. This table is then appended to the LODES table of Work Area Characteristics at the block group level. This process is repeated for all UTM zones containing U.S. states. All the block group files, one for each state, are then merged into a single data table. This process is repeated to produce three total tables—one for each year: 2005, 2010, and 2015.

The data table is then summarized for each Principal City, according to Eq. (2). Here, job accessibility is calculated as the number of jobs in the block group containing the Principal City's central point, plus the inverse-distance weighted count of jobs in all block groups for which Principal City i is the nearest. Following these calculations, the results are compared for Shrinking Principal Cities and Non-Shrinking Principal Cities. All analyses are completed in *R*.

$$ACC_{it} = JOBS_{j,DIST=0} + \sum_{j=0}^{n} \frac{JOBS}{DIST/1000} \quad (2)$$

where:
ACC = Job accessibility,
i = Principal City,
t = year (2005, 2010, or 2015),
j = block group for which i is the closest Principal City,
$JOBS$ = total jobs within the block group, by place of work,
$DIST$ = Distance, in meters

4. Results

4.1 Regression-based results: The generalizable effects of a context of decline

Table 2 presents the regression-based results for auto-based job accessibility in U.S. Principal Cities. Models have been checked for multicollinearity using VIF scores and showed no issues (scores are all below 2). The models do, however, show heteroscedasticity and are thus presented using robust error terms calculated using *R*'s "lmtest" and "sandwich" packages. Plots were used to test for linearity, which was found. All models show F-statistics with *P*-values lower than 0.01.

Table 2 is presented as a series of four models, each building on the last, allowing a more nuanced interpretation of results that helps to connect the model to existing literature. The final panel, Model 4, shows the key finding: the context of decline lowers job accessibility by, on average, 7485 jobs, or 6.9%, *ceteris paribus*.

The first three models show intermediary results which warrant discussion. The first panel shows that virtually all of the final model's explanatory power is accounted for by a single variable: the number of jobs in the MSA. It makes sense that the number of jobs in an MSA would explain most variation in job accessibility when the dependent variable is the number of jobs within 45 min by car (with a distance decay). In all but the largest and/or most congested MSAs, the majority of jobs in the MSA are reachable within 45 min by car from any other point in the MSA. In Model 2 the non-white alone share is added and shows a statistically significant, negative effect on

Table 2 Auto-based job accessibility models.
Dependent variable: Auto-based accessibility

	Model 1			Model 2			Model 3			Model 4		
	Estimate	Std. error	*P*-value	Estimate	Std. error	*P*-value	Estimate	Std. error	*P*-value	Estimate	Std. error	*P*-value
(Intercept)	57336.550	413.687	***	61122.598	654.384	***	108113.645	2145.805	***	108200.788	2143.473	***
CBSA_EMP	0.076	0.000	***	0.076	0.000	***	0.075	0.000	***	0.074	0.000	***
NWA_PC				−10510.111	1800.809	***	7344.566	1872.439	***	9937.214	1915.460	***
LOWWG							−189173.746	7978.480	***	−186495.317	8016.395	***
SC										−7485.246	762.180	***
R^2	0.7673			0.7716			0.7741			0.7742		

***P-value < 0.01.

job accessibility, a finding consistent with the literature. However, once *LOWWG* enters in Model 3, the non-white alone share bears a positive coefficient, which persists through the final model. Several interaction variables were created and tested in exploratory work but did not clarify interpretation of these inter-related variables. Overall, the auto-based accessibility models show strong model fit, especially considering their basis in block group data.

Table 2 supports the hypothesis given: that the context of urban decline worsens job accessibility. However, the model does not suggest causal mechanisms. Is it, in fact, a result of job suburbanization that is not replaced by new growth? The following section tests this hypothesis—that job movement within the region disproportionately harms job accessibility in Shrinking Principal Cities, when compared to Non-Shrinking Principal Cities.

4.2 Descriptive hypothesis testing: Suburbanization of jobs, 2005–2015

This section tests the hypothesis that job accessibility is lower in Shrinking Principal Cities because as jobs suburbanize away from the urban core successors are less likely in the context of decline than in strong market cities. Taking Cleveland, OH as an example, news stories from as long ago as 1997 proclaimed that "only 20 percent of the current crop of low-skill job opportunities that open up every year are in the city. The others are in the suburbs and adjoining counties, in places poorly served by mass transit or not served at all" (No author, 1997). The same article goes on to argue that companies should consider their responsibilities when selecting suburban locations. Another article similarly expressing concern about the suburbanization of jobs appeared in 2017 (Truog, 2017). In other words, this trend is observed at the local level and has been for a long time.

Job accessibility was calculated according to Eq. (2) for all Principal Cities for 2005, 2010, and 2015. The results were then divided into two groups: Shrinking Principal Cities and Non-Shrinking Principal Cities. Outliers unduly challenge interpretation of the estimates at the mean; Table 3 shows the results using the median. The table also shows the median number of jobs for each type of Principal City. As given in the methods, this number includes all jobs within the block groups for which the given city is the closest. As such, the region as defined does not match regional definitions given by the Office of Management and Budget or the U.S. Census Bureau.

According to Table 3, the total number of jobs in block groups closest to Shrinking Principal Cities declined by (at the median) 6.1% between 2005

Table 3 Median job accessibility and median total jobs from Cities' Central Point, 2005, 2010, and 2015.

	Job accessibility				Total jobs			
	2005	**2010**	**2015**	**% Change, 2005–2015**	**2005**	**2010**	**2015**	**% Change, 2005–2015**
Shrinking Principal Cities	122,391	108,533	105,926	−13.5%	183,196	163,257	172,074	−6.1%
Non-Shrinking Principal Cities	81,620	82,302	84,153	3.1%	114,661	114,902	120,748	5.3%

and 2015, although significant growth is observable following the recession (2010–2015). However, job accessibility from the city's central point declined 13.5%. Importantly, while the total number of jobs grew post-recession, job accessibility from the core of Shrinking Principal Cities continued to decline, reflecting a marked suburbanization process. In contrast, the total number of jobs in block groups closest to Non-Shrinking Principal Cities increased (at the median) by 5.3%, and this growth was shared with the central city. Job accessibility from the city's central point increased by 3.1%, with accessibility gains both before/during (2005–2010) and after (2010–2015) the recession.

The results support the hypothesis: jobs are suburbanizing across cities of both types (Shrinking and Non-Shrinking Principal Cities). There continues to be growth/replacement in the core of non-shrinking cities. Yet in shrinking cities, suburbanization of jobs results in disproportionate losses for the core, suggesting full replacement of suburbanizing jobs is not occurring. Over time this would result in lower job accessibility for central city residents, even when the size of the region's economy is held constant.

Of course, declines in job accessibility and declines in population are inter-related. Previous research (e.g., Partridge et al., 2007) finds that in the spatial deconcentration process within regions, households move first and jobs follow. Shrinking cities are, by definition, cities that have lost occupied housing units (and in all cases, also population). However, it is not necessarily the case, and it often is not the case, that the MSA around a shrinking city is also declining. Therefore, it stands to reason that the process of Principal City population decline itself may initiate the declines in job accessibility for workers living in those cities; households suburbanize, jobs suburbanize, neither sees replacement (in aggregate) in the core (causing decline), and job accessibility declines for those who are left behind.

Given these results, from an economic development perspective, the assumption that suburban development is just that—development—only holds in a highly localized sense in a shrinking city context. In other words, to avoid market failure, suburban development proposals in shrinking city regions might account for the deleterious effects they will have on the central city. When jobs are leaving the central city (meaning, the City of Cleveland, for example), generally they are not being replaced by new ventures. Jobs are simply moving farther away—from the city and from its resident-workers.

For economic development practitioners, adopting a regionalist approach can be difficult. In part, the difficulty stems from the fact that suburban development's benefits *are* highly localized, meaning there will be local pressure to engage in development even if it draws investment away from the core. In part, in many regions the incentives and/or legal structures (i.e., Home Rule/Dillon's Rule provisions) for regionalism are insufficient to produce economically efficient outcomes. Galster (2012) has written extensively about the sociological norms within the Detroit region that have compounded the challenges raised by Home Rule authority.

For transit agencies in shrinking cities, these results support what they already believe: jobs are moving farther away from city residents. Connecting workers who live in the central city to those jobs is, in fact, an increasing challenge—and one for which increased budgets are not necessarily available. The Greater Cleveland Regional Transit Agency (GCRTA), although only one example, depicts this clearly. In Ohio (and other states), changes to Medicaid resulted in reduced sales tax revenue. While this situation is evolving, as of this writing the changes in tax revenue threaten to affect the GCRTA financially, potentially resulting in a decrease of 7% in the annual operating budget, reductions in service levels, and the elimination of up to 200 jobs (Calabrese, n.d.).

The GCRTA and others have proposed strategies to overcome the need to cover more territory with lower operating revenues. Some of those ideas include using public transit dollars to pay for ride sharing services and working with employers to more strategically select locations, among other ideas (for a fuller discussion, see Ganning and Tighe, 2017). Yet there is little if any evidence that these strategies can overcome the effects of job suburbanization fully; research remains to be done to explore the effects of such efforts.

5. Conclusion

This paper set out to estimate the effect that the context of urban decline has on job accessibility for residents of Principal Cities, then to descriptively test one causal pathway by which that context might challenge job accessibility. The first, regression-based analysis shows that while the size of the region's economy influences job accessibility more than other factors, being in a Shrinking Principal City lowers job accessibility by about 6.9%, *ceteris paribus*. The descriptive analysis provides initial support for a hypothesized causal mechanism: job suburbanization without replacement in the core distinguishes Shrinking Principal Cities from Non-Shrinking Principal Cities. In Non-Shrinking Principal Cities, where the total number of jobs grew between 2005 and 2015, central cities shared in the growth, enjoying increased job accessibility over the period. However, in Shrinking Principal Cities, where (at the median) jobs decreased by 6.1% over the period, job accessibility at the city's center declined by 13.5%. It follows that while the region shrank, it also pushed outward, away from the central city.

Further research might more closely examine the causal mechanisms for job deconcentration in shrinking cities, although qualitatively this area is covered nicely by Galster (2012). In economic development, the prevention of market failures will require fully incorporating the effects on central cities into the cost-benefit analyses of suburban development projects. Programming to encourage regionalism, and the development and protection of incentives for regional collaboration must be vigorously pursued. In transportation, the results presented herein support the belief that jobs are getting farther away in shrinking cities, and that connecting to them will likely become more difficult.

George Galster recently wrote that "Processes experienced by shrinking cities are not merely the mirror images of those manifested in growing cities" (Galster, 2017, p. 13). The results of this paper support that assertion. In an urban growth context, development that pushes economic activity outward may be necessary to accommodate demand. It is conceivable that such deconcentration could even be done in a fashion that promotes node-based development and strategic polycentricity, helping regions work toward sustainability goals (e.g., Ganning, 2018). If the context of decline provided mirror image urban processes, economic activity would retract back toward the core, pulling the urban footprint inward as it grew smaller. Instead, in the context of decline, the core suffers an order of magnitude more than does the region. The process itself, let alone its causal mechanisms, are only beginning to be understood by planners, regional scientists, and economists. Yet, the effects of these processes are likely to be felt for generations.

Acknowledgements

I would like to acknowledge Matt Miller for providing feedback on an earlier draft of this paper and Sherry Poe and Lydia Benish for their work as Graduate Assistants.

Appendix

Table A1 Shrinking cities as identified by Ganning and Tighe (2018).

Gadsden, AL	Covington, KY[a]	Rome, NY	Lima, OH
Birmingham, AL	Monroe, LA	Schenectady, NY	Springfield, OH
Pine Bluff, AR	New Orleans, LA	Utica, NY	Dayton, OH
Inglewood, CA[a]	Holyoke, MA[a]	Troy, NY	Cincinnati, OH
Hartford, CT	Towson, MD	Albany, NY	Scranton, PA
Bridgeport, CT	Baltimore, MD	Syracuse, NY	Erie, PA
Macon, GA	Dundalk, MD[a]	Rochester, NY	Wilkes-Barre, PA
Chicago, IL	Saginaw, MI	Niagara Falls, NY	Reading, PA
Berwyn, IL[a]	Flint, MI	Buffalo, NY	Philadelphia, PA
Cicero, IL[a]	Pontiac, MI	Binghamton, NY	Harrisburg, PA
Rock Island, IL	Detroit, MI	Euclid, OH[a]	Altoona, PA
Decatur, IL	Dearborn, MI	Cleveland Heights, OH[a]	York, PA
East Saint Louis, IL[a]	Dearborn Heights, MI[a]	Cleveland, OH	Pittsburgh, PA
South Bend, IN	Lincoln Park, MI[a]	Lakewood, OH[a]	Chester, PA[a]
Gary, IN	Saint Louis, MO	Warren, OH	Providence, RI
Hammond, IN[a]	Paterson, NJ[a]	Toledo, OH	Galveston, TX[a]
Anderson, IN	East Orange, NJ[a]	Youngstown, OH	Norfolk, VA
Terre Haute, IN	Newark, NJ	Akron, OH	Milwaukee, WI
Evansville, IN	Trenton, NJ	Canton, OH	Charleston, WV
Kansas City, KS	Camden, NJ	Mansfield, OH	Huntington, WV

[a]Denotes cities not included in analysis.

References

Beauregard, R.A., 2013. Strategic thinking for distressed neighborhoods. In: Dewar, M., Thomas, J.M. (Eds.), The City After Abandonment. University of Pennsylvania Press, Philadelphia, pp. 133–150.

Calabrese J., State of 2018 Operating Budget, Available online http://www.riderta.com/budgetchallenges, n.d., Accessed 20 May 2018.

Cheng, J., Bertolini, L., 2013. Measuring urban job accessibility with distance decay, competition and diversity. J. Transp. Geogr. 30, 100–109.

Department of Housing and Urban Development, 2018. Location Affordability Index. Available online: https://www.hudexchange.info/programs/location-affordability-index/. Accessed 9 April 2018.

Department of Housing and Urban Development, Data and Methodology: Location Affordability Index Version 2.0, Retrieved (12/20/17) from http://www.locationaffordability.info/LAPMethodsV2.pdf, n.d.

Environmental Protection Agency, 2018a. Smart Location Mapping. Available online: https://www.epa.gov/smartgrowth/smart-location-mapping#SLD. Accessed 9 April 2018.

Environmental Protection Agency, 2018b. About Smart Growth. Available online: https://www.epa.gov/smartgrowth/about-smart-growth. Accessed 9 April 2018.

Galster, G., 2012. Driving Detroit: The Quest for Respect in the Motor City. University of Pennsylvania Press.

Galster, G., 2017. Why shrinking cities are not mirror images of growing cities: a research agenda of six testable propositions. Urban Aff. Rev. https://doi.org/10.1177/1078087417720543 (online first).

Ganning, J., 2018. The effects of commuter rail establishment on commuting and deconcentration. Reg. Stud. 1–10. https://doi.org/10.1080/00343404.2018.1437898.

Ganning, J., Tighe, J.R., 2017. What Do We Know About Location Affordability in US Shrinking Cities? (No. NITC-RR-872). National Institute for Transportation and Communities. Portland State University.

Ganning, J., Tighe, R., 2018. Moving towards a shared understanding of the U.S. shrinking city. J. Plan. Educ. Res. https://doi.org/10.1177/0739456X18772074.

Geurs, K.T., Van Wee, B., 2004. Accessibility evaluation of land-use and transport strategies: review and research directions. J. Transp. Geogr. 12 (2), 127–140.

Geurs, K.T., Montis, A., Reggiani, A., 2015. Recent advances and applications in accessibility modelling. Comput. Environ. Urban. Syst. 49, 82–85.

Gobillon, L., Selod, H., 2014. Spatial mismatch, poverty, and vulnerable populations. In: Handbook of Regional Science. Springer Berlin Heidelberg, pp. 93–107.

Goldsmith, W.W., 2016. Saving Our Cities: A Progressive Plan to Transform Urban America. Cornell University Press.

Halás, M., Klapka, P., 2015. Spatial influence of regional centres of slovakia: analysis based on the distance-decay function. Rendiconti Lincei 26 (2), 169–185.

Halás, M., Klapka, P., Kladivo, P., 2014. Distance-decay functions for daily travel-to-work flows. J. Transp. Geogr. 35, 107–119.

Kain, J.F., 1968. Housing segregation, negro employment, and metropolitan decentralization. Q. J. Econ. 82 (2), 175–197.

Keohane, N.O., Olmstead, S.M., 2016. Markets and the Environment, Second ed. Island Press.

Mallach, A., 2014. Parallel histories, diverging trajectories: resilience in small industrial cities. Chapter 7In: Wachter, S., Zeuli, K. (Eds.), Revitalizing American Cities. University of Pennsylvania Press, Philadelphia, pp. 125–146.

Margulis, H.L., 1998. Predicting the growth and filtering of at-risk housing: structure ageing, poverty and redlining. Urban Stud. 35 (8), 1231–1259.

Martinez-Fernandez, C., Wu, C.T., 2009. Shrinking cities: a global overview and concerns about Australian mining cities cases. In: The Future of Shrinking Cities: Problems, Patterns and Strategies of Urban Transformation in a Global Context. Center for Global Metropolitan Studies, Institute of Urban and Regional Development, and the Shrinking Cities International Research Network, pp. 29–36.
McMillen, D.P., 2006. Testing for monocentricity. Chapter 8 In: Arnott, R.J., McMillen, D.P. (Eds.), A Companion to Urban Economics. Blackwell Publishing Ltd., pp. 128–140.
Merlin, L.A., Hu, L., 2017. Does competition matter in measures of job accessibility? Explaining employment in Los Angeles. J. Transp. Geogr. 64, 77–88.
Myrdal, G., 1957. The drift towards regional economic inequalities in a country. In: Economic Theory and Under-Developed Regions. Gerald Duckworth, London, pp. 23–38.
Neudorf, J., 2014. Understanding Accessibility, Analyzing Policy: New Approaches for a New Paradigm. Master's ThesisUniversity of Waterloo.
No author, 1997. A case of jobs too far. The Plain DealerEditorial, page 2E.
Northeast Ohio Sustainable Communities Consortium, 2014. Vibrant, N. E. O. 2040. A Vision and a Framework for Our Future. Available online: http://vibrantneo.org/wp-content/uploads/2014/04/Vibrant-NEO-Final-Report_3-31-14_lowres_ALL.pdf. Accessed 10 January 2018.
Pallagst, K. (2009). Shrinking cities in the United States of America. 81-88 in The future of Shrinking Cities: Problems, Patterns and Strategies of Urban Transformation in a Global Context. Karina Pallagst, Jasmin Aber, Ivonne Audirac, Emmanuele Cunningham-Sabot, Sylvie Fol, Cristina Martinez-Fernandez, Sergio Moraes, Helen Mulligan, Jose Vargas-Hernandez, Thorsten Wiechmann, Tong Wu (Eds.) and Jessica Rich (Contributing Ed.). Center for Global Metropolitan Studies, Institute of Urban and Regional Development, and the Shrinking Cities International Research Network Monograph Series. University of California Berkeley.
Partridge, M., Bollman, R.D., Olfert, M.R., Alasia, A., 2007. Riding the wave of urban growth in the countryside: spread, backwash, or stagnation? Land Econ. 83 (2), 128–152.
Riemets, T., 2009. Shrinking cities: causes and effects of urban population losses in the twentieth century. Nat. Cult. 4 (3), 231–254.
Tasic, I., Bozic, C., Hanss, E., 2017. Towards true multimodal transportation accessibility: data, measures, and methods. In: Proceedings of the 96th Annual Meeting of the Transportation Research Board (TRB), Washington DC. Transportation Research Board.
Thomson, D.E., 2012. Targeting neighborhoods, stimulating markets: the role of political, institutional and technical factors in three cities. In: The City After Abandonment. University of Pennsylvania Press, Philadelphia, pp. 104–132.
Tighe, J.R., Ganning, J.P., 2015. The divergent city: unequal and uneven development in St. Louis. Urban Geogr. 36 (5), 654–673.
Truog, P., 2017. Urban-focused transit must also bring people to suburban jobs. The Plain Dealer E2.
Wang, C., Chen, N., 2015. A GIS-based spatial statistical approach to modeling job accessibility by transportation mode: case study of Columbus, Ohio. J. Transp. Geogr. 45, 1–11.
Wiersma, J., Bertolini, L., Straatemeier, T., 2016. How does the spatial context shape conditions for car dependency? An analysis of the differences between and within regions in the Netherlands. J. Transp. Land Use 9 (3), 35–55.

CHAPTER EIGHT

Commuting behavior and local population loss: Means of transportation to work as an indicator of urban decline

Christopher Graziul[a,b,*], Eric Seymour[a], Daniel Schleith[a]
[a]Spatial Structures in the Social Sciences, Brown University, Providence, RI, United States
[b]Department of Comparative Human Development, University of Chicago, Chicago, IL, United States
*Corresponding author: e-mail address: christopher_graziul@brown.edu

Contents

Abstract

Prominent urbanists have recently claimed that demographic trends and changing lifestyle preferences will generate population gains in communities whose built environments encourage non-automotive transportation. However, given increasing recognition of the frequent and often persistent appearance of population loss, we assess the converse: Do neighborhood-level affinities for alternative modes of transportation, which we term commuting culture, protect communities from population loss? Through an analysis of census tracts nested within the 50 largest metropolitan areas in the United States, we test whether increasing use of alternative modes is associated with (1) population change and (2) changing odds of population loss as a dichotomous outcome variable. We further examine the interaction between population density and commuter mode choice on population change 2000–2010. We find higher utilization of alternative modes of transportation have different effects, particularly when examined across density levels. We find that bus use and biking are associated with increased odds of population loss in all but the densest neighborhoods, where walking is associated with decreased odds of loss. Light rail utilization, on the

Advances in Transport Policy and Planning, Volume 2
ISSN 2543-0009
https://doi.org/10.1016/bs.atpp.2018.09.005

contrary, insulates against loss regardless of tract density. These findings should be relevant for planners and place makers promoting accessibility-first programs of neighborhood renewal.

Keywords: Commuting behavior, Neighborhood change, Urban planning

1. Introduction

In 2011, the influential urbanist Christopher Leinberger penned an opinion piece for the *The New York Times* in which he declared the death of the "fringe suburb" (Leinberger, 2011). Leinberger, long a proponent of walkable urbanism, argued the effects of the recession and the changing lifestyle preferences of empty-nest baby boomers and young adults were driving a demographic shift away from remote auto-dependent suburbs with giant homes and large lot sizes back to smaller units in dense, mixed-use communities. According to Leinberger (2011), "there has been a profound structural shift—a reversal of what took place in the 1950s when drivable suburbs boomed and flourished as center cities emptied and withered." The strength and durability of this trend have been remarked upon by a number of notable urbanists, who variously refer to this phenomenon as "The Great Inversion" (Ehrenhalt, 2012) and "The Fifth Migration" (Fishman, 2005). This trend overlaps with what some researchers refer to as the "back-to-the-city" movement (Hyra, 2015), with many remarking on the migration of high-skilled young professionals to urban neighborhoods near tech jobs and stimulating settings (Florida, 2003; Lawton et al., 2013). But migration from fringe suburbs is also directed toward walkable suburbs, particularly mature inner-ring suburbs, but also to younger communities developed according to neotraditional design principles (Katz et al., 1994) and those developed around transit hubs (Anderson, 2011; Cervero, 2004).

Among the numerous factors driving the reverse migration from far-flung suburbs, transportation plays an integral role, particularly the growing rejection of long commutes or automobility altogether. Rising gas prices since the late 1990s and worsening highway congestion in many metropolitan areas greatly increased the costs of living in remote suburban communities. From 2000 to 2011, the cost of unleaded gasoline rose from 1.5 to 3.5 dollars per gallon, an increase of >130% (U.S. Energy Information Administration, 2012). Researchers have also noted substantial increases in peak-hour traffic congestion since the 1980s, driven by a combination of population growth, suburban residential preferences, and the intensive use of automotive vehicles this entails (Downs, 2000). The historical ease of reaching centrally located jobs from peripheral residential enclaves was enabled by cheap gas and high-speed highways. These low transportation costs were integral to millions of middle-class households' decisions to spend more on larger suburban housing in the post-war decades (Jackson, 1987). Low transportation costs were central to creating the "drive til you qualify" scenario of the 1990s and early 2000s, in which households priced out of centrally located communities would purchase lower-cost peripheral housing. In short, the rising costs of automotive travel have begun to erode the incentive structure central to fringe-suburban residential preferences.

The changing transportation preferences of the millennial generation are argued to have an even more pronounced effect on population increases in non-auto-dependent communities. Millennials are more likely than members of older generations to prefer public transportation and other alternatives to private automobile use. Millennials are purchasing cars in smaller numbers than young persons in the past for a number of reasons, including financial and credit reasons, but also because of changing preferences for living in locations accessible to jobs and amenities without long commutes by car (National Association of Realtors and Portland State University, 2015; Ross, 2011). These trends are reinforced by findings from studies of the intra-urban residential preferences of creative class workers and the ongoing class restructuring of cities through gentrification (Bereitschaft, 2014; Frenkel et al., 2013; Hess, 2018; Hyra, 2015). Regardless of whether it is attributable to the "soft" or "hard" amenities driving locational preferences, young creative workers are clearly congregating in urban neighborhoods and abandoning private automobile use as their primary or even secondary means of transportation (Klein and Smart, 2017; McDonald, 2015).

Less studied is the relationship between commuting behavior and population loss, however, despite recent attention paid to the causes and consequences of urban depopulation in the literature on so-called shrinking cities (Martinez-Fernandez et al., 2012). In this chapter we address the understudied question of how patterns of modal choice among commuters, which we term commuting culture, relate to population loss. If certain types of commuting behaviors, particularly mode choices other than private automobile, correspond with an influx of young professionals, empty-nest baby boomers, and others, to what degree, if any, is mode choice linked to population loss? Are neighborhoods populated by public transit users less susceptible to loss than those with large numbers of individuals driving to work? These questions move beyond assessing the effect of mode accessibility on neighborhood desirability by highlighting decisions made net of the practical costs associated with mode choice, and thus provide a window into the practical relationship between commuting behavior and locational decision making.

The relationship between commuting culture and population change is also tied to the spatial mismatch of home and work, particularly for low-income households (Gobillon et al., 2007). Neighborhood outmigration leading to net population loss likely reflects, at least in part, residential sorting to improve access to jobs and proximity to employment. During the late 2000s, for instance, some low-income households took advantage of the foreclosure crisis and plummeting home values to relocate to amenity-rich suburbs (Howell and Timberlake, 2014; Pfeiffer and Lucio, 2015). These patterns of relocation suggest a larger question: To what extent, if any, are alternative modes of transportation a pull factor for groups beyond those already studied? Put another way, can urban planners assume that greater alternative mode usage indicates something about the overall attractiveness of a neighborhood? If so then we conjecture a commuting culture oriented around these alternative modes should, on average, correlate with net population gain (and, conversely, insulate against population loss). On the other hand, if the utilization of alternative modes of transportation indicates a neighborhood is more attractive to only a select population then we would expect commuting culture to exhibit a selective relationship to population change (i.e., no global relationship would be apparent). We can test for these selective effects by asking whether neighborhoods with a commuting culture oriented around alternative modes of transportation are more or less likely to experience population loss. Contexts where such neighborhoods are more likely to experience population loss challenge the assumption that increased accessibility to alternative modes represents a planning panacea to population decline (Mallach and Brachman, 2013).

2. Background

Since the 2000s, demographic trends and changing neighborhood preferences have lead urbanists to anticipate return migration from remote auto-dependent suburbs and the attraction of young professionals (Ehrenhalt, 2012). Population and real estate research has long assumed a strong relationship between aging, tenure, and neighborhood and location preferences (Clark et al., 1994; Doling, 1976; Kendig, 1984). Young childless individuals and couples often economize by living in smaller low-cost apartments, often in central city locations dense with employment opportunities and multi-family rental housing. As couples have children, they are likely to become homebuyers, seeking larger dwellings in municipalities and neighborhoods with high-quality schools and amenities like parks and playgrounds. This transition is often linked to suburban migration flows. Once the adult children of suburban parents have left home, empty-nest parents have an incentive to downsize to smaller condo or rental units and move to walkable neighborhoods. This later transition is linked to the reurbanization of older working households and young retirees. Between 2005 and 2015, the number of baby boomer renter households climbed from 10 million to 15 million, accounting for half of the nation's renter growth in that period (Joint Center for Housing Studies, 2017). There are numerous media accounts of boomer households selling their homes and renting apartments in locations near shopping and entertainment (MarksJarvis, 2016). In addition to growing rentership and reurbanization of boomer households, Generation X households have broken with historical family life cycle and homebuying patterns as many have remained renters in part due to the lingering effects of the foreclosure crisis and recession (Joint Center for Housing Studies, 2017).

The large size of Millennial birth cohorts combined with changing preferences for urban living and automobile ownership in a context of economic recession is argued to have led to a substantial back-to-the-city movement with young urban inhabitants making fewer and shorter trips by car (Cortright, 2014; McDonald, 2015; Myers, 2016; Polzin et al., 2014). Not only has the size of the Millennial generation exceeded Generation X, but so has the percentage of highly educated young adults, propelling population gains in central city areas dense with jobs in the advanced services like design and finance. Even chronic population loss cities like Buffalo and Cleveland saw increases in the number of young adults with college degrees living in centrally located neighborhoods since 2000 (Cortright, 2014). Further, research has found that a larger share of Millennials live in urban areas compared to the previous generation, with 77% of 25–30 year old households living in urban areas in 2009 compared to 69% in 1995 (McDonald, 2015).

The reurbanization of young workers is related to changing transportation preferences, with an increasing share of Millennials eschewing automobiles and long commutes from suburban bedroom communities. According to a 2014 on-line survey conducted by transportation-focused foundation TransitCenter, people under 30 were substantially more likely to use public transportation than older respondents (TransitCenter, 2014). A 2015 joint survey by the National Association of Realtors and researchers at Portland State University found that Millennials prefer walking over driving far more than older generations. Further, Millennials expressed stronger preferences for using public transit and living in attached housing (National Association of Realtors and Portland State University, 2015). Millennial preferences for centrally located neighborhoods and those well-served by public transit, particularly light rail, have fueled concern over rising gentrification, as relatively more affluent and predominantly white in-movers bid up rental demand and price out incumbent inhabitants (Baker and Lee, 2017; Dawkins and Moeckel, 2016; Dong, 2017; Hess, 2018; Luckey et al., 2018; Nilsson and Delmelle, 2018).

From research on Millennial location patterns and neighborhood and transportation preferences we might conclude that neighborhoods with a commuting culture oriented around alternative modes of transportation, particularly those in central city locations, are most attractive to Millennial households and therefore likely to experience population growth. But what is the relationship between neighborhoods with regard to mode choice and population loss? Can we infer that neighborhoods with a commuting culture based on private automobile use are those most likely to lose inhabitants? This would be the corollary derived from extant literature on transportation-related pull factors, at least as far as young adults are concerned. This relationship likely depends on metropolitan structure, particularly the correspondence between home and work locations.

While creative class and financial sector jobs tend to be clustered in central cities, much employment remains located outside the central city. In Detroit, the city that perhaps best illustrates this pattern, the majority of resident's jobs are located outside the city (Grengs, 2012). Despite the large distances between home and work for these residents, many depend on public transportation, in spite of the serious deficiencies in regional transit in many sprawling metropolitan areas. In this sense, commuting culture reflects decisions made net of costs associated with commute distance and mode accessibility, decisions that may be related to ideological commitments or aesthetic preferences for some commuters but grounded in more practical concerns for others. But these relationships remain understudied, suggesting it may be premature to tout the benefits of bike lanes, improvements to pedestrian infrastructure, and highly localized public transit if they do little to better connect residents to employment.

3. Data and methods

To analyze the relationship between commuting culture, specifically the utilization of alternative modes of transportation, and local population loss, we employed tract level data from the 2000 Decennial Census and 5-year population estimates from the American Community Survey (ACS) for the 2006–2010 period for the top 50 Metropolitan Statistical Areas (MSAs) in 2000 by population. While the 2006–2010 ACS data utilize tract boundaries based on the 2010 Decennial Census, the Census Bureau publishes files that indicate the relationship between Census geographies in 2000 versus 2010. The tract relationship file allowed us to estimate population change from 2000 to 2010 using consistent geographic boundaries by providing data on the proportion of a tract's population falling within the 2000 or 2010 boundaries. This feature made it possible to estimate population change in tracts whose boundaries have changed. To test the robustness of this strategy, we also estimated models including only tracts whose boundaries did not change and found no substantive differences in our results.

We examine the relationship between commuting culture and population change with two different dependent variables. Notably, tracts in our sample gained an average of 304 residents from 2000 to 2010, and so the experience of population loss cannot be captured through a simple continuous measure of change. To capture change in population as well as real population loss, our dependent variables are both the difference in the logarithm (base 10) of tract population in 2010 versus 2000 as well as a dichotomous variable indicating whether the tract experienced population loss during this period. Analyzing a dichotomous indicator for tracts that experienced real population loss removes the overall bias toward population growth exhibited across all tracts. These two measurement strategies thus allow us to more fully disaggregate the magnitude and direction of population change.

Commuting culture is measured in 2000 using three variables constructed from identical survey items: Percent of commuters in tract commuting via (1) bus, (2) light rail (streetcar, trolley car, subway or elevated subway), (3) bicycle, or (4) walking. These survey items capture the behavior of local residents and reflect both preferences for particular modes of transportation and the costs associated with those mode choices (e.g., mode availability/accessibility). In this regard, we view mode utilization as an indicator of a neighborhood's commuting culture, since the availability/accessibility of alternative modes also does not guarantee residents utilize those modes.

In multivariate analysis, we also include a number of potential/likely confounding variables from the 2000 Census: percent black or African American, percent Hispanic, percent Asian or Pacific Islander, percent other race/ethnicity, percent with some college education, percent with a Bachelor's degree, percent with an advanced degree, a Gini-Simpson index of racial diversity, a Gini-Simpson index of educational diversity, unemployment rate, population density (log10) of tract, population density (log10) of MSA, and whether the tract is located in a "central" county within the MSA, according to the Census Bureau. These measures help to capture neighborhood context in terms of economic conditions, racial makeup, and educational attainment, as well as associated levels of diversity. Each is likely to shape the aggregate needs, preferences, and costs associated with certain mode choices (Dugundji and Walker, 2005). As a result, we believe that each will also influence aggregate patterns in modal choice (i.e., commuting culture).

Descriptive statistics for our dataset may be found in Table 1. Our analytic strategy was to assess bivariate relationships using *t*-tests before probing the robustness of these relationships using three-level mixed effects modeling (nesting tracts within counties within MSAs) via the *mixed* and *xtmelogit* commands found in Stata 15. To decompose these global trends further, we also estimated mixed effects models including multiplicative interactions between mode utilization and tract population density, as the practical ability to bike or walk to work (as well as the availability of bus or light rail service) will often depend on the geographic concentration of residents. This strategy helped to mitigate the fact that patterns in mode choice may reflect other contextual factors we do not measure while also serving the substantive purpose of providing insight about highly dense neighborhoods.

Table 1 Descriptive statistics for all variables.

Variable	*N*	Mean	SD	Min	Max
Population loss (1 = loss)	42,649	0.42		0	1
% Population change (2000–2010)	42,649	16.72	91.52	−98.95	3340.32
% Black of African American	42,649	15.11	24.93	0	100
% Asian or Pacific Islander	42,649	4.87	8.14	0	93.54
% Other race/ethnicity	42,649	2.60	2.71	0	100
% Hispanic	42,649	14.78	20.50	0	100
Median household income	42,649	50,777	23,273	0	200,000
% Some college education	42,648	27.34	7.84	0	84.93
% Bachelor's degree	42,648	17.26	10.66	0	100
% Advanced degree	42,648	10.01	8.98	0	69.19
Racial diversity (Gini-Simpson)	42,649	0.80	0.13	0.46	1.00
Educational diversity (G-S)	42,648	0.52	0.05	0.45	1.00
Unemployment rate	42,631	6.28	5.99	0	100
Tract population density	42,649	2681	5372	0.10	89,657
% Bus	42,625	4.56	7.35	0	100
% Light rail	42,625	2.90	9.51	0	93.56
% Bike	42,625	0.41	1.22	0	100
% Walk	42,625	3.26	6.12	0	100
Central county (1 = central)	42,261	0.10		0	1
MSA population (log10)	42,649	6.68	0.42	6.00	7.33

4. Results

Table 2 indicates a significant, if modest, inverse relationship between population change and each of the four modes of transportation to work explored in this chapter. Similarly, Fig. 1 shows that there are statistically significant differences between tracts that exhibited net population loss versus those that exhibited net population growth in terms of the percentage of

Table 2 Correlation matrix for key variables of interest ($N = 42{,}649$).

	(1)	(2)	(3)	(4)	(5)
(1) Population change (2000–2010)	1.000				
(2) % Bus (2000)	−0.208	1.000			
(3) % Light Rail (2000)	−0.078	0.230	1.000		
(4) % Bike (2000)	−0.064	0.112	0.050	1.000	
(5) % Walk (2000)	−0.098	0.269	0.260	0.219	1.000

Note: All correlations significant at the $P < 0.001$ level.

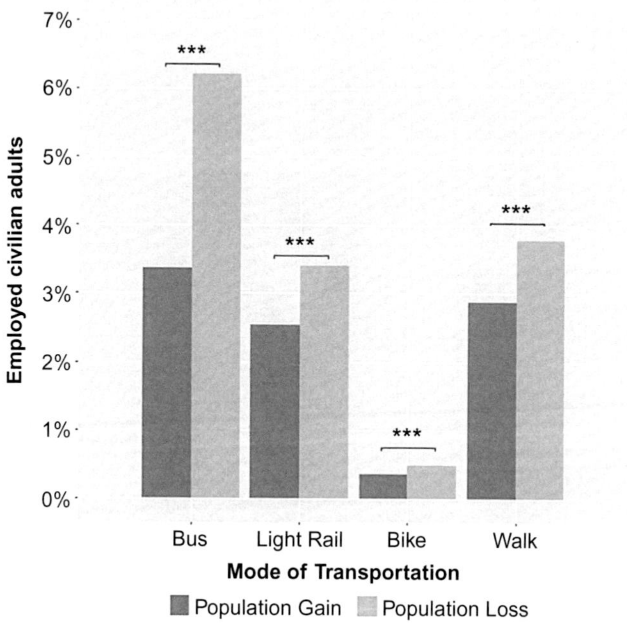

Fig. 1 Mode of transportation use in neighborhoods experiencing population gain/loss.

the adult employed population using an alternative mode of transportation to work. For each mode, population loss tracts exhibit higher utilization compared to population growth tracts. This in part reflects the continued growth of suburban areas and the dominance of automobile use among workers living in those areas (Glaeser et al., 2008). The greatest difference between gain and loss tracts comes from bus use, with >6% of the adult employed population in loss tracts using the bus to commute to work compared to roughly 3.5% in population increase tracts.

Examining the conditional effect of transportation mode, net confounders, reveals a more complex relationship (see Table 3). Fig. 2 depicts

Table 3 Mixed models for change in population and odds of experiencing population loss (2000–2010).

	% Change in population		Odds of experiencing population loss	
Variables	**Model 1**	**Model 2**	**Model 3**	**Model 4**
% Black or African American(2000)	−0.001	0.001	1.142***	1.127***
% Hispanic origin (2000)	0.011***	0.010***	1.004	1.011
% Asian or Pacific Islander (2000)	0.001	0.001	1.011	1.019
% Other race (2000)	−0.004***	−0.004***	1.093***	1.091***
Median household income (2000)	0.008***	0.007***	0.905***	0.912***
% Some college (2000)	0.006***	0.005***	0.895***	0.900***
% Bachelor's degree (2000)	0.020***	0.020***	0.836***	0.839***
% Advanced degree (2000)	−0.013***	−0.013***	1.095***	1.093***
Racial diversity (Gini-Simpson, 2000)	−0.012***	−0.014***	1.233***	1.248***
Educational diversity (G-S, 2000)	0.000	0.000	0.970	0.971
Unemployment rate (2000)	−0.001***	−0.001***	1.005*	1.004
Central county in MSA (1 = central)	−0.027***	−0.034***	0.684***	0.719***
Population, MSA (log10, 2000)	0.014	0.017	0.871	0.857
% Bus commuters (2000)	0.002*	−0.052***	0.992	1.334***
% Light rail commuters (2000)	0.010***	0.006	0.922***	0.797*
% Biking to work (2000)	0.000	−0.017***	1.027*	1.232***
% Walking to work (2000)	0.002***	−0.045***	0.992	1.699***
Population density (log10, 2000)	−0.090***	−0.086***	2.241***	2.237***
Population density × % bus		0.015***		0.922***
Population density × % light rail		0.001		1.038
Population density × % bike to work		0.006***		0.946**
Population density × % walk to work		0.014***		0.851***

Continued

Table 3 Mixed models for change in population and odds of experiencing population loss (2000–2010).—cont'd

	% Change in population		Odds of experiencing population loss	
Variables	**Model 1**	**Model 2**	**Model 3**	**Model 4**
(Constant)	0.188*	0.150	0.175	0.206
Var(MSA)	0.0006	0.0006	0.1694	0.1675
Var(county)	0.0016	0.0016	0.1864	0.1710
Level-1 units (counties)	419	419	419	419
Level-2 units (MSAs)	50	50	50	50
Log-likelihood	30,846	31,225	−25,400	−25,320

Note: $*P<0.05$, $**P<0.01$, $***P<0.001$.

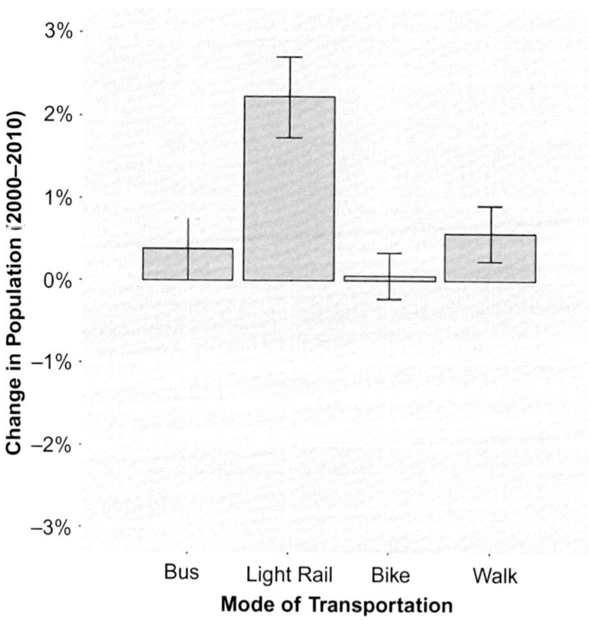

Fig. 2 Conditional effect of mode of transportation on change in population.

coefficient estimates suggesting that while commuting by bus or bicycle now exhibit little to no relationship with population change, it is clear that light rail usage (2.2% increase per standard deviation increase in utilization) and walking (0.5% increase per standard deviation increase in walking to work)

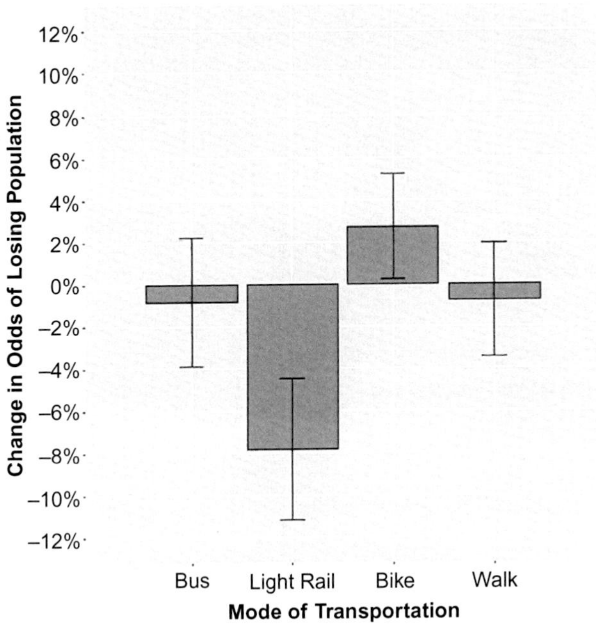

Fig. 3 Conditional effect of mode of transportation on odds of experiencing population loss.

are directly related to population change. Conversely, Fig. 3 reveals that tracts where more commuters bike to work had slightly higher odds of losing population (2.7% increase per standard deviation increase in biking to work) but we observed no relationship between walking to work and net population loss at the tract level. However, light rail usage, in addition to being associated with population growth, appears to also insulate tracts from population loss (7.8% decrease in odds of population loss per standard deviation increase in the use of light rail).

Figs. 4 and 5 present the marginal effect of transportation mode by local population density. Both figures tell a largely similar story, though with some notable differences. In each case, commuting by bus, bicycle, or walking is associated with relative as well as absolute population loss in tracts with low population density, while light rail usage is associated with population gain and insulates against population loss regardless of tract population density. However, Fig. 4 suggests that commuting by bus or bicycle is associated with population growth in the densest tracts, while Fig. 5 suggests no relationship.

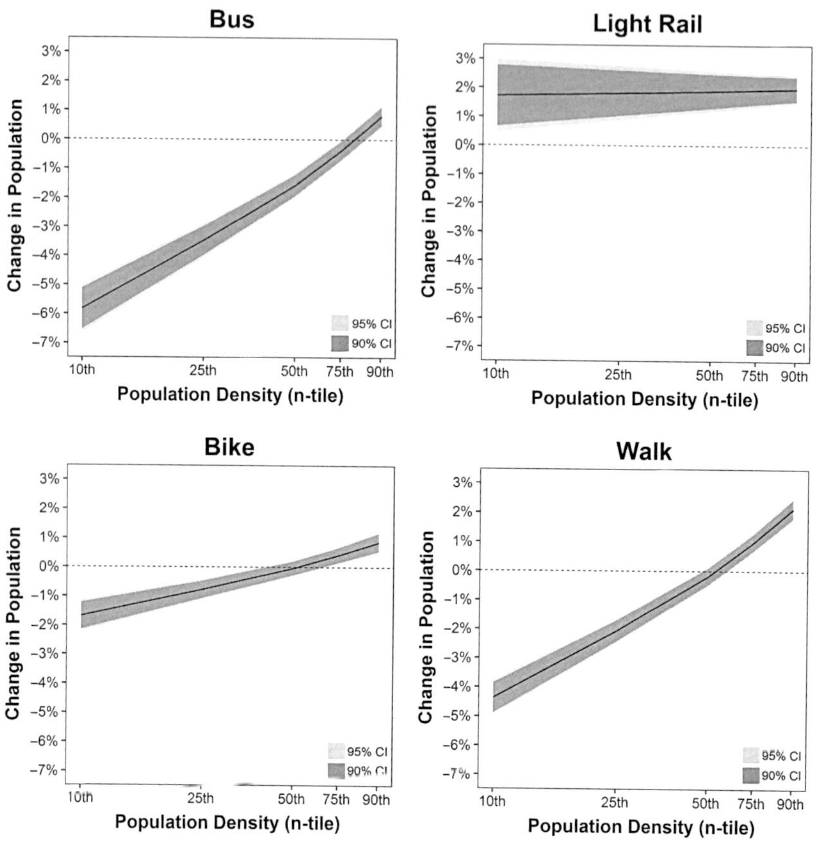

Fig. 4 Marginal effect of mode of transportation on change in population by population density.

5. Discussion

Overall, these results suggest that commuting culture, defined here as the patterned use of alternative modes of transportation, exhibits a surprisingly nuanced relationship with population change, with its effects often mediated by other features of the local context, such as population density and the demographic makeup of local residents. Without accounting for these features, we observed bivariate relationships indicating that (1) utilization of alternative modes of transportation to work was inversely related to population change, and (2) neighborhoods experiencing population loss exhibited greater utilization of alternative modes of transportation compared

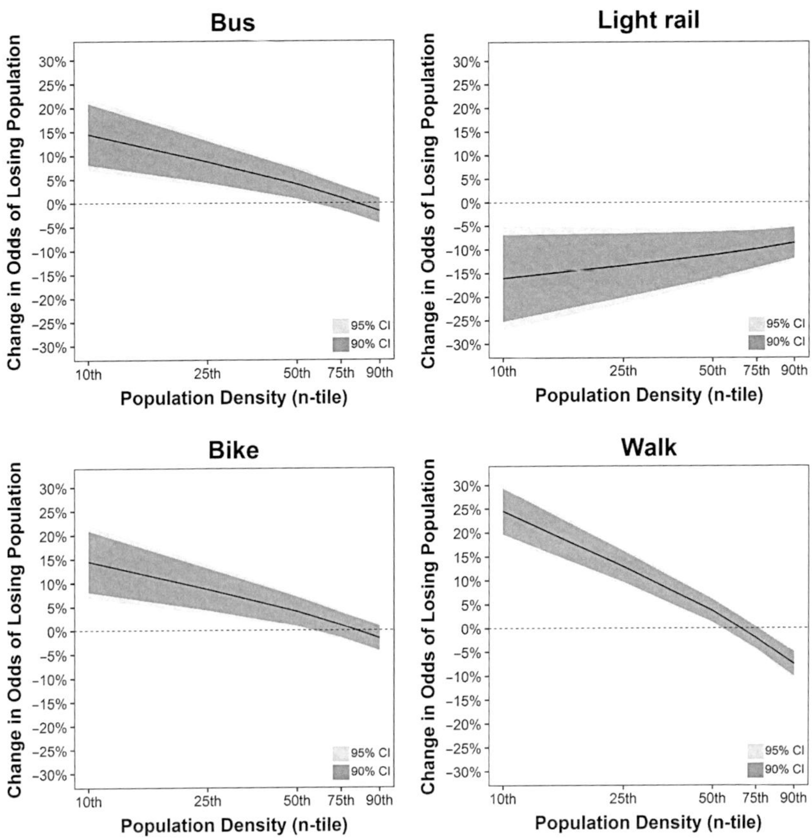

Fig. 5 Marginal effect of mode of transportation on odds of population loss by population density.

to neighborhoods experiencing population growth. The consistency of this pattern suggests a global trend where commuting culture relates to both the likelihood and magnitude of population decline.

These bivariate associations were particularly strong for bus use as compared to the share of workers using light rail, biking, and walking as their primary means of transportation to work. Examining our dichotomous variable for population growth/loss, population growth neighborhoods are linked to far higher rates of the employed population driving to work relative to population loss neighborhoods. These findings are consistent with conventional accounts of post-WWII growth occurring principally in auto-dependent suburban communities, with urban inhabitants continuing to flee older inner-city neighborhoods where a greater share of the employed population is likely able to commute to work without a car (Beauregard, 2006; Downs, 2000). Conversely, low-income transit-dependent households are more likely to remain in place as more affluent households move out to consume new housing in growing suburbs where public transportation is limited, if at all present (Glaeser et al., 2008). These bivariate associations, therefore, provide no evidence for the global effect of greater neighborhood-level utilization of alternative modes of transportation—of any type—generating population gains in the past decade.

However, when we accounted for the nesting of geographic regions (an indicator of both mode availability and labor market structure), and a basic set of variables characterizing local residents and their neighborhoods, we found a markedly different pattern. For example, regression analysis revealed that the share of employees walking and taking the bus to work both had modest (but statistically significant) positive associations with population growth but no association with the odds that a tract experienced net population loss. These conditional relationships differ substantially from the bivariate relationships observed in each case, though comport with popular accounts of bus availability and walkability as desirable neighborhood features for potential residents. Yet this effect does not extend to preventing net population loss, representing an asymmetry in how these modes of transportation may contribute to neighborhood change.

In a similar departure from our bivariate analysis, the share of employed residents biking to work exhibited no relationship with overall population change. Yet, as before, biking to work was associated with higher odds that a tract experienced net population loss. Another asymmetry in results comparing population change versus experience of population loss, biking to work may be an indicator of spatial mismatch and thus presage relocation of those workers to neighborhoods closer to their workplace.

These results indicate that neighborhoods dense with employees using non-motorized modes of transportation (biking and walking) were no less likely to experience population loss than neighborhoods with lower shares of workers using those modes. Thus, all else being equal, a commuting culture based on non-motorized transportation modes, which we suspect to be associated with real-world jobs accessibility via those modes, is unable to stave off population loss as other push and pull factors have greater influence.

Neighborhood-level utilization of light rail, however, stands apart from other alternative travel modes through its association with not only population growth, but also with substantially lower odds of population loss, all else being equal. These findings are consistent with recent scholarship examining demographic changes around light rail corridors (Hess, 2018). It is important to recall that we measure light rail utilization in 2000 and not its change over time or its level in 2010. New light rail development during the 2000s is certainly linked to population growth in nearby communities, particularly in historically low-density suburban areas (Federal Transit Administration, 2014). Our results, however, do not directly measure the relationship between these new developments and population gains during the past decade, but rather the gains accruing to neighborhoods likely already well-served by light rail. This makes the results even more remarkable because they do not capture the likely sizable increases in areas where new systems and transit oriented developments were constructed in recent years.

Our initial multivariate analysis thus suggests that utilization of alternative modes of transportation, outside of light rail, is not so much positively associated with loss, as indicated by simple bivariate analysis, but rather that they fail to insulate against loss. Our second set of mixed models address the fact that our measures are also capturing mode availability and that mode availability will be shaped by population density. Given the focus of prior research and urban punditry on densely populated neighborhoods, principally in inner-city locations, our research also sheds interesting new light on the relationship between neighborhood walkability and transit usage and population change across the spectrum of population densities exhibited across metropolitan space in our sample of the 50 largest MSAs.

Overall, we find biking, walking, and bus use are associated with population growth only in the densest neighborhoods, likely those centrally located in inner-city or dense suburban nodes. This is particularly the case for bus use and biking, where these modes are associated with growth when density is greater than the 75th percentile. Below these thresholds, increasing shares of employees biking, walking, or commuting by bus are associated with population loss, with bus use and walking linked to larger losses in low-density neighborhoods, net of demographic characteristics.

These findings suggest that only in already dense neighborhoods that are already gaining population are biking, bus use, and walking indicative of higher neighborhood desirability (i.e., attractive to new inhabitants and/or incumbent residents). However, in low-density suburban or losing inner-city neighborhoods similar patterns of mode utilization do not indicate higher neighborhood desirability (i.e., utilization is not associated with either population gain or a lower likelihood of real population loss). In other words, utilization of these alternative modes of transportation likely means different things in different contexts, suggesting that increased alternative mode availability, even if utilized, will not have a universal effect on neighborhood attractiveness or, in turn, population change. Light rail usage, unlike other alternative modes, is consistently positively associated with population gain regardless of density and consistently negatively associated with tracts experiencing net population loss.

6. Conclusion

In this chapter, we choose to examine how patterns in commuter mode of transportation in 2000, defined here as commuting culture, related to neighborhood population change from 2000 to 2010. This work was initially inspired by existing research that suggests utilization of alternative modes of transportation may be associated with broad patterns of population growth (e.g., the "back-to-the-city" movement). To study this topic, we measured tract level population change two ways, first in terms of percent change from 2000 to 2010 and then in terms of whether tracts experienced net population loss over this period, and tested its relationship to the use of four alternative modes of transportation (bus, light rail, biking, and walking).

Our analysis revealed three distinct patterns in the relationship between commuting culture and neighborhood-level population change. First, even though it implies the presence of potentially significant spatial mismatch between residential and workplace locations, light rail utilization is a robust predictor of population growth and insulator against net population loss. This effect may be due to lower commute times despite distance traveled, granting similar access to both dense (e.g., inner city) and less dense (e.g., suburban) neighborhoods. Second, utilization of other modes of transportation that suggests the presence of spatial mismatch (i.e., bus use and biking) exhibits a more complex relationship to population change. Low-density neighborhoods with higher utilization of these modes exhibited population loss (or, more accurately, lower population growth) and higher odds of net population loss, a fairly predictable result. However, in high density neighborhoods such utilization was associated with population growth but did not insulate against net population loss. The third and final pattern we observed was that walking to work exhibited a consistent relationship with population change based on neighborhood population density: Walking to work was an indicator of lower population growth and higher odds of net population loss in less dense neighborhoods, but an indicator of higher population growth and lower odds of net population loss in denser neighborhoods. These results are consistent with percent of residents walking to work serving as a proxy for walkability and low spatial mismatch.

Finally, we can partially answer a question that broadly motivated our research: Are residents leaving neighborhoods that lack easy access to alternative modes of transportation? We did not measure mode availability directly, but we did capture the commuting culture of a neighborhood. In that sense, we can provide a qualified answer: Commuting behavior, in particular the utilization of certain alternative modes of transportation, is associated with population loss in less dense neighborhoods located within the top 50 MSAs. Light rail being the exception, we have reason to believe that this trend is tied to spatial mismatch, but further research is necessary to pinpoint the exact cause of this relationship, in particular the independent effect of mode availability and the mechanisms linking commute mode and residential location choice. However, our results suggest the presence of broader patterns in the relationship between transportation decisions and neighborhood change beyond inner-city neighborhoods and beyond particular demographic groups, patterns we believe are worth further study given their implications for urban planning, specifically, and regional governance, more generally.

Acknowledgment

This material is based upon work supported by the National Science Foundation under Grant No. 1561060.

References

Anderson, G., 2011. Walkable Neighborhoods Gaining Popularity—Even in the Suburbs. Huffington Post.

Baker, D.M., Lee, B., 2017. How does light rail transit (LRT) impact gentrification? Evidence from fourteen US urbanized areas. J. Plan. Educ. Res. 1–15. https://doi.org/10.1177/0739456X17713619.

Beauregard, R.A., 2006. When America Became Suburban. University of Minnesota Press.

Bereitschaft, B., 2014. Neighbourhood change among creative–cultural districts in mid-sized US metropolitan areas, 2000–10. Reg. Stud. Reg. Sci. 1 (1), 158–183.

Cervero, R., 2004. Transit-Oriented Development in the United States: Experiences, Challenges, and Prospects. vol. 102. Transportation Research Board.

Clark, W.A.V., Deurloo, M.C., Dieleman, F.M., 1994. Tenure changes in the context of micro-level family and macro-level economic shifts. Urban Stud. 31 (1), 137–154. Sage Publications Sage UK: London, England.

Cortright, Joe., 2014. Young and Restless. City Observatory. http://cityobservatory.org.

Dawkins, C., Moeckel, R., 2016. Transit-induced gentrification: who will stay, and who will go? Hous. Policy Debate 26 (4–5), 801–818.

Doling, J., 1976. The family life cycle and housing choice. Urban Stud. 13 (1), 55–58. Sage Publications Sage UK: London, England.
Dong, H., 2017. Rail-transit-induced gentrification and the affordability paradox of TOD. J. Transp. Geogr. 63, 1–10.
Downs, A., 2000. Stuck in Traffic: Coping with Peak-Hour Traffic Congestion. Brookings Institution Press.
Dugundji, E., Walker, J., 2005. Discrete choice with social and spatial network interdependencies—an empirical example using mixed generalized extreme value models with field and panel effects. Transp. Res. Rec. 1921 (1), 70–78.
Ehrenhalt, A., 2012. The Great Inversion and the Future of the American City. Vintage.
Federal Transit Administration. 2014. Trends in Transit-Oriented Development 2000–2010.
Fishman, R., 2005. Longer view: the fifth migration. J. Am. Plan. Assoc. 71 (4), 357–366. Taylor & Francis.
Florida, R., 2003. Cities and the creative class. City Commun. 2 (1), 3–19.
Frenkel, A., Bendit, E., Kaplan, S., 2013. Residential location choice of knowledge-workers: the role of amenities, workplace and lifestyle. Cities 35, 33–41.
Glaeser, E.L., Kahn, M.E., Rappaport, J., 2008. Why do the poor live in cities? The role of public transportation. J. Urban Econ. 63 (1), 1–24.
Gobillon, L., Selod, H., Zenou, Y., 2007. The mechanisms of spatial mismatch. Urban Stud. 44 (12), 2401–2427.
Grengs, J., 2012. Equity and the social distribution of job accessibility in Detroit. Environ. Plan. B: Plan. Des. 39 (5), 785–800.
Hess, C.L., 2018. Light-rail Investment in Seattle: gentrification pressures and trends in neighborhood Ethnoracial composition. Urban Aff. Rev. 1–35. https://doi.org/10.1177/1078087418758959.
Howell, A.J., Timberlake, J.M., 2014. Racial and ethnic trends in the suburbanization of poverty in U.S. metropolitan areas, 1980–2010. J. Urban Aff. 36 (1), 79–98.
Hyra, D., 2015. The back-to-the-city movement: neighbourhood redevelopment and processes of political and cultural displacement. Urban Stud. 52 (10), 1753–1773.
Jackson, K.T., 1987. Crabgrass Frontier: The Suburbanization of the United States. Oxford University Press.
Joint Center for Housing Studies, 2017. America's Rental Housing 2017. Harvard University, Cambridge, MA.
Katz, P., Scully, V., Bressi, T.W., 1994. The New Urbanism: Toward an Architecture of Community. vol. 10. McGraw-Hill, New York.
Kendig, H.L., 1984. Housing careers, life cycle and residential mobility: implications for the housing market. Urban Stud. 21 (3), 271–283. Sage Publications Sage UK: London, England.
Klein, N.J., Smart, M.J., 2017. Millennials and car ownership: less money, fewer cars. Transp. Policy 53, 20–29.
Lawton, P., Murphy, E., Redmond, D., 2013. Residential preferences of the 'creative class'? Cities 31, 47–56.
Leinberger, C.B., 2011. The Death of the Fringe Suburb. The New York Times. Nov. 25.
Luckey, K.S., Marshall, W.E., Durso, C., Atkinson-Palombo, C., 2018. Residential preferences, transit accessibility and social equity: insights from the Denver region. J. Urban 11 (2), 149–174.
Mallach, A., Brachman, L., 2013. Gateway Cities Don't Need a Silver Bullet. The Boston Globe.
MarksJarvis, G., 2016. More Older Americans Becoming Renters. Chicago Tribune.
Martinez-Fernandez, C., Audirac, I., Fol, S., Cunningham-Sabot, E., 2012. Shrinking cities: urban challenges of globalization. Int. J. Urban Reg. Res. 36 (2), 213–225.

McDonald, N.C., 2015. Are millennials really the 'go-nowhere' generation? J. Am. Plan. Assoc. 81 (2), 90–103.
Myers, D., 2016. Peak millennials: three reinforcing cycles that amplify the rise and fall of urban concentration by millennials. Hous. Policy Debate 26 (6), 928–947.
National Association of Realtors and Portland State University. 2015. NAR & Portland State University: 2015 Community and Transportation Preferences Survey. www.nar.realtor. https://www.nar.realtor/reports/nar-2017-community-preference-survey.
Nilsson, I., Delmelle, E., 2018. Transit investments and neighborhood change: on the likelihood of change. J. Transp. Geogr. 66, 167–179.
Pfeiffer, D., Lucio, J., 2015. An unexpected geography of opportunity in the wake of the foreclosure crisis: low-income renters in investor-purchased foreclosures in Phoenix, Arizona. Urban Geogr. 36 (8), 1197–1220.
Polzin, S.E., Chu, X., Godfrey, J., 2014. The impact of Millennials' travel behavior on future personal vehicle travel. Energ. Strat. Rev. 5, 59–65. US energy independence: Present and emerging issues.
Ross, D., 2011. Millennials Don't Care About Owning Cars, and Car Makers Can't Figure Out Why. Fast Company.
TransitCenter. 2014. Who's on board: 2014 Mobility Attitudes Survey. http://www.trb.org/Main/Blurbs/171428.aspx.
U.S. Energy Information Administration. 2012. Retail Motor Gasoline and On-Highway Diesel Fuel Prices, 2949–2011.

Kolibri 360 GmbH
Ferdinand-Jühlke-Straße 7
99095 Erfurt, Deutschland
produktsicherheit@kolibri360.de